Charlie Peace
His Amazing Life
and Astounding Legend

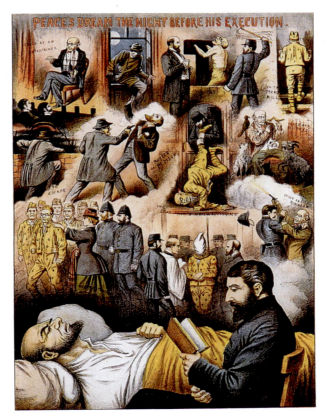

A Kaleidoscope of True
and Not-so-True Crime

Charlie Peace:
his amazing life and astounding legend

Published in 2017
by Five Leaves Publications,
14a Long Row, Nottingham NG1 2DH
www.fiveleaves.co.uk
www.fiveleavesbookshop.co.uk

ISBN 9781910170304

Printed in Great Britain

Dedication

To Forgotten Forebears: Anonymous penny-a-liners; Grub Street scribblers; gin-shop scriveners; public bar poetasters, shabby genteel strivers struggling to put food on the table and drink in their bellies; underpaid in their labours; neglected in their lives; ignored in their deaths, scratching what passed for a living in the ignoble business of bringing cheap entertainment to the masses who devoured their derided fruit in their hundreds of thousands without ever knowing their names; every last one of them doubtless believing themselves the equal, certainly not of Dickens but surely of Thackeray or Bulwer Lytton, the doors to whose Pall Mall clubs were firmly barred to the likes of them; lurching from one impossible deadline to the next; copy surrendered before the ink was dry. And to an unremembered army of threadbare bohemians: illustrators; etchers; type-setters; fairground family thesps; cinematographic adventurers; penny-gaff exhibitors; wax-figure modellers; *Boys Own* bamboozlers; ambulance-chasing pressmen; crankers-out of comic-strips; midnight oil burners; brown bottle breakfasters; liverish lunchers; coffee-shop habitués and chop-house diners... My cousins, my peers.

Michael Eaton
Nottingham, 2017

Contents

A NEW SONG ON THE TRIAL AND SENTENCE OF CHARLIE PEACE —
For the Murder of Mr. Arthur Dyson, at Bannercross Sheffield, Nov. 29, 1876

A NEW SONG ON
The Trial and Sentence
OF
PEACE,

For the Murder of Mr. Arthur Dyson,
at Bannercross Sheffield, Nov. 29, 76.

Charles Peace, the Blackheath burglar is sentenced now
to die.
For Mr. Dyson's murder long ago,
He has been wild and reckless, but his day it has gone
by,
For in the grave he'll soon be lying low.
He has led an evil life, of robbery and strife,
But his days are numbered in this world
The only friend that's left him is that poor neglected
wife
Now in the depths of misery she's hurled.

CHORUS.

In heavy irons lying he is condemned to die,
Charles Peace, the murderer, none can save,
Broken down and dejected his wild career's gone by
His crimes will soon be ended in the grave

Of all the bold highwaymen in the history of the land,
He never had an equal in his time,
The riches of the wealthy he stole with cunning hand,
He has been the terror of those modern times,
He feared no living foe, with his pistol he would go.
Determined to escape or to die,
The life of Peace the burglar I'm sure will plainly show.
That from justice he could not always fly.

For nearly fifty years he has pursued a life of crime,
Such as no one ever knew before,
Confined within a prison he has been many times,
But still he always would defy the law.
Tho' guilty he has been, by many it has been seen,
True affection sometimes he could show,
He loved his pictures and his birds, they were a joy to
him
And his pony loved its master as we know.

He shot poor Mr. Dyson there cannot be a doubt,
There's no excuse for murder you will say
Mrs. Dyson he pretended he could not live without
But he'd no right to take her husband's life away.
Every crime beneath the sun perhaps he may have done,
But if with blood he had not stained his hand,
He may have passed the last few dayshis life had to run
In preparing for a better land.

He has fought for life many times, especially on the
line,
Although he's getting old and full of years,
If upon the scaffold his life he must resign,
There's sure to be a friend to drop a tear.
The poor he did befriend, and money he would spend,
In helping those around him who were poor,
Altho' the laws of England we know he did offend,
Many things untrue have been said at his door.

His days will soon be over, the hangman soon will come
The body of the murderer to demand,
To suffer for the many crimes that often he had done,
Against the peace and welfare of the land,
His doom will teach us all that guilt will have a fall,
We cannot escape the convict's fate,
When once a crime's committed it is beyond recall,
And repentance perhaps may come for us too late.

Who is Charlie Peace?

'To follow Crime with reasonable impunity you simply <u>must</u> have a parallel, ostensible career — the more public the better... Mister Peace, of pious memory, disarmed suspicion by acquiring a local reputation for playing the fiddle and taming animals. Fill the bill in some prominent part and you'll never be suspected of doubling it with another of equal prominence... That's the one and only reason why I don't burn my cricket bats for firewood.'

Gentlemen and Players E.W. Hornung, 1899.

'A complex mind. All great criminals have that. My old friend Charlie Peace was a violin virtuoso.'

The Adventure of The Illustrious Client Arthur Conan Doyle, 1927.

This is Charlie Peace:

This is Charlie Peace:

This is Charlie Peace:

Charles Peace, as he appeared sitting in the dock when I defended him for murder in 1879.

Charles Peace on Trial.
(From a Sketch by Frank Lockwood.)

And this, too, is Charlie Peace:

These are the only known photographs of the most celebrated criminal of the late nineteenth century — well, at least until the arrival, a decade after Peace's execution, of a multiple killer in Whitechapel whose identity remains open to the outer limits of speculation. All of them are police pictures, 'mug-shots' for cataloguing and identifying known miscreants. However, as the man in question looks remarkably different in each, it's doubtful whether they would have been much use, proving Peace's reputation as 'a master of disguise' to be well-founded. The first three images at least give the lie to later descriptions of the old lag as being remarkably unprepossessing in his facial characteristics, 'more monkey than man'. His very appearance is an enigma: shifting, unstable.

The earliest is the Ticket of Leave issued to one George Parker, one of Charlie's many aliases, who was released in June 1864 after serving a six year stretch for receiving stolen goods. The latest was taken on his final arrest in November 1879 when he was described as a 'mulatto' and gave the name John Ward. The final reliable image of him is the sketch by Frank Lockwood, his defending counsel, taken at his trial for murder in January 1879 when he was in his late forties but could pass for twenty years older.

8

My fascination with this unlikely anti-hero began at an early age. When I was a little lad my grandma would sing me music-hall songs of her youth. Among them was this fragment, the provenance of which remains unknown:

I used to be Napoleon in the waxworks show
All the people they admired me so
But now I've had bad luck
They've melted down my grease
They've put me in the Chamber of Horrors
And called me Charlie Peace.

Tales of this night prowler had the desired scarifying effect, though I believed him to be a fairy-tale bogey man, a made-up creature of folklore. Only when I saw his terrifying effigy in the Chamber of Horrors did I realise Charles Peace had been all too real.

Was it Peace the girls were chanting of when the skipping-rope twirled in the playground?

I loved Charlie, Charlie was a thief
Charlie killed a copper, Charlie came to grief
Charlie came to your house, stole a leg of beef
Charlie came to our house, stole some bread and jam
Ate me mother's pudding, ate me father's ham
When the coppers caught him hung him on a rope
Poor old Charlie... hasn't got a hope.

Nana told me that he had lived in our town, near where she grew up down in the warrens of Narrow Marsh, site of notorious slums long-since cleared. But when I looked up his entry in the essential reference work, Colin Wilson and Pat Pitman's *Encyclopaedia of Murder*, there was no mention of Nottingham. So I faithlessly supposed she must have made it up — we have a long-standing habit of embracing legendary criminals round here.

Peace further impinged upon the sensibilities of children of my generation when he made a startling appearance as the star of a strip in *Buster* comic. This began in 1964, when I was ten, and ran for over a decade, during which cartoon Charlie gradually transformed from a violent 'criminal terror of Victorian London' into a lovable 'arch-rogue', a grown-up Artful Dodger whose antagonists were not so much the 'Crushers' (police) as Scrooge-like exploitative capitalists and criminals far more hard-hearted than himself.

From this,
in 1966:

To this, in 1980:

If Charles Peace had simply been the most successful cat burglar of his day and age then why was his name being used to frighten children almost a century later? Why did this robber and double-murderer become in popular consciousness a legendary trickster, a Robin Hood of the public prints? Why did the process of metamorphosis into a folk-hero begin even before his execution?

A few brief facts: The man they called 'The King Of The Lags' was born in Sheffield, possibly on May 14th, 1832. His father worked on a travelling fairground show with trained caged lions and tigers before he settled down and became a zealous convert to evangelical Christianity. If Charlie had inherited his dad's show-business career would he have turned to the bad? When his father passed away Charlie penned this tribute:

> In Peace he lived, in Peace he died
> Life was our desire, but God denied.

When his childhood was over he was apprenticed in the hell of a South Yorkshire steel mill. Charlie had an unexpected fourteenth birthday present when a length of white-hot metal shot through his leg. His very survival was amazing, the saving of his limb little short of miraculous. He not only learned to walk again but became a contortionist of immense agility.

This accident was the turning point. He made a pledge to himself that henceforth no man would ever be his mester. He would never do an honest day's work again. Peace declared war upon respectable society.

He was a fine musician, playing, appropriately, the fiddle, billed in low music halls as 'The Modern Paganini'. But his musicianship acted as a cover for a much more profitable trade: house-breaking and cat burglary, when his violin case hid the tools of his trade.

Not only a master of disguise but a ferocious fighter with no fear of anyone, Charlie eluded a disorganised police force until his inevitable capture.

Peace was in and out of gaol for eighteen years under various aliases and prison regimes. Finally released in 1872, now aged about forty, he determined never to see the inside of a prison again. During one of these stretches in November 1871 his only son, John, died at the age of five, causing the remorseful father to pick up his pen for another epitaph:

> Farewell, my dear son, by all us beloved
> Thou art gone to dwell in the mansions above
> In the bosom of Jesus who sits on the throne
> Anxiously waiting to welcome us home.

His wife, Hannah, had remained loyal to him whilst he was banged up and now they outwardly maintained a respectable existence in the patriotically named Victoria Terrace on Britannia Road in Darnall near Sheffield — a fine location for a man who gave 'darn all'.

And then he met the beautiful Missis Dyson. Peace had always exerted a charismatic charm over the opposite sex and Katherine Dyson was far from immune to his blandishments. She was an Irish-American woman who moved in next-door-but-one with her husband, Arthur, who was twice her age and had been a railroad engineer in the States. Though later, somewhat unconvincingly, she publicly denied intimacy, their torrid affair must have been conducted right under the noses of their respective spouses. In time, however, the magnetic attraction Katherine once felt for this villainous neighbour turned into terror. Peace did not take easily to being spurned. His lust mutated into obsession. Like a man possessed his twisted passion began to affect the delicate balance of his work.

One night, on a job in Whalley Range Manchester, he slipped up and was about to be caught, when he took out his pistol and shot a policeman. Now he had crossed the line. He was a cop killer. His luck held out though. The police pinned the shooting on an innocent Irish labourer: a case of 'Round up the usual Fenians!' But this was not an act of political terrorism but Ordinary Decent Criminality.

Peace brazenly attended the trial of young William Habron for the murder of Police Constable Cock. He was even heard complaining that the evidence against the young Irish lad was merely circumstantial as he sat, supposedly in disguise as a clergyman, in the Public Gallery. Habron was found guilty and sentenced to death despite his desperate pleas of innocence. Fortunately the jury recommended mercy because of his youth and the verdict was commuted to imprisonment for life.

The Dysons moved out of the area, but if Arthur thought he could evade his wife's tormentor he was sorely mistaken. Peace tracked them down to Banner Cross on the posh side of town, the western edge not far from the Peaks, where they lived in a house still standing today. One November night Charlie appeared like a wraith, collaring Katherine as she stepped out to the privy and finally blowing away poor Mister Dyson in his own back yard as his wife looked on in horror.

Banner Cross

Peace was on the run with a considerable reward of One Hundred Pounds on his head.

That was when he came to Nottingham — I should never have doubted my grandma. He holed up in a cheap lodging-house in the crime-ridden no-go zone of Narrow Marsh, shamelessly continuing to pursue his chosen profession. And there he fell in lust again.

Susan Gray was one of her names, another was Sue Bailey. She shared a love of music with the man she came to know as 'Jack Thompson'. Saturday night was the Music Hall; Sunday morning was the Chapel. Her singing voice must have been a great attraction to this supposed travelling salesman. When they set up as man and wife neither of them thought it significant to tell the other they were both already married. Did Sue know what Jack was up to when he went out to work whilst the city slept? She soon found out when the knock on the door came early one morning. She opened up to find two policemen standing there. Her 'husband' leapt out of an upstairs window and legged it into the lawless warrens.

POLICE NOTICE.

AMENDED DESCRIPTION OF

CHARLES PEACE,

alias GEORGE PARKER, *alias* ALEXANDER MANN, *alias* PAGANINI,

WANTED FOR

MURDER

AT SHEFFIELD;

He is thin and slightly built, 46 years of age but looks 10 years older, 5 feet 4 or 5 inches high, grey (nearly white) hair, beard, and whiskers, (the whiskers were long when he committed the murder but may now be cut or shaved off), has lost one or more fingers off left hand, cut mark on back of each hand and one on forehead, walks with his legs rather wide apart. speaks somewhat peculiarly, as though his tongue was too large for his mouth, and is a great boaster.

He is a joiner or picture-frame maker, but occasionally cleans and repairs clocks and watches, and sometimes deals in oleographs, engravings, pictures, &c. Associates with loose women and has been twice in penal servitude for burglaries near Manchester. He has lived in Manchester, Salford, Liverpool, and Hull.

Be good enough to make vigilant enquiries and communicate with

MR. J. JACKSON,
Chief Constable.

CENTRAL POLICE OFFICES,
SHEFFIELD, DEC. 4th, 1876.

Later a message came for her to join him in London. A brass plaque outside his Peckham house proclaimed him: 'Dealer In And Repairer Of Musical Instruments'. They shared their genteel South London home with another woman. 'Jack' told the uncomplaining Sue this was his 'mother', Missis Ward — actually she was none other than long-suffering Hannah Peace. Sweet Sue was unknowingly sharing a *ménage à trois*!

Inhabitants of the suburbs of South London found themselves victims of a one-man crime wave. The Thompsons were popular neighbours, holding soirées presided over by the Master of the House on his violin accompanying Sue in hymns and sentimental parlour songs. Sometimes he would make his excuses to be called out on an important matter of business only to return home later when his guests were somewhat worse for wear from the generous gin-soaked hospitality doled out by the old lady. Coincidentally, some guests would return home to find their homes had been burgled.

One day Sue must have accidentally discovered not only that 'the mother' was really 'the wife' but that the man in her life was, in fact, the notorious Banner Cross Murderer! From that day forth Hannah kept her under virtual house arrest, plying her with spirits and snuff to keep her quiet and befuddled.

And then, on an autumn night in 1878, Peace was caught in the act by Constable Edward Robinson whilst robbing a villa in Blackheath.

Blackheath

Charlie's revolver flashed and the policeman was wounded, shot in the arm. The heroic Blue Lobster managed to keep hold of his murderous assailant. Upon arrest the burglar gave his name as 'John Ward' but otherwise kept silent. Heavily disguised, his face dyed with walnut juice and his lower jaw extended, none of the London police thought to connect the man in the holding cells with the name on the wanted poster still displayed in every cop shop in the land.

A pretty young woman, it would seem, turned up at the Greenwich police station, claiming the Hundred Pound Reward for the Sheffield killer. Only then did the police realise that the man sitting calmly reading the Bible in their holding cell, the man they thought was a 'half-caste', might be the infamous Charles Peace: The Banner Cross Murderer.

Peace made a daring escape from the train taking him back up north for his hearing. But he was caught once again and finally convicted after a trial at the Crown Court in Leeds which galvanised Victorian society. For Katherine Dyson was brought back from the States to testify against him, branding the prisoner in the dock 'a devil', fulsomely denying she had ever had an affair with the monster who had killed her darling husband. The jury returned a verdict within minutes: Guilty!

Charlie was an untroubled prisoner who, in the death cell, made a model of a cardboard Gothic monument, which he wished to be his tomb, rather resembling the Albert Memorial. But before his last day on this earth he made an astounding admission. He confessed that it was he who had shot the young policeman in Whalley Range. The Manchester coppers had committed perjury to convict that young Irish lad. William Habron was released from hard labour as Peace walked to the gallows.

Before the drop Charlie addressed the assembled gentlemen of the press: 'You know what my life has been. Tell all my friends I feel sure that I am going into the Kingdom of Heaven. Goodbye and Amen!'

But that was far from the end of the story. Charlie Peace's life and crimes instantly struck a chord amongst the labouring populace; they certainly kept his memory green.

One thing is certain: the effort of the Baker Street consulting detective to garner reflected glory from an acquaintanceship with Charlie must be considered entirely bogus. Notwithstanding the fictionality of Holmes (despite the convictions of his more committed devotees) and the all-too-reality of Peace, young Sherlock would surely still have been in short trousers when Charlie lived incognito in South London. And, if Holmes really had been in possession of Peace's true identity, he would have been in dereliction of a law-abiding citizen's duty by not dobbing in the miscreant to Inspector Lestrade. More convincing is that Peace might well have been looked up to by the Old Etonian, Raffles, the Amateur Cracksman, the creation of Doyle's brother-in-law.

So Charlie Peace was memorialised, not only in cheap, sensational, quickly-produced penny bloods for the lower classes and apprentice boys but in more elevated literature as well as waxwork shows, travelling fairground theatres, then later in films and comic strips.

It has been my destiny to present the latest contribution to the mythology.

The Land Learns —
The Illustrated Police News

From the woodcuts on the covers of the *Illustrated Police News*, the abiding image of Charles Peace was forged.

The paper was a product of developments technological (the rotary printing press was developed in the 1840s) and fiscal ('taxes on knowledge' were progressively abolished throughout the mid-century: Advertisement Duty in 1853; Stamp Duty on newspapers in 1855; Excise Duty on paper in 1861).

Prior to its first appearance in 1864 the following advertisement appeared:

NOTICE TO THE PUBLIC!

ON SATURDAY, the 20th of February will be published
PRICE ONE PENNY, NO.I of the ILLUSTRATED POLICE NEWS AND
LAW COURTS AND CRIMINAL RECORD.

THIS WEEKLY NEWSPAPER, handsome in appearance and highly interesting in the novelty of its principal features, will contain Special Reports of all cases of public interest in
THE LONDON AND PROVINCIAL POLICE COURTS

The Court of Divorce and Matrimonial Causes, The Court of Bankruptcy, the Court of Chancery, the Court of Exchequer, the Court of Common Pleas, the Court of the Queen's Bench, the Criminal Courts, and all the Courts of Justice in the United Kingdom.

THE ILLUSTRATED POLICE NEWS will also contain
THE LIVES AND TRIALS of
CELEBRATED CRIMINALS OF ALL NATIONS
who by their Atrocious Deeds have rendered themselves Notorious
On Land and on the High Seas.

These truthful and yet thrilling narratives, compiled at the cost of much research and expense from Ancient Records, and from the Private Journals of the Governors and Chaplains of the
GAOLS OF THE GREAT CITIES OF EUROPE AND AMERICA
will be accompanied by numerous and graphic illustrations which will be facsimiles of the pencil and water-colour sketches actually laid before the Juries in support of evidence while the trials were proceeding, and thus will prove of the highest historical interest to the purchasers of the Paper.

'The Worst Newspaper in England'

Twenty years later, in November 1886, a journalist from the *Pall Mall Gazette* ('written by gentlemen for gentlemen') was dispatched to interview the proprietor.

On perceiving that the readers of the Pall Mall Gazette... had voted the Police News to be the 'worst English newspaper,' one of our representatives betook himself to the office of the journal which has required so unique a distinction, in order to learn something as to its character, career, and circulation, and to discover what points its conductors could plead in defence of the publication. He was without delay introduced to the proprietor, Mr. George Purkess, who received the 'verdict of the jury' with great good temper, not to say complacency, readily answered when put to the question, and urbanely volunteered much interesting information as to the history and position of his illustrated weekly calendar of crimes, casualties, and curious incidents.

THE PREMISES AND THE PROPRIETOR
The office of the Police News is situated in 'the neck' of the Strand, and the presence of a small crowd, gathered in front of the pictorial placard (really the first page of the paper) descriptive of the new issue, caused it to be 'spotted' yards away. The premises are not of the princely and palatial order. A small shop, in fact, does duty as a publishing office, and the editorial rooms on the upper floors are diminutive and dark, and certainly, late on a wet November afternoon, also somewhat dismal... The proprietor himself is a stout, comfortable-looking man of middle age, medium height, and dark complexion. He has just sold 'a pretty house' by the Thames, and confesses that he 'would be telling a lie' if he did not acknowledge that good fortune had been meted out to him in very generous measure.

WHAT THE PAPER IS LIKE
The *Police News* is a paper of four pages, about the size of a morning journal; the price a penny. The first page only is devoted to pictorial blocks. The remaining three pages are devoted principally to articles descriptive of the leading murders, suicides, offences, and casualties of the week... The staff — an editor and sub-editor — cut the bulk of the contents of the paper from the daily journals, and it is cast together with scarcely an attempt at an attractive arrangement. The illustrations on the front page are for the most part vivid representations of tragedies and horrors of all kinds. These are vividly portrayed and strikingly executed.

Here are the titles of the illustrations that have appeared in the last five weeks: "Tragic Occurrence in the Borough," "Suicide in a Railway Carriage," "Desperate Encounter between English and French Fishermen at Ramsgate," "Gored to Death by a Bull," "Fatal Accident at the Toxteth Workhouse," "Suicide and Murder of Four Children at Fulham,", "The Girl in Boy's Clothes," "The Affray at Gerard's Cross, Slough," "Stabbing a Performing Bear," "Shocking Discovery at Lambeth," "Burned to Death through Reading in Bed," "The Irish Poisoning Case," "A Lunatic Baited by a Mob," "A Runaway Horse in the City," "Fatal Occurrence at Shadwell," "Extraordinary Suicide," "The Burglary at the Residence of the Comte de Paris," "Fatal Gun Accident," "Savage Assault," "Double Murder at Lytham," "Shocking Tragedy in Bloomsbury," "Thief Captured by a Cabman," "Suicide of a Woman at Islington," "Tragic Murder at Paris: a Desperate Death-struggle," "Sad Death at Bowes Park," "The Late Fred Archer, Champion Jockey: Portrait and Scenes," "Fatal Fire at Ramsgate, Loss of Five Lives," "Wife Murder at Norwich."

Mr. Purkess assured me that he has half-a-dozen artists on his staff in London; and he produced a book containing the names and addresses of from seventy to a hundred artists in various parts of the country whom he employs on occasion. Whatever else his journal may be, Mr. Purkess claims credit for the fact that it is 'the cleanest paper in the country,' bar none... He declared that even reports of indecent assault cases are rigorously excluded from the columns of the *Police News*. An examination of the last five issues discloses two cases of an indelicate nature, not to mention Divorce Court cases; but so far as can be determined by an inspection of these last numbers, Mr. Purkess's paper is certainly freer than the ordinary daily and weekly journals from reports of the character described. This favourable impression, however, is scarcely strengthened when our glance is extended to the advertisement columns...

AN ENORMOUS CIRCULATION
The paper is printed on the Tuesday under Saturday's date. On the Wednesdays it is sent to the country, on Thursdays it is despatched to town agents. It is printed on the flat, from six stereo formes. The machines are kept at work until the Saturday, in order that whatever demand may exist may be adequately met. Six thousand pictorial placards are printed every week, three thousand of which are sent to agents in direct communication with the publisher's office. W.H. Smith and Son send out the paper to agents whom they supply with other periodicals; but they do not show it on their stalls, and Mr. Purkess has not cared to open a hopeless controversy by asking them to do so...

The paper is most highly circulated in Manchester and Liverpool; Birmingham and the Black Country stand next; then Scotland (Glasgow and Edinburgh) and the North of England about rank together in appreciation of the journal; the London circulation is only about one-eighth of the entire issue. The lowest weekly circulation ranges from 150,000 to 200,000 copies; it often runs much higher; and it has two or three times reached the enormous number of 600,000, as when the case of Peace excited popular interest...

'People run away with the idea that the circulation lies entirely among the lower classes, but that is somewhat of a mistake. I have had even the name of a dowager-marchioness on my subscription list; an earl has written me for a "Life of Calcraft," [the erstwhile public hangman] and I have a number of letters from reverend gentlemen asking for copies. The police are also purchasers of the paper. The police lend our staff every assistance; yes, even the higher officers. That, I suppose, is on account of the goodness of our portraits. My artists get into every court... The paper, in fact, is found all over the world. Recently Mr. Du Val, the entertainer, sent me a copy which he had picked up in Hyderabad... I don't advertise nor send out placards; people buy it for what it is worth; it seems to sell for some reason. Unless it had merit, it could never have lived.'

THE PROPRIETOR'S DEFENCE
'Now, Mr. Purkess, the popular impression is that your paper makes for criminality, that many of your patrons are apt to believe that they will have attained to the heights of heroism and glorification when their portrait appears in the Police News.'

'Certainly not,' answered the proprietor, 'it rather tends to prevent crime. Ten years ago, a murderer said to his friends, "If you would do me a service, keep my portrait out of the Police News." People really don't like to have their portraits in the paper, and a prisoner will try all he can, by making a wry face or otherwise, to prevent my artists from securing a good portrait. As to the illustration of crime, what do Miss Braddon and other novelists do? Don't they illustrate crime?'

The figure of six hundred thousand copies might perhaps be an exaggeration but even the conservative estimate of two hundred thousand makes one wonder whether the soubriquet of 'The Worst Newspaper In England' might not have been coined by jealous rivals — Dickens's monthly instalments rarely sold above forty thousand by comparison.

'Nothing Like Example'

Hardly surprising, then, that *All the Year Round,* which at twopence per week cost twice as much and was devoid of pictures, couldn't resist a pop at Purkess and his ilk. The author of the article 'Nothing Like Example' from the issue of May 30th 1868 is unknown, but there is no doubt the scorn expressed would have echoed the sentiments of the 'Conductor' Charles Dickens, whose style, in its persistent deployment of the bizarre inventory and facetious disdain if not superabundant dark humour, the anonymous contributor attempts, not entirely convincingly, to emulate:

> There is to be found in many of what we call the low parts of London, and in the back regions of higher neighbourhoods as well, a shop, established for the sale of cheap periodicals and newspapers, bottles of ink, pencils, bill-files, account books, skeins of twine, little boxes of hard water colours, cards with very sharp steel pens and a holder sown to them, Pickwick cigars, peg-tops, and ginger-beer. Cheap literature is the staple commodity...
>
> One of the leading features in these second-rate news-venders' windows — perhaps *the* leading feature... is always a great broadsheet of huge coarsely executed woodcuts, representing, in a style of art the badness of which has never been surpassed at any period of our uncivilisation, every kind of violent and murderous act, every foul and diabolical crime, every incident marked by special characteristics of noisomeness, horror, or cruelty, which the annals of the week preceding the publication day of this grievous sheet have furnished for the benefit of the morbidly disposed part of the British public.
>
> Only the worst crimes are commemorated here. Has some wretched child been tormented with rare ingenuity by an unnatural parent; has some miserable woman been assaulted with more than common ferocity by her husband; has a father been murdered by his son, or a son by his father; has an ardent lover blown out his sweetheart's brains, or his own, or both his sweetheart's and his own; here, as surely as the Saturday comes round, we have thrust before our eyes, certain great woodcut illustrations of such horrors, the original ghastliness of the subjects being supplemented by the additional grimness which the vilest and rudest execution can impart...

This protégé of The Inimitable fully realised it was pictures of maleficent celebrities which fascinated avid eyes of half-educated, barely-literate potential consumers:

> The greater the crime, the larger the woodcut. This seems to be the simple rule of the artist who furnishes these illustrations. It is not uncommon, in the cases of very distinguished criminals indeed, to follow out the story of his crime from beginning to end; showing him first in the act of committing the murder, then in the condemned cell taking leave of his friends, then on his way to the scaffold or in the pinioning-room,

and lastly actually on the scaffold with the noose suspended over his head...

[In] these illustrations there is strong suggestion of a tendency, conscious or unconscious, on the part of the designer to impart something of the aspect of a hero, or a martyr, to the figure of his principal performer... there is an indescribable air about him of knowing that he is famous, and enjoying the consciousness of fame...

But the revolted *All the Year Round*-er could never have anticipated that it was precisely the bizarre weekly pictorial juxtapositions which might well, in latter days, be appreciated as proto-surrealism:

There is no want of variety in these works of art. In one respect, it is true, they are alike — they deal always in horrors. But the horrors are various. Here is a huge design showing the assassination of the Deputy-Lieutenant of Westmeath, on the same page with a smaller cartoon representing the ruinous results of a race between a couple of costermongers' donkeys, and a third in which one of the costermongers, who has managed to kill a gentleman's horse with the shaft of his barrow, is captured by a particularly able-bodied woman, who holds him down on the ground until the tardy policeman arrives on the scene. A man holding a child by the waistband, over the mouth of a well into which he is about to drop it, is shown on another of the broadsheets, side by side with a most horrible representation of a pauper, with a long beard, chopping at his own throat with a huge dinner-knife. The pauper is described in the literary notice which accompanies the woodcut as holding aside his beard while in the act of cutting his throat; and the gusto with which the artist has laid hold of this incident is very marked...

It is curious to observe how utterly devoid of power are these woodcuts, one and all. There is not the slightest token of the commonest and most widely diffused power of observing, on the part of the artist...

And here it comes: the hand-wringing class-biased scorn, the condescending calumny of the supposed sociological 'influence' of truly popular culture upon minds evidently less elevated than those of himself and his only-just bourgeois readership:

But it is not in a critical examination of these precious works of art that we are now engaged. It is the moral rather than the technical result achieved by the artist with which we have to do. What is their effect on the group of men and boys, who always congregate round a fresh sheet as soon as it makes its appearance in the shop-window of the small news-vender? This is the really grave question. That audience of men and boys is never wanting. They stand in little knots gazing at the shocking reproductions of shocking scenes, with every manifestation of profound interest, if not of extreme enjoyment. They seem to gloat over these horrors, and always to enjoy the worst and most violent atrocities the most keenly; and especially is this so with the younger amateurs. They will compare notes one with another on the merits of the art treasures thus liberally exhibited to them free of charge. They make an excellent audience. No especially malignant bludgeon stroke, no exceptionably wide-gaping wound, no more than commonly generous flow of the vital fluid — and the wounds gape very wide, and the vital fluid flows very freely in most of these pictures — is lost upon them. On the contrary, all these delicate touches find in this special public to which they appeal, a keen and sympathizing appreciation. Nor, to judge by appearances, is the infliction of the punishment awarded to crime, less attractive as a subject for art illustration to these morbidly disposed youngsters than the commission of the crime itself. The prison scenes, and especially those which represent the transactions which immediately precede the last scene of all, are invariably popular; while as to that really last scene, with its prurient display of nooses, and night-caps, and the other horrible paraphernalia of the scaffold, it is always regarded as a thing of beauty beyond the rest, and a joy — if not for ever, at least for a considerable part of the current week.

It is impossible for any thoughtful man to come upon one of these little groups, and not to ask himself whether the habitual contemplation of such representations is a good and wholesome thing for any human being under the sun. Before those who stand thus and absorb with their eyes, are displayed a succession of transactions, in which the desire of vengeance, the lust of plunder, the gratification of ferocity or cruelty, appears as the instigating motive of all sorts of enormities. Blows, stabbings, shootings, violent acts of every kind, are made familiar to all who choose to look, by these prints. Is it good for men — still more is it good for boys — to be familiarised with these things? We do not say that a man or boy will, after scrutinizing one of these representations of active crime simply go and do likewise, because of what he has seen; but we do say that when the time of temptation comes his nature will be all the less ready to resist, because of the habitual familiarity with violence...

These grim representations of cruel and savage deeds spread out before his eyes, and appealing thus, by the strongest appeal of all, to his understanding — such as it is — tend, plainly, to the utter, utter debasing and degrading of his nature, and tend likewise to a horrible imitation of a long series of horrible examples...

[W]hat this particular public seems to like best of all, is a detailed history of the last hours of some well-known malefactor — a kind of murderers' Court Circular... The description of the machinery of punishment is executed with an especial relish. At last we get to 'the pinioning': a scene which gives an opportunity for a little of that hero-worship which the true penny-a-liner almost always indulges in when describing the last hours of a malefactor. We get to the hangman too now, and have occasion to mention him by name more than once: which seems in these cases always to afford infinite satisfaction both to writer and reader.

The concluding moral is as familiar today as it was one hundred and fifty years ago — that which we do not understand we must perforce condemn:

Now who can be the better for all this? Who can be the better for discovering that by committing a great crime a man instantly starts into celebrity, becomes the observed of all observers, has his doings described, his sayings recorded, his bearing, looks, and manner, made the subject of careful investigation and comment?

Is any one deterred from the commission of a misdeed by reading in nauseous and minute detail that some one else has been similarly guilty? Is any one kept from blood-guiltiness, by reading those morbid scaffold chronicles? The influence of such reading is, as events have proved, exactly the other way. We are imitative creatures, and the influence of bad example is notoriously great in the criminal world. Any offence of an exceptional kind, and distinguished by exceptional characteristics, is sure to be followed by another, and another, wonderfully like the first in all respects.

If not envy then hypocrisy might well be detected here. For Dickens himself was throughout his career, whether as a journalist or a story-teller, continually attracted to the repulsion of crime and punishment, of courts and condemned cells. The most popular, certainly the most gruesome, of his public readings was the unforgettable account of the bloody murder of Nancy by Bill Sikes. Who would dare to suggest that the habitués who made up his audience were prompted by higher motives than those of the True Crime amateurs crowded round the windows in the Strand?

Ever a champion of his readership's predilections, George Purkess was, on more than one occasion, forced to defend himself against this species of quasi-sociological embryonic 'effects study' peddled in periodicals apparently more presentable than his own; against scribblers who considered themselves his betters, ever-ready to accuse the paper of inciting the half-educated and impressionable to commit the kind of violent deeds reported in its pages.

In *Cruel Deeds and Dreadful Calamities — The Illustrated Police News 1864-1938* (British Library 2011) Linda Stratmann cites a letter in *The Times* of March 31st 1870 headed 'Criminal Literature' and penned by a correspondent who had become particularly incensed by the report of a murderer named Mobbs blaming the inspiration for his homicidal behaviour on seeing a picture in the *Illustrated Police News* of 31st August 1867 of the murder of Sweet Fanny Adams by Frederick Baker 'with the severed head of the girl in one hand and a bloody knife in the other'.

A few days later, on April 4th, Purkess, never ashamed of his mission to provide 'the toiling masses' with hebdomadal diversion to 'beguile their leisure hours' and with illustrations to 'assist in fixing on the memory the remarkable occurrences of the times', took up his pen in reply. Stratmann writes:

> He denied that police news came under the category of criminal literature, and pointed out with regard to Mobbs' confession [that] if a picture representing the tragedy had acted as an incentive then: 'in an equal degree did the book to which the prisoner alludes in the following passage: "I had a book about Cain and Abel in my dinner basket." '

As a gazetteer of gore Holy Scripture gives *The Newgate Calendar* or *The Terrific Register* a rapid run. Surely no-one could have been influenced to brutality by exposing themselves to the Old Testament... or could they?

The *Illustrated Police News* accounts take us into a grubby world far different from that recounted in High Victorian literature — even of the most sensational stamp.

Charles Peace in the Police News

As George Purkess himself admitted, Charlie Peace was a gift that kept on giving. The proof of this fascination is evident as he made the lurid front page for an unprecedented eight weeks. From the time of his capture until after his execution the penny-a-line writers progressively reported each new facet of this tale on its emergence as the artists worked overtime. This remains by far the best contemporary source of information about the Case of Charles Peace for, if read in weekly chronological order, the gradual unfolding of the story can be experienced in exactly the same way as it would have been revealed to eager readers nearly one hundred and forty years ago.

August 12, 1876. No. 652

From the short account headlined MURDER OF POLICEMAN NEAR MANCHESTER no-one would have suspected that this report of the inquest into the shooting of P.C. Nicholas Cock could have referred to a murder committed by someone who, a few months later, would be Public Enemy Number One. Dr. John Dill, physician and surgeon residing at Chorlton Road, was routinely quoted: 'The cause of death was the integral haemorrhage produced by the wound caused by the bullet.' The report of this outrage was confined to page 3, column 4.

December 16, 1876. No. 670

Unfortunately, existing copies of the paper are so degraded that the first picture of the murder of Dyson cannot be reproduced. Nevertheless, this issue deserves mention as it marks Peace's entrance onto the stage of public consciousness — in the densely packed type of page 2, columns 3 & 4, under the headline: THE MURDER AT ECCLESHALL. There is full report of the inquest at The Stag, Sharrow Head, in which Mary Ann Gregory, a near neighbour of the Dysons, is quoted:

> 'After the murder I heard Mrs. Dyson say, in answer to a question, if she knew who had done it, meaning who had shot her husband. His name was Peace and she knew him very well... I think I could identify him if I saw him again... He was creeping in front of the house... It was a light night, the moon was shining brightly.'

A verdict of wilful murder was returned against him. A wanted poster was displayed in every police station with a description he had already changed and which offered the massive reward of a hundred pounds upon his head. Peace has arrived.

The First Ballad

By the time Charlie Peace was flourishing, the Broadside Ballads — the 'Chorus From The Gallows' which had been sold in their thousands in the streets and at the foot of the scaffold in the earlier decades of the century — were long since on the wane. In some ways the *Illustrated Police News* took up the baton of Gallows Literature. Nevertheless, the production of such verses at such a late date signals the immediate importance of this man and helps to determine his legacy. The earliest known was knocked out by a provincial poetaster in Peace's home town of Sheffield shortly after he had murdered Arthur Dyson, the husband of his lover. It was published by William Rose, Letter-press Printer, Steelhouse Lane, Sheffield.

THE NOTORIOUS BLACKHEATH BURGLAR.

PEACE,

THE MURDERER OF Mr. ARTHUR DYSON, Civil Engineer, Banner Cross.

THE HORRIBLE MURDER OF ARTHUR DYSON BANNER CROSS ECCLESHALL NEAR SHEFFIELD

On Wednesday Night November 29th 1876.

A most cruel murder we have to relate
And how a poor man met an untimely fate
The murder in Eccleshall has startled us all
But that fatal night everyone must recall.

The victim is dead and soon laid in his grave
No-one had time his dear life to save
The moments flue past when he receiv'd his death wound
For alas! he was found nearly dead on the ground.

CHORUS: Arthur Dyson was murdered deny it no-one can
Charles Peace they say that he is the man
Eccleshall near Sheffield was the scene of the strife
When poor Mr Dyson lost his dear life

It was on Wednesday night this deed it was done
Murder! it struck terror in the heart of each one
Charles Peace met his poor victim at night
With a loaded pistol he took his dear life
It has brought grief and trouble on many minds.
Almost heart-broken are those left behind
The poor wife is left in this world forlorn,
For the one that she loved is now dead and gone.

At Banner Cross the foul deed was done
Peace tried to decoy Dyson's wife from her home;
How shocking to think he met such a fate
His poor loving wife her grief must be great.
May God sooth her sorrows in this world of care
For the loss of a loved one we know is sincere.
But we hope that his soul took its flight that night
With the angels above in the realms of night.

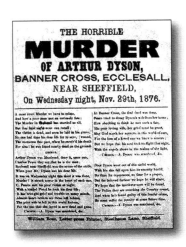

Poor Dyson went out of this sinful world
With his sins full upon him to eternity hurled;
No time for repentance, no time for a prayer
But the beloved Saviour we hope he will share.
We hope that the murderer soon will be found
The police they are searching the country round
And when he's found guilty of this fearful crime
He must suffer the penalty at some future time.

Two Years Later

There was, understandably, no more mention of Peace during the months in which he pseudonymously evaded capture as John Thompson — first in Nottingham and latterly in the seething metropolis. However, A POLICEMAN SHOT BY A BURGLAR did surely warrant a report and a dynamic front page illustration of a generic gonif with a sharpened jemmy in his right hand and a pistol in his left firing at a bearded copper as he is bodily restrained from front and rear by two of the capital's uniformed finest.

A POLICEMAN SHOT BY A BURGLAR.

October 26, 1878. No. 767

Naturally, there was no knowledge at this time that the burglar in custody for the shooting of daring P.C. Robinson, was the Banner Cross Murderer or that the notorious portico thief Charles Peace had been solely responsible for the one-man crime wave sweeping the more salubrious suburbs of South London.

> Burglaries have been frequent in the neighbourhood of Blackheath... the houses selected being generally those with a garden in the rear... It is thought that the man who shot the constable is the principal actor... and that from his mode of procedure and the housebreaking tools found upon him, it is evident he was no novice at his work... On being charged with the offence, the prisoner refused to give any name or address and, as his face was stained with walnut juice, he was mistaken for a time for a mulatto.

Having previously refused to give any name he was eventually brought up on remand at Greenwich police court as 'John Ward, aged sixty.' Little did they know...

November 16, 1878. No. 770

On page 2, column 5, comes the startling revelation. THE GREENWICH BURGLAR AND ALLEGED MURDERER. At last the connection is made, though no knowledge of how his real identity was discovered is reported.

> The police then became aware that night after night the most audacious depredations were committed in the district. Scarcely a night passed but a burglary was announced. The value of the booty was exceedingly great and thieves — for they were then believed to be a gang — were said to be well rewarded for their audacity.

And now the first appearance of a core motif in the legend: his double life at Peckham: 'a gentleman of independent means' by day while 'night after night the houses of leading residents in the locality were broken open, and quantities of plate, jewellery and other valubles were stolen.' The furnishings of the Evelina Road villa become necessary props to stimulate working-class aspiration. The reader peeks in through the lace curtains of suburbia at possessions only dreamed of, never affordable by the slim pickings of honest toil.

> His home at Peckham was a most beautifully furnished abode. In the drawing room was a suite of walnut worth fifty or sixty guineas, a Turkey carpet, mirrors, and all the etceteras which are considered necessary in the house of a gentleman in his position. Upon the bijou piano was an inlaid Spanish guitar, worth about thirty guineas — the result of some depredation. His sitting-room was a model of comfort.... Charles Peace prospered. He added to his store of wealth and music.

Within a week of this and other such reports the home life of our dear Peace at his *cottage ornée* was already the subject of comedy.

CELEBRITIES AT HOME.
(In anticipation of the " World.")
Mr. Charles Peace, Cracksman, Equipped for a Burglary, enjoying "a Musical Evening" at his Cottage Ornée at Peckham.

This cartoon appeared in Issue 208 of *Funny Folk* on November 23rd with the artist paying especial attention to the sumptuous décor. Though the image of Peace is not yet fixed, the 'musical evening', details recounted by dumbfounded neighbours, has already become *de rigeur*. In the absence of firm knowledge of the true domestic arrangements in Peckham, the Peaces are depicted as a more conventional family unit, with the wife seated at the piano and a young son presumably packing the tools of his father's trade. The puzzling contradiction between musical connoisseurship and portico thievery was crucial in raising the reputation of Charles Peace above that of every other professional criminal. The song on the music stand is, appropriately, *I Am Coming*. His *soirées* would continue to occupy an obligatory role in future representations.

There is an element of suspense in this week's report. 'The whereabouts of Mrs. Dyson, the widow of the murdered man, are at present unknown and it supposed that she may have returned to America... every effort will be made to discover [her] and when she is found a writ of *habeas corpus* will be applied for to secure the presence of Peace at Sheffield to answer the capital charge.' *Cherchez la femme.*

November 23, 1878. No. 771

Little to report on the Peace front this week but the *Police News* scribes keep the pot boiling in the secure knowledge that juicer revelations must perforce soon emerge. On page 4, column 4, THE BURGLARIES IN SOUTH LONDON AND THE SHEFFIELD MURDERER, another leading member of the *dramatis personae* is introduced: Hannah. She was 'brought up on remand charged with receiving stolen property obtained by Peace' having 'returned to Sheffield with two boxes filled with stolen property'. Her first recorded words are: 'I am innocent of receiving the property knowing it to be stolen... I don't care what you do with me.' It would become crucial to her defence to establish herself as the legitimate spouse of the accused as, under law, a wife cannot be treated as accessory.

In the absence of hard fact there is recourse to anecdote:

> A Sheffield gentleman has communicated an extraordinary story to Peace's adventures in 1853, when he was a member of an amateur dramatic society, connected with which were several young men who have now attained very good positions in the town. The dramatic company made their first public appearance at Worksop, where they obtained the use of the theatre for a week for £5, which they could not raise after all, and one of the members of the company had to leave his watch for security. The bill announced the opening of the theatre for six consecutive nights during the Christmas season of 1853 [and] described Peace as 'the star of the company... who would perform six tunes on one string of his violin.' The performances were announced under the patronage of the nobility of Worksop and the neighbourhood, and the prices were fixed at 3s. 6d. and 1s, and for this sum the public enjoyed the acting of 'two lady professionals' specially engaged by the company. The first night was a great success. The house was crowded and Peace, after the screaming farce, was introduced to the audience by Mr. A. Clarke, now of Springwood Road, Sheffield, who said: 'Ladies and gentlemen, this is Mister Peace, the Modern Paganini, who will now play a number of solos on the violin on one string. If any gentleman doubts his ability to do so he is at liberty to examine the violin.' Peace then played the violin under his leg, behind his back, and in many other positions, but in the midst of his performance the lights went out, and the entertainment was concluded by candlelight. The house realised £10 that night, but the dramatic venture was a failure for the remainder of the week and some members of the company were so reduced that they had to subsist on turnips. Mr. Clarke states that Peace borrowed the violin he used at Worksop, and when he returned to Sheffield he pawned it, instead of returning the instrument to its owner.

The legend begins to form.

November 30, 1878. No. 772

Just over a month following the arrest of a 'half-caste' in Blackheath and here he is occupying an iconographic space for which he was destined. Granted, it's only the top third, but in the forthcoming weeks he will knock off every possible competitor and make the front page of the *Illustrated Police News* his own. This is the Parnassus of Criminal Celebrity. Only one accolade could possibly trump this dubious honour: a permanent fixture in Madame Tussaud's Chamber of Horrors. Don't fret, Charlie, this is just a matter of time.

The layout of the images of PASSAGES IN THE LIFE OF CHARLES PEACE THE BURGLAR suggests nothing less than an iconostasis, a hagiographic reversal where scenes from the life circulate around a depiction of the anti-saint.

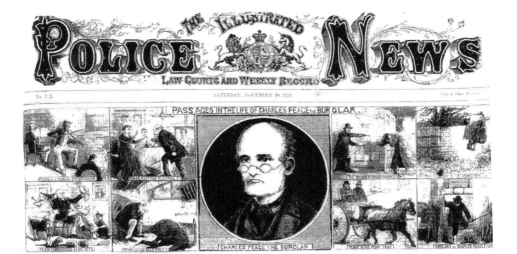

THE ILLUSTRATED POLICE NEWS
LAW COURTS AND WEEKLY RECORD
SATURDAY, NOVEMBER 30, 1878

PASSAGES IN THE LIFE OF CHARLES PEACE THE BURGLAR

CHARLES PEACE THE BURGLAR

This central image is of CHARLES PEACE THE BURGLAR, 'the respectable gentleman', bespectacled with receding hairline, stiff wing-collar, resembling a non-conformist minister. How was this icon obtained? He looks nothing like any of the police mug-shots which, presumably, have not yet gained wider circulation, nor like his image on the wanted poster which he had gone out of his way never to resemble. This is the nightmare next-door neighbour — he seemed like such a nice man, so normal.

The eight images, four on either side, confirm and secure what is already in the process of becoming public property, binary oppositions foreshadowing Freud's 'discovery' of the unconscious. On the left, Peace as he must have appeared in accounts by Peckhamites: PEACE AS A PUBLIC ENTERTAINER; PEACE A LITTLE PLAYFUL; PEACE SURROUNDED BY HIS PETS; PEACE AND HIS DEAD PONY. On the right is the Shadow Self which can only be generically imagined: THE BANNER CROSS MURDERER; ESCAPE OF THE MURDERER; PEACE IN HIS PONY TRAP; BURGLARY BY CHARLES PEACE. Some might cavil that these woodcuts might have been reversed — after all crime is 'the left-handed side of human endeavour.' But we read from left to right: the overt appearance and the hidden reality. It's Jekyll and Hyde, not vice versa.

This is what the eager public could have absorbed *gratis* in the newsagents' windows. Should anyone have invested a penny for a copy they would have seen that now he's invaded page 2, occupying all four columns, and that the pictures are far from fanciful but all founded upon forensic actuality.

First comes an account of his trial for the assault on P.C. Robinson, the policeman who is fast becoming a popular hero as, although severely wounded, he 'manfully stuck to his prisoner, although the latter was armed with a sheath knife, and used all but superman effort to stab the plucky officer.' Peace ('altogether an unlikely looking man for deeds of such desperate enterprise') pleads: 'I have this to say, my lord, I have not been fairly dealt with, and I declare before God that I never had the intention to kill... all I meant to do was to frighten him in order that I might get away.' Mister Justice

Hawkins will have none of it: 'Notwithstanding your age... I should fail in my duty to the public if I did not pass upon you the extreme sentence of the law for the offence of which you have been convicted, which is that you be kept in penal servitude for the rest of your natural life.'

The irresistible cliché cannot be avoided: 'The old adage that "truth is stranger than fiction", is forcibly exemplified by the career of Charles Peace — that is, if the extraordinary accounts given of his doings are to be relied.' Details to titillate the prurient begin to surface, adding sex to the mix: 'He lived latterly in style in London, occupying a large and elegantly furnished house. He also indulged in two lady "housekeepers".'

It is now even conjectured that 'Mrs. Thompson, the prisoner's housekeeper, whose statement first led the police to suspect that the Blackheath burglar was Peace, is none other than Mrs. Dyson herself'! How cracking would that revelation have been for a publication which could say what few novelists would dare? Sadly, this dramatic trope was not to be confirmed. Though we do learn that the so-called Mrs. T. must have been the one who 'peached' on him, supposedly prompted by jealousy to betray him. The plot thickens and she, as yet without a name of her own, must have disappeared immediately after making the revelation and the police have not been able to find her... although, as they always say in these cases, they 'have a clue.' Another *femme* to be *cherchez*ed. Now there are three.

Evidence of life at Evelina Road continues to be unearthed by one intrepid reporter who has evidently personally pounded the thoroughfares of London SE and who buttonholes his audience in the first-person. They coagulate around three indispensable recurring themes of 'rare rascality':

(i)   His music: frequently Moody and Sankey's *Sacred Hymns and Solos*, a legacy of his evangelical past with, on the guitar, his seventeen-year-old stepson Willie Ward (the introduction of another bit player whose role will remain marginal) and with the harmonium preferred for sacred music. Mister Knight, who delivered the milk, was inspired by this odour of sanctity: 'in days of doubt there are still those who give us hope of a return of the age of faith.' The milkman also gives a rather different account of the appearance of the house in the early morning: 'things were higgledy-piggedly — all the kitchen utensils seemed in a mess.'

(ii)   His fondness for dumb creatures: 'When Tommy his pony died he is said to have burst into tears... He had four dogs of the white Maltese terrier breed, two goats, two cats, a number of rabbits and half a dozen Guinea pigs.' And a new element:

(iii)   His scientific ingenuity, attested to by his attempt to take out a patent for raising sunken vessels — presumably a more legitimate method of getting his hands on hidden treasure.

Out-of-town readers might take some pride: 'Never before has a provincial scamp jumped so suddenly and completely into Metropolitan conversation.'

Stop Press: MRS. THOMPSON DISCOVERED. 'I have been informed where she is but for obvious reasons have promised not to state it... She is in safe keeping... She is not Mrs. Dyson... but who she is I know not yet... She is in a state of fear and trepidation'.

December 7, 1878. No. 773

Nothing new to report, but Purkess blows on the glowing embers with this small ad on the top of column 1, page 4:

December 14, 1878. No. 774

True to last week's announcement, FURTHER INCIDENTS IN THE LIFE OF PEACE THE BURGLAR take up the central section of the front page with MRS PEACE (SKETCHED IN COURT) in the middle. Hannah, three-quarter profile, looks rather demure in her flowery bonnet. Above her are three scenes from 'the extraordinary charge against Lady Gooch' — doubtless a forgotten scandal of crim con — whilst underneath is a block depicting A MAN MISTAKEN FOR AN ESCAPED GORILLA and THREE DAYS AT SEA IN A CHEST. Such proto-surrealist juxtapositions are par for the course in the layout of these *faits divers*.

Flanking Hannah are four square pictures on either side beneath a cameo of, on the left, Hero CONSTABLE ROBINSON (artistically evoked in traditional portraiture style by defining objects: lantern, rattle and truncheon) and, on the right, Villain PEACE THE BURGLAR (with mask, revolver, violin and harp). The vignettes do not have the detail of *Police News* illustrations at their most graphically lurid, they're rather scratchy, ill-defined, uncharacterised. Beneath the copper: ARREST OF MRS PEACE (could be anyone); THE HOME OF PEACE (could be anywhere); PEACE AND PLENTY (pun waiting to happen); WHERE THE BANNER CROSS MURDER TOOK PLACE (some house somewhere). Beneath the burglar: DETECTIVES EXAMINING STOLEN PROPERTY; WHERE PEACE USED TO LIVE; PEACE SETTLED; MRS PEACE AT BOW ST STATION. Only the first of these attracts attention: One detective strums a banjo while his colleague blows a clarinet — something of the erstwhile anti-estab-lishment radicalism of the Purkess stable might be encoded in this squib. It was only recently that high-ranking members of the Metropolitan Detective Force had tarnished their reputation when they stood trial for corruption, taking back-handers from organ-ised criminal gangs and fitting up less well-connected felons. Charlie was the one-man crime-wave who cocked a snook at London's Finest.

The Burglaries at Blackheath and Greenwich

Scraping the barrel of Peckham revelations on page 2, columns 2 & 3 this week but there is one enticing tit-bit:

> A rather extraordinary fact has come to light since the conviction of the prisoner — namely, the tracing to him of a most elaborate plan of the residence of the ex-Empress Eugenie at Chislehurst, and there appears to be little doubt that if this notorious culprit had made his escape... the public would have been startled by a report of a similar attempt being made at this residence... [A]ll the corridors and principal apartments of the building were correctly marked out and evidently for some dishonest purpose.

Had Charlie really set his sights on the exiled consort of Napoleon III? Readers are likely to be more interested in news of a different widow: 'It is said that Mrs Dyson... is on her way to this country from America for the purpose of identifying the prisoner as the man who shot her husband.' Katherine Dyson is the only one whose testimony can put a rope around Charlie's neck.

December 28, 1878. No. 776
Page 3, column 3: THE BLACKHEATH BURGLARIES. The sound of water being trod as attention is shifted to Hannah. Was she really married to him? There seems to be no proof at Somerset House, so she could be charged as accessory. She mounts a spirited defence: 'What she did was done from compulsion, and she had no guilty knowledge — she was truly married.'

Future criminologists ought to find material here, as other burglaries in the posh houses of south-east London are attributed to Peace.

January 25, 1879. No. 780

Nothing to report for almost a month... but that will soon change. For on page 3, column 5, THE BANNER-CROSS MURDER, it is reported that the crucial witness has been located — Peace will surely be indicted for murder.

Police Constable Walsh, who has passed ten years in Cleveland and is acquainted with Mrs. Dyson's relatives there, was sent to America a few weeks ago in order to ascertain her whereabouts and, if possible, to induce her to return to England to give evidence... The officer has succeeded in his efforts and is now on his homeward journey accompanied by Mrs. Dyson.

Charles Peace and the Hull Burglaries

More back-story and the emergence of another bizarre detail which will become essential to the depiction:

In order to disguise himself he made a gutta-percha instrument, which he wore on the left hand, and which gave him the appearance of a man with one arm.

February 1, 1879. No. 781

At last a real scoop; no speculation or hearsay, no dredging up the past. When it was all becoming a trifle predictable... Good Old Charlie never fails to deliver. His reckless leap from the train window on the journey north towards his committal in his home town has an inherent three-act structure: cunningly confounding his captors through indelicate bodily request, running down the line despite severe physical injury, inevitable recapture. He doesn't disappoint!

Almost the whole of the front page is taken up with THE BANNER CROSS MURDER — ESCAPE & RECAPTURE OF PEACE. Four small blocks document recent events: PEACE IN PRISON DOING THE CONSTITUTIONAL; PEACE AT BREAKFAST AT THE POLICE STATION; PEACE BEFORE THE MAGISTRATE; PEACE IN GOOD SOCIETY, WAITING FOR THE TRAIN.

And in the centre the iconic moment PEACE'S DESPERATE ATTEMPT AT ESCAPE.

The unknown *Police News* artists and engravers excel themselves in this intrinsically mobile, graphic moment. This scene will join other essential incidents in the developing narrative: the outrageous burglaries; the shooting of Dyson; the musical evenings; the fond affection for dumb animals; the suburban harem. With this desperate act he has conspired in his own future representational ambiguity. Vicious villain? Loveable rogue? Notorious outlaw? Warped polymath? Increased circulation assured; mythical miscreant metamorphosised. Thank you, Charlie.

But, always surprising, the bottom rank of pictures shows scenes from WESTON'S GREAT TOUR THROUGH ENGLAND — the American Edward Payson Weston was one of the nineteenth century's great walkers, known as 'The Father of Pedestrianism' Memory has not been so kind to this 'Man in a Hurry'

Charlie's daring exploit is recounted on page 2, columns 2 & 3: ESCAPE AND RECAPTURE OF PEACE:

33

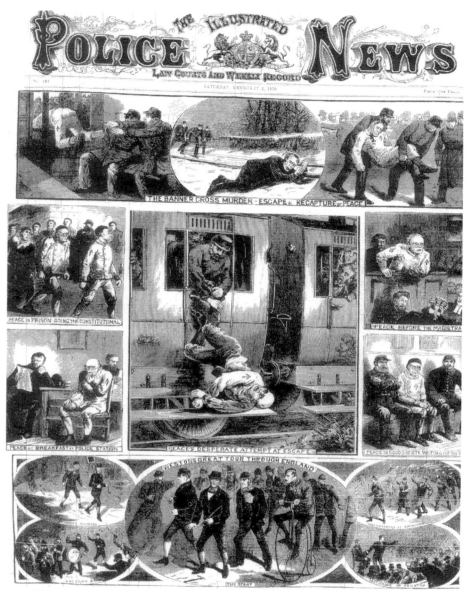

This appears to be the crowning act of his career... He was known to be a bold and reckless man, but few if any were prepared for the exhibition of intrepidity which he displayed on Wednesday morning when he succeeded in escaping from the window of an express train going at full speed...

At Peterborough he was allowed to leave the train for a necessary purpose and when he was requested to return to the carriage he refused. Considerable confusion was thus caused. A large crowd immediately collected, and it was with considerable difficulty that the warders were able to force him into their compartment... As the train neared Sheffield the convict became more restless; and when they passed Shireoaks, a small colliery station... he asked that one of the windows might be opened for his convenience. His request was complied with, and immediately, with a kind of harlequin's leap, Peace jumped through the open space...

He is in the process of becoming a pantomime character: Harlequin, the Trickster who transforms ordinary objects to further his needs with a whack of his magical slapstick, leaping and bounding through trapdoors to confound and elude representatives of conventional society to the envious delight of those not so labile or audacious as himself.

The euphemisms masking the indelicacy of Charlie's subterfuge ('for a necessary purpose', 'for his convenience') only add to the ingenuity of his wiles, deploying bodily functions as the pretext for escape. But the motive is essentially ambiguous, ever open to interpretation. Was this an attempt at flight or suicide?

> A startling discovery was made on Thursday night. It was found that Peace's object in jumping from the train was not to escape, as had been imagined, but that his deliberate purpose was to kill himself... One of the warders found in his pocket a note written in pencil as follows: 'Bury me at Darnall. God bless you all. Charles Peace.'

From now on there is a weekly propulsion towards the inevitable closure: trial, repentance, execution. Charlie is put on suicide watch, then taken to Wakefield Prison — a nick from which he had also tried to escape when confined there in his life before Katherine. His growing popularity is becoming an insult to his captors:

> As he was being carried he moaned piteously, and continued groaning until he was on his temporary bed and covered up under his rugs. In spite of the exertions of the police a great many people gathered about the van in a very short time; hundreds crowded the railway bridge and every point from which a view could be obtained... As the train moved off one person remarked 'He's a plucky dog; give him a parting cheer.' The only response was the retort from several persons, 'Give him a rope, rather.'

Fortunately the forces of law and order can produce their own champion to challenge Charlie's anti-heroic status. For who should be present but Constable Robinson:

> He was the centre of an admiring knot of spectators. He came forward and talked with the convict, whom he little expected to have become so notorious. To the remark of a bystander that Peace could not be a strong man, Robinson replied, 'No, he is not so very strong, perhaps, but he's as slippery as an eel.'

Little did the young copper know on that fateful November night on a lawn in Blackheath that he'd bagged the most notorious villain in the land, ensuring him an enduring role in a continuing popular drama.

Notice of his prowess as a fiddler has become mandatory:

> Peace's friends are doing their utmost to raise money for his defence. They have commissioned a Mr. Harvey, a Sheffield auctioneer, to sell two favourite violins which the convict has been in the habit of using. The largest is a copy of what is known as the Duke fiddle, and Peace has played upon it in various towns.... This small instrument is described as a perfect model, and being very small was preferred by him, as he could manage to play it with his little finger.

The other fascination concerns his complex sexual couplings. 'Mrs. Peace, in spite of all that has transpired, leans strongly to her husband and blames both Mrs. Dyson and Mrs. Thompson.' The intrepid reporter somehow manages to secure an exclusive interview with Charlie and, for the first time, details emerge of his life in Nottingham with the elusive Susan:

In a short time I became acquainted with Mrs Thompson and then I had to exert myself more than I had done. I took a shop in a quiet street and gave it out that I was a 'manufacturer of marking ink' and no suspicion attached to me. After the silk robbery — and my escape through a bedroom window from an inspector — I thought... I had done well, and had money, and could afford to take a holiday. So I went and took Mrs. Thompson with me.

Charlie would make the front page for the next seven weeks.

February 8, 1879. No. 782

Under the banner THE BANNERCROSS MURDER — THE CONVICT PEACE the central cameo shows the only known picture of MRS DYSON SKETCHED IN COURT. In profile she looks far from the alluring beauty of imagination. In a black dress with a lace collar she adopts the role of the grieving widow she will play to such fine effect at the trial.

> Mrs. Dyson... arrived in Leeds on Thursday... dressed in deep mourning having a thick veil over her face... She attracted much attention and curiosity. Afterwards she proceeded to a temperance hotel, and will remain there until the trial.

Peace is now a cowering felon and the other pictures show: PEACE AND THE CHAPLAIN; PEACE AND HIS SON; PEACE READING MRS THOMPSON'S LETTER and PEACE LEAVING WAKEFIELD.

Charlie is not the only game in town, however. For, true to form, these miserable moments are accompanied by illustrations of the *Police News* artists at their bizarre best: DEVOURED BY SHARKS; A PAUPER WITH TWENTY CATS and AN ENCOUNTER WITH A MONKEY.

The trial took place on the 4th of February and, naturally, occupies the bulk of this week's edition. 'The case has excited great public interest, and the court was densely crowded, among those present being a distinguished party from Lord Houghton's, the Vicar of Leeds, the Mayor &c.' But this advertisement comes at the top of page 2 before the process itself is reported:

IMPORTANT NOTICE TO NEWSAGENTS

The entire Front Page of next Week's (Feb. 15, 1879)
ILLUSTRATED POLICE NEWS
Will be devoted to Illustrations in connection with
THE BANNERCROSS MURDER.
TWO LARGE PORTRAITS OF
CHARLES PEACE
One Portrait will present him in his Convict Dress, and the other will be
a representation of him disguised as a Burglar;
with other illustrations connected with this Extraordinary Case.

No. 782   SATURDAY, FEBRUARY 8, 1879.   Price One Penny.

THE BRUTAL MURDER NEAR SANDWICH.

Mr ARTHUR GILLOW.   STEPHEN CAMBRILL.

PEACE AND THE CHAPLAIN.

THE BANNERCROSS MURDER—THE CONVICT PEACE

PEACE AND HIS SON.

PEACE READING MRS THOMPSONS LETTER.

Mrs DYSON SKETCHED IN COURT.

PEACE LEAVING WAKEFIELD.

DEVOURED BY SHARKS.   A PAUPER WITH TWENTY CATS.   AN ENCOUNTER WITH A MONKEY.

The trial itself is something of anti-climax. Mrs. Dyson appears veiled and in mourning to firmly refute any intimacy with the accused; to assert that the apparent love-letters were certainly not in her own hand and to deny the only defence of the counsel for the prisoner could put forward which was that he shot to defend himself as he was under attack from her husband. Her performance evidently sways the jury:

37

After a considerable amount of further evidence had been given, the jury retired. After some time they returned and recorded a verdict of GUILTY. Sentence of Death was passed. Peace uttered not a word.

How can the publisher continue to mine this seam now sentence is passed and execution will take place before three weeks has elapsed? Fear not, Purkess knows his game and would never allow the goose that lays the golden egg to expire along with the guilty party. For another ad appears on page 4, interrupting the account of the proceedings:

NOTICE TO NEWSAGENTS

Will be ready on Wednesday next, February 12th
(Published in Penny Weekly Numbers)

A NEW AND STARTLING ROMANCE ENTITLED
'CHARLES PEACE

OR THE ADVENTURES OF A NOTORIOUS BURGLAR'
WRITTEN BY A WELL-KNOWN AUTHOR

This Novel will disclose Scenes and Adventures
of this Criminal never before published.

EACH NUMBER WILL BE HANDSOMELY ILLUSTRATED.
All purchasers of No. I will be presented Gratis
With No.2 in a beautifully coloured Wrapper.

*The trade are requested to send Early Orders
for the First Numbers of this Extraordinary Romance
which will be Ready on Wednesday next Feb. 12th
Applications for Bills &c. to be sent to the Publisher.*
G. PURKESS, 286 STRAND LONDON W.C.

If real life has a sell-by date and refuses to deliver indefinitely then Peace must be transformed into a fictional character, the protagonist of a Penny Dreadful which will hit the streets before the trapdoor opens for the long drop and can sustain weekly publication for as long as the public continue to show interest. Life will become Legend, Man will become Myth. To few others has this honour been granted — Charlie will join Robin Hood, Jack Sheppard, Dick Turpin in the pantheon of transgression. Henceforth who will know where truth ends and story starts?

February 15, 1879. No. 783
As advertised, the entire front page is taken up with nine pictures of which the middle two are: PEACE THE BURGLAR DISGUISED and PEACE IN HIS CONVICT DRESS (SKETCHED IN COURT). On the left Peace's lower jaw seems extended over his upper lip, presumably with his face dyed, he carries a revolver in his right hand whilst his left is equipped with one of his false arms with a hook at the end — this will

become an iconic representation. In his arrowed convict garb he seems twenty years younger, sprightly even — very different from the sketch his counsel made in court. The top row shows THE TRIAL — MRS DYSON EXAMINED, flanked by cameos of Hannah and Robinson. Along the bottom are four woodcuts showing incidents apparently from THE HISTORY OF PEACE BY MRS THOMPSON but not referred to anywhere in the text: PEACE AND HIS BRADFORD GIRLS (un-named); STEALING WATCH (from a sleeping woman — another conventional image open for continual reproduction); DISGUISED AS A ONE-ARMED MAN and PEACE AND THE JEW FENCE (a stereotypical depiction which will be expanded upon in the Penny Dreadful.)

Page 2 is taken up with an editorial in which, at last, a genuine attempt is made to explain the unique charisma of someone who was, in reality, little more than a common career criminal:

> The peculiar interest in the burglar Peace, says the *Spectator*, is due, we imagine, mainly to an unusual courage and the notion that he was a kind of criminal gladiator, always staking himself against society; but there was a reason for intellectual interest about him, too. He was a man of a type in some ways unusual amongst violent criminals — a man with something of the artist's organisation about him, which is usually accompanied by sensitiveness and is often supposed to be inconsistent with the callousness which is the most marked characteristic of Peace. He was a very fair musician... He was a good carver and gilder, and very proud of his proficiency in those arts, once carving the wood pulpit for the prison chaplain. His favourite device in prison, indeed, for obtaining lenient treatment was to exhibit a kind of universal 'handiness' which conciliated the officials until, though he had once headed a mutiny, he twice obtained remissions of his sentences.
>
> He was ingenious too, as well as artistic. He was mechanical, of some skill, having invented and made the false arm on which he greatly relied to conceal his crimes, as no-one would suspect a one-armed burglar...
>
> He had, moreover, very considerable histrionic faculty, acting all sorts of characters to the police, whom he specially liked to deceive, and 'changing his face' in a way which astonished those who knew him best and made them declare that even they could not recognise him as he passed in the street. He certainly could effect remarkable change in a moment... by bringing the blood into his face till he looked bloated, instead of thin, and this without holding his breath or any preparation... While as an engineer, with his gift for invention and his very peculiar daring (which was not so much courage as a force of will, enabling him to do exactly what he intended to do) he might, had he possessed any virtues, have risen to competence and credit. He was just the man for a mining engineer in a dangerous mine, or to superintend torpedo experiments, or in fact to perform any of the functions in which ingenuity and recklessness have to be displayed at one and same time. He had the power, as he showed in his daring leap from the railway carriage at Darnall, of compelling himself to accept any risk, however appalling, that stood in the way of his design... That form of courage is very rare... Peace's daring never failed him by day or night, under any circumstances of danger or solitude, any more than it fails a ferret or an otter. That such a man should have deliberately elected to lead a life of unsuccessful crime, and violent crime, can only be explained by an inborn propensity to evil...
>
> The man, in fact, liked crime, the double life it involves, the excessive danger it created, the cynical enjoyment yielded... [W]e find no trace of generosity of mercy, such as was attributed to highwaymen, and a spirit of animal ferocity shown to all who interfered with him — rare even in the criminal classes and the more noteworthy because Peace had that love for living pets which, in Europe, is supposed to suggest tenderness of nature — though it was found in several of the French terrorists... He made burglary his business. He was in no temptation from want but robbed on without a reason, except for the pleasure of robbing, the excitement of his business...
>
> There has seldom been a criminal more dangerous to society or one who has misused more various faculties and means... He had perfect courage, great inventiveness and unusual thrift; and used all those instruments of happiness in order to be a completely unsuccessful criminal, who never even secured the fidelity of the woman he seduced, who passed half his manhood in penal servitude and ended it under sentence to the gallows.

All in all, he's a conundrum to Victorian values.

Mrs. Dyson, the 'woman he seduced' is also something of an enigma. Judgment is passed that: 'she was a foolish woman of a vulgar type who accepted attentions from vanity, and was concealing something in her evidence.'

In the news pages there is also a transcription of a letter sent by another mysterious woman in his life: Susan Bailey a.k.a Mrs. Thompson. Making no mention of the fact that she had applied for the reward money, she writes:

> 'My dear John,
> I have had my weary journey from London to this place only to be disappointed. It is too cruel, more almost than I can bear...
> They said only your relatives would be allowed to see you, as if I were not nearer to you than anyone else. I said I wanted to see you on important business, but they thought my going would disturb you. Oh dear Jack, would it be so? For if it be true then I won't ask to go any more. I know, dear, that my visit would do us both good. I should like to see you once more... I, as much or more, wish for mercy for your unhappy soul.
> Bless you — I am your most unhappy SUE.'

What was this important business? Did she wish forgiveness for revealing his true identity?

There is also a tantalising extract from a letter 'said to be written by the convict from Armely Gaol', but to whom is not revealed, in which he gives a first-hand account of his time in Nottingham, heretofore shrouded in mystery:

> 'I went to Nottingham and took lodging at a little shop three or four doors from the police-station in Burton Road right opposite a timber yard where I was stopping and the police-station is on the corner of Leanside.
> I remained with them until they left there and went to live in a yard a bit lower down that led out of Leanside into Narrow Marsh... I remained some time, working Nottingham and the towns round about. I then went to live with Mrs. Adamson, a buyer, next door to the Woodman Inn in Narrow Marsh. It was there I became acquainted with Mrs Thompson...
> At Nottingham I done a big tailor and draper establishment for a lot of overcoats and cloth. I think it is in Castle Gate; it is not far from the end of Bridlesmith Gate... I done a great many gentlemen's houses. I then went to Melton Mowbray and done a lord's house and brought away a great quantity of valueably (sic) jewels besides silver plate... Back in Nottingham I did a large silk robbery in the market place next to the new Post Office. Some short time after this the detectives got some idea that it was me that had done it; one morning they came to Mrs. Adamson's to inquire if I was lodging there; she told them yes; and I was in bed with Mrs. Thompson and Detective Golden came upstairs into the bedroom and awakened me as I lay in bed with Mrs. Thompson, asking me what my name was and where I came from and what I was doing for a living; and I told him my name was John Ward and I came from Bridgewater in Somerset and that I was hawking spectacles. I said if he would go downstairs till I had dressed me, I would show them to him. He went downstairs and I got out of bed and put on my things that I had upstairs and went through the window bars down into the Woodman's public house yard. I went through the house, right round a lump of buildings till within about three doors of Mrs Adamson's house, where the detectives were at, asking the Mrs to go into Mrs. Adamson's and fetch out my boots and clothes, and she went in for them, just at the time the detective was finding out that I had gone through the window bars and made my escape.'

This marks the first appearance of Ma Adamson, landlady and fence.

The tale is gradually revealed in dizzying, kaleidoscopic fashion.

February 22, 1879. No. 784

In its effort to understand, the entire front page shows the PHRENOLOGICAL HEAD OF CHARLES PEACE, THE BURGLAR. NUMBERING AND DEFINITION OF THE SUBJECTS OF THE VARIOUS ORGANS. Magnificent! The acme of pseudo-science!

In the Phrenological Head the various organs are pictorially represented in a series of small illustrations on the cranium. The fundamental principle of phrenology, and those in which it chiefly differs from other psychological systems, are that the manifestations of each of the several faculties of the mind depend on a particular part of the brain, as represented in the several subjects mapped out on the large head in our front page.

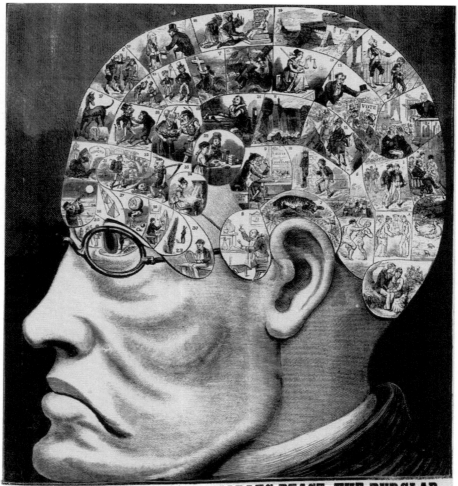

PHRENOLOGICAL HEAD OF CHARLES PEACE, THE BURGLAR.

NUMBERING AND DEFINITION OF THE SUBJECTS ON THE VARIOUS ORGANS.

ORGANISM AS FUNCTION
HEREDITARY ORGANISM AS AFFECTING MENTALITY

Hereditary organic quality is congenital and is imparted by the parentage along with life itself... It depends mainly on the original nature of the parents, yet partly also on their existing state of body, mind and health, their mutual love or want of it... It lies behind and below and is infinitely more potential than education... Each creature much resembles a galvanic battery and its life-force depends mainly on how that battery is 'got up'...

We do not think that anyone will dispute the soundness of phrenology.

Taken altogether Peace's head is a most remarkable one. We are not able to give a definition of the various organs of it at present; but it is to be hoped, in the interests of science, that the authorities will permit a cast to be taken of the notorious criminal.

From a psychological point of view, says the *Medical Press*, the character of this man presents rather a curious study. He seems to be one of those exceptional beings in whom there is an almost innate criminal propensity, and whose famous practices are in themselves as great a source of pleasure and satisfaction as the booty derived from them. Not long ago a distinguished German psychologist asserted that his studies led him to regard the impulse of criminal nature in the light of natural laws. He said that an 'anthropological change' or, in other words, a defective organisation of the brain, lies at the foundation of the criminal propensity of habitual thieves, murderers &c; that the cerebral changes were of so gross and palpable a nature as to admit of easy demonstration in the post-mortem room and that they might even be recognised during life by a careful examination of the criminal's head.

Whether the conformation of Peace's cranism or brain is different from that of most people, we will not venture to say, but, judging from his photographs, a man like Professor Benedkt of Vienna might certainly find some further data for his doctrines in an examination of the prisoner. Be this as it may, we have no doubt that the cerebral organisation of an hardened and determined fellow like Peace must be very different from that of ordinary individuals... None the less true, however, is the materialistic view of the criminal propensity — a view which, unfortunately, precludes all hope of our ever permanently ridding society of such characters. As long as human nature is as it is, we shall have amongst us thieves, murderers, forgers *et id genus omna*. No armour of education, no penal codes, no force of example, or religious or moral suasion, will deter such men from the evil courses, or induce them to lead an honest life. Indeed the very propensity which seems to be 'born and bred' in their flesh is fanned and encouraged by the morbid interest and sympathy of society, which considers itself outraged by their acts. When well-dressed ladies contend for the opportunity of looking at these villains through their opera-glasses, and special correspondents 'are told to watch and record every change in the features of the criminal, and every word and whisper that escapes his lips' can we wonder that such men may even feel as much pleasure and pride in being infamous as their more discreet neighbours do in being honest?

The rest of the reporting in this issue concerns THE BURGLAR'S LETTERS.

To an unnamed correspondent, Peace writes expressing a contrition — real or feigned — that seems to belie the essentialist interpretation of the phrenological experts:

'I shall do my best to prepare myself to meet my God and to obtain his forgiveness, if it is possible, for the sins of my past... imprisonment is much harder now than it has been ever known... I should never have gained my freedom but should have died a miserable death on a prison bed, surrounded by a class of men anything but good and God-fearing...

I am neither a fool or idiot to say that we think there is no God, but on the contrary I know there is a merciful God, whom I have sinned against and broken all his commandments all the days of my life. I hope and trust that I feel that my great load of sins shall be forgiven me by His granting me free repentance, and by my blessed Lord Jesus Christ washing me and cleansing me from my sins and raising my poor soul into the kingdom of heaven where I hope to meet you and all my dear family at the last great day. If any people are so mean as to sneer at you because of me put it down to their badness and take my advice and leave it to their foolishness and God to deal with them.'

The abuses of celebrity reporting then, as now, took their toll on anyone connected with the case, including his Peckham neighbour Mr. Brion. 'In consequence of being so much annoyed by the frequent visits of reporters and others he has been compelled to affix the following notice to his door: "Visitors are requested to communicate their business in writing. No person admitted under any circumstances. (Signed) Henry F. Brion."'

March 1, 1879. No. 785

For the second week running the front page is taken up with one full-page design, the EXECUTION OF PEACE on the 25th of February when 'the last dread sentence of the

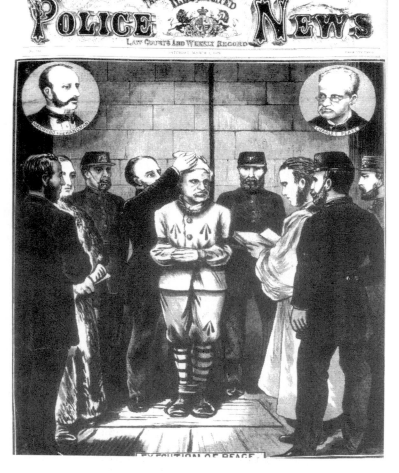

law' was passed; with a vignette of MARWOOD THE HANGMAN in one corner and CHARLES PEACE facing him on the other. This bold design provides the invariable template for future scaffold scenes in the paper.

Public executions had only stopped in England eleven years before; now the scaffold was erected behind prison walls. Journalists privileged to witness the grotesque ritual of the law become the readers' surrogates, taking them close to the dread scene which a decade before they could have witnessed with their own eyes:

> In the old Tyburn days the great attraction of the gallows was for many not so much the sight of a fellow-creature dangling from a rope as his dying speech and confession. The British public supped full with the mere horror of executions in times when stealing from the person any trifle value for twelve pence was grand larceny, punishable by death, and offenders were turned off every day. But there was always the prospect that the criminal would 'die game' — that is, meet his end with bravado and blasphemy... The inventive writers who purveyed the literature of the gallows made his biography their care and hawked his miserable chronicle among the eager crowd for whom his hanging made a holiday... Justice had her revenge, but her victims lived in the ballad poetry of the nation, for even at this very day the songs made upon some of these ancient marauders are sung in parts of Great Britain. All that is over now, fortunately... if Peace is reserving himself for a display he will have to do without an audience... Capital punishment would lose its terror and pain for men of Peace's temperament if it were not ignominiously private... He has continued to be a pest to society after it might be thought that society had disabled him... The life of Charles Peace is just now among the current literature of the London kerbstones and if some condemn many admire him as a superlative villain... It is raking in the sink to publish every shred of evidence between the condemned brigand and his paramours... [I]f, as it appears, there are some who admire the man and his career it will be a corrective of their admiration to know that the peculiarities of procedure which give their hero his notoriety are especially repugnant to the laws and revolting to the people of this country.

One such instance of gallows pamphleteering is *The Life And Notorious Adventures Of Charles Peace*. A one-sheet folded to produce four pages, it has a woodcut of the hanging on the front, far cruder than the *Police News* version, and, on the back page, a poem with a terrible, tasteless pun in the penultimate line of the chorus. It almost scans to the tune of *Grandfather's Clock*, entirely plausible as the song was written three years before in 1876.

At last Charlie Peace is laid on the shelf
Of robberies he's done many a score
He murdered and plundered all by himself
He has gone, he will never do it more.

They've stopped his little game
He will never do it again
To plunder was his joy and pride
He had an artichoke at the end of a rope
When old Peace died.

In death he lies a slumbering: Peace, Peace, Peace, Peace
Half his life he's been plundering: Peace, Peace, Peace, Peace
He had an artichoke at the end of a rope
When old Peace died.

To rob and murder night and day he'd go
He seemed to be Mrs. Thompson's joy
The town and the country old Peace seemed to know
He was a very crafty old boy.

By the windows or the door he'd enter I am sure
He'd fire if for help any cried
But he had an artichoke at the end of a rope
Then old Peace died.

To try and cheat the law it was his desire
Not a burglar like him could be found
He'd as leave shoot a poor man as he would a squire
For he looked on the world with a frown.

From the railway train he tried to get that's plain
As along the line a prisoner he did glide
But he fell down and broke his head
And they thought old Peace would have died.

It fills us with alarm I don't think it's right
They say another murder Peace has done
If he knew he was guilty he kept out of sight
And an innocent had to suffer for the guilty one.

His death bell told the time, he left dear friends behind
The hangman stood by his side
He gave him a hearty choke, but he forgot to grease the rope
When old Peace died.

The reference in the eighth verse to 'another murder' relates to a final shocking revelation. Who could ever have anticipated this unexpected surprise? For shortly before his final walk Peace made an astounding, confession: It was he, not young William

Habron, who had murdered P.C. Nicholas Cock at Whalley Range in August 1876. The Purkessite contingent must have rubbed their hands with glee.

This show will run and run.

Students of criminology are directed towards the interview with Executioner William Marwood of Horncastle, Lincs. where verbatim reflections upon his singular craft occupy several paragraphs. As the self-styled 'inventor' of the 'long drop', the 'scientific' style of strangulation, Marwood is proud that his new-fangled method is a distinct improvement upon the often brutal dispatches of his predecessor.

> It is his business to ply the ghastly trade upon the trap-door of a gibbet. He is the artful manipulator of certain hempen ropes that proclaim in no mean or unmeasured manner the signal supremacy of the British law. His name has earned in many parts of the world an unenviable notoriety. He declares that his mode of hanging is the most merciful one ever known...
>
> He is a man of more than ordinary intelligence, and is highly conversational, never appearing happier than when engaged in his relation of some incidents connected with his calling. He is a veritable fund of anecdotes, and is not at all without a keen sense of the humorous. Marwood has wooed and wed a woman, but no blessings have been vouchsafed the hangman and his wife.
>
> May I inquire what first induced you to your peculiar calling?
>
> Well, from my earliest childhood I evinced a strong fancy for anatomy and when I read that the old 'un, Calcraft, was giving way in years I sent in my application for the first job and so adopted the business.
>
> How many have you dispatched?
>
> A little over one hundred.
>
> What is the difference in the way you execute a culprit and that adopted by Calcraft?
>
> Mr. Calcraft placed the rope differently on the neck. I place it so as the neck may at once be broken and the spinal cord either snapped or wrenched.
>
> What drop do you generally allow?
>
> I never decide upon that until I see the culprit and hear his weight... It is my duty to dispatch them and hope that I will not give them more pain than I can help... At my hands you will suffer very little pain.

The journalist is clearly impressed:

> The hangman answered all my inquiries in a smart, cheerful, business-like manner. In that respect he is far ahead of Calcraft (who) was never at any time disposed to be communicative or familiar with strangers, more especially if he thought they were connected with the press.
>
> Only four reporters were admitted to witness the execution. It appears, from what we have been informed, that as the fatal hour approached Peace broke down and was completely prostrated. He, however, prayed fervently and gave every outward demonstration of sincere penitence. Marwood gave him a long drop which appeared to be efficacious, for insensibility or death appeared to be swift and sudden. There were a vast number of persons outside the walls of Armley Gaol when the black flag was hoisted.

Before his last penitent words were reported the *IPN* lathers up the public with a trailer for the coming feature:

It always pains me to read the words from the gallows of Armley Gaol, Leeds, that bitter Tuesday morning in February 1879. His appeal to the mercy of heaven threatens to undermine the anarchic, excessive, transgressive figure I confess I somehow have come to expect. Don't misunderstand, I would have been terrified to meet the old lag in person, especially in the course of his professional pursuits, divesting our house of cherished possessions.

THE EXECUTION OF CHARLES PEACE THE MURDERER
The chaplain entered the cell at six o'clock this morning and prayed with the convict until a quarter to seven when Peace was served with breakfast, consisting of bacon, eggs and tea. He ate heartily and appeared quite resigned to his fate.
The culprit walked along pretty steadily; he was ghastly pale but he looked remarkably well. While Marwood proceeded to adjust the fatal noose Peace was observed to tremble slightly, but whether from nervousness or the biting cold, as he was but thinly clad, it was impossible to say. Marwood got ready the white cap to place on Peace's head. At this point Peace looked round and spoke to Marwood. 'Stop a minute,' were his words; 'Don't put it on — I want to hear this read.' The chaplain read,
'God have mercy upon us.' Peace responded, 'Lord have mercy upon me. Christ have mercy upon me.'

Did Charlie really revert, at heart, to the evangelical beliefs his zealous father would always have wished him to espouse? Was there truly a genuine death-bed conversion? With some reluctance, these tin tabernacle sentiments of his last-minute piety must be put on the record:

When the chaplain ended his reading Peace, bracing himself up, said, 'Now, gentlemen, you reporters, I want you to notice a few words I am going to say. You know that my life has been base and bad; I wish you to learn I have been a bad man. But when you find that I died in the fear of the Lord you will see what sustained me. I wish to ask the world, after you have seen my death, what man could die as I die if he did not die in the fear of the Lord? Tell all my friends that I feel sure that they sincerely forgive me and that I am going into the Kingdom of Heaven, or else to that place prepared for us to rest until the day of judgement. I have no enemies that I feel anything against on earth. I wish that all my enemies would do so to me. I wish them

48

to come to the Kingdom of Heaven at last. I hope to meet you all in Heaven. I am thankful all my sins are forgiven. Say that my best thoughts, say that my best wishes on earth were to my dear wife and children. Dear gentlemen, I hope that no paper will disgrace itself by taunting them and jeering at them on my account, but will have mercy upon them. I hope that nothing is said hereafter in the press or papers about me to bring distress on my family. Oh, my friends, God bless you, tell my dear wife and children God bless them and may God in Heaven bless you all. Goodbye and Amen.'

Flying in the face of all known facts, I might venture to propose that the reported clichéd homiletic might not be an expression of his own opinion but could possibly have been constructed by the press, complicit with the forces of authority to ensure the condemned man might never serve as a 'role-model' for the easily impressed.

I struggle in vain to re-interpret these pious platitudes as one last cocking of a sarcastic snook — which is why I felt obliged to go so far as to rewrite his speech, putting words into his mouth that I wish he had spoken. But this is what seems to have really happened:

Peace turned around to Marwood and the others on the scaffold and said,
'I am ready if you are.' The chaplain's voice was then heard loudly crying, 'In the midst of life we are in death.' Marwood at this moment adjusted the white cap. When it had been pulled down over the face of Peace, and whilst the executioner was busily adjusting the rope, Peace again spoke to Marwood. 'Take care, I have got but little wind. It is too tight.' 'No, no,' said Marwood, 'be quiet, it is all right. I won't hurt. Are you ready?' 'Yes. God bless you all.' Marwood instantly sprung to the lever and removed the string holding it in position. The Chaplain cried, 'Lord Jesus, receive his soul.' The bolt was withdrawn, the drop fell, and Peace died without a struggle.

But the tale is far from told.

DEPARTURE OF MRS. DYSON FOR AMERICA
Mrs. Catherine Dyson... left Sheffield last week for Liverpool, on her way to America. Her notoriety as the chief witness against Peace has caused her such annoyance that she has determined to leave England. Whenever she appeared in the streets she was followed by large crowds, and once or twice had to take refuge in the police station to escape their attentions... Since the murder of her husband a large fortune has been left to her son, a boy about twelve years old, by a relative on the Dyson side.

This is the first mention that she had a child. Where was this forgotten lad, whose very name remains unknown, when his mother was cavorting with Peace at Sheffield Fair and in the taverns of the town? What became of him back in the USA? We shall never know.

March 8, 1879. No. 786
PEACE'S DREAM THE NIGHT BEFORE HIS EXECUTION. ARMLEY GAOL — FEBRUARY 25 1879 establishes another magnificent full-page front cover template. This engraving, showing 'many of the incidents and events in his sinful career floating before him like the fragments of a hideous nightmare' also became the basis of the beautiful colour print given gratis with a later reprint of the serial novel.

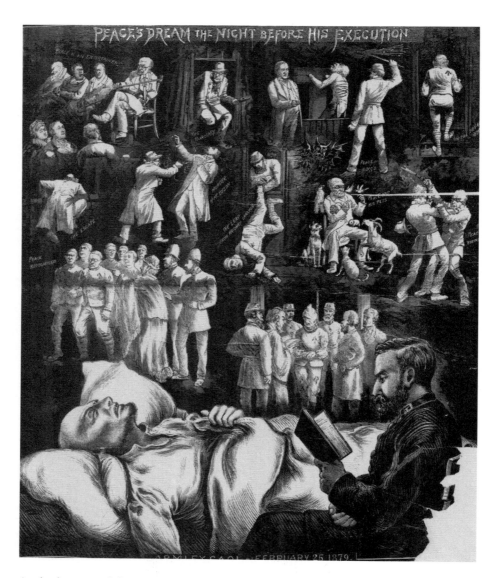

At the bottom of the page a Warder reads, presumably from the Good Book, to the convict lying on his pallet in troubled sleep; with grim visage and unshaven jaw, he bears scant iconographic resemblance to Peace as hitherto represented. Over his head, in three columns, swirl ghostly visions reminding the purchaser of incidents already frozen into folklore. Across the top: PEACE AS AN ENTERTAINER; THE BURGLARY; PEACE FLOGG'D; ON THE TREADMILL. In the middle rank: THE ESCAPE; MURDER OF MR. DYSON; THE LEAP FROM RAILWAY CARRIAGE; PEACE AND HIS PETS; PEACE AND ROBINSON. Immediately above his head: PEACE RECOGNISED and THE EXECUTION (untitled). Should there be any doubt that these are supposed to represent haunting scenes a stylised caricature of a winged devil peeps out.

There is an ironic literary precedent for his 'not particularly edifying religious turn' in a Dickensian character: 'The repentance of Uriah Heep was not a whit more thorough than that of Mr. Peace.' Quilp has transformed into Heep.

The *Police News* was not the only publication to compose an epitaph.

LINES ON A CARD ISSUED AFTER DEATH
Farewell, immortal Peace, farewell
Thy chequered life is o'er
Thy cunning brain, thy nerves of steel
Will trouble us no more.

For thee no pain or grief is felt
No tears of sorrow now
Uncared for by kind or gentle hands
They now have laid thee low.

The Executioner's Story — a Quiet Chat with Marwood

Fascination with the man 'the Irish call the Prince of Executioners' is unabated; the contrast between his grisly vocation and his 'benevolent' demeanour, between 'the great skill attained in the science of hanging' and his 'voice sweet and low — almost as gentle as a woman's' makes him even more unfathomable. An interview given to the *Sheffield and Rotherham Independent* is reprinted in full to expand upon his dealings with Peace:

> A firmer step never walked to the scaffold. I admired his bravery. He met his fate like a man; he acknowledged his guilt; and his hope in God with regard to his future was very good… During the seven years I have officiated as an executioner I never met a man who faced death with greater calmness... It's true he shivered a bit, but not through fear. It was a bitter winter's morning and he complained of the cold... The night before his execution he said to one of the warders 'I wonder whether Mr. Marwood can cure this bad cough of mine?' And I can tell you that a man who jokes about getting hanged is no coward... When I appeared in the doorway he seemed pleased and holding out his hand said, 'I am glad to see you, Mr. Marwood. I wish to have a word with you. I do hope you will not punish me. I hope you will do your work quickly.' 'You shall not suffer pain from my hand.' 'God bless you. I hope to meet you in Heaven. I am thankful to say my sins are all forgiven.'
>
> He was not at all nervous and quietly submitted to my operations. Pinioning is a very ingenious process. I run a main strap round the body; and connected with it are two other straps which take the small of the arm so that the elbows are fastened close to the body, and the hands are free. Peace complained, saying, 'The straps fit very tight.' I replied, 'It is better so; it will prevent you from suffering.' [H]e made a beautiful speech. Such a speech has never come from a condemned man I have executed.
>
> My process is humane... My principles are rapidity and dislocation... I am doing God's work according to the Divine command and the laws of the British Crown. I do it simply as a matter of duty and as a Christian, and I think no more of it than I do of chatting to you now... I sleep as slightly as a child and am never disturbed by phantoms... I work in my shoe-shop near the church day after day until such time as I am required elsewhere.

The demands of the genre have been fulfilled, though the reporter reveals: 'I am not easily frightened, but I find this dissertation on the science of hanging oppresses me. I have a desire to get out of the house, to get into a freer atmosphere; I can almost imagine that if I don't, and that speedily, I shall not escape the long drop myself.'

Charlie is becoming public property. Under the headline THE LATE CHARLES PEACE — ADDRESS AT BARNSLEY there follows a report of the Rev J.F. Hallows, pastor of the Congregational Church, preaching a sermon to between two and three thousands souls on the topic 'Some lessons from the Life of Charles Peace'. He takes as his text Jeremiah ch. 2 v. 19 'Thine own wickedness shall correct thee.' He may be the first, but will not be the last divine to exploit the memory, concluding 'by exhorting those present to learn some lessons for good even from the life of such a bad man.'

March 15, 1879. No. 787

Is there no end to the purposes to which this life can be put? Or was there ever a villain as posthumously generous as Charles Peace? He donated his story to generations of parasitic tale-tellers, of which the present writer is, of course, but the latest. And with his confession of the murder of P.C. Cock he allowed the *Illustrated Police News* to keep his misdeeds on the front page for a few more lucrative weeks. This front page is a mopping up exercise, with a PLAN OF THE BANNER CROSS MURDER DRAWN BY PEACE IN PENTONVILLE PRISON below the masthead.

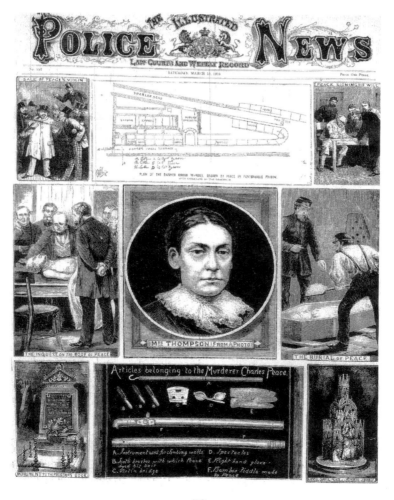

The trade in Peaceiana, vestiges of the dead sinner, is represented by SALE OF PEACE'S VIOLIN (one of many) and ARTICLES BELONGING TO THE MURDERER PEACE. These tools of his trade were purchased by Madame Tussaud's which lost no time in putting them on display. Also in their possession was the MODEL CARVED BY PEACE AS A MEMORIAL TO HIMSELF. This monumental relic of vanity was made using cardboard by Peace in his death-cell in the days between trial and execution. No-one now seems to know whether these precious relics have survived. The macabre reality of his interment is depicted in THE INQUEST ON THE BODY OF PEACE and THE BURIAL OF PEACE — cut up by anatomists and rotting in a lime pit in the grounds of the prison, rather than reposing beneath his memorial.

Such gruesome images flank the only known picture of MRS THOMPSON (FROM A PHOTO) who appears in a full face cameo.

> Mrs. Thompson is a woman of gaunt stature and altogether the very antithesis of the saucy Mrs. Dyson for whom Peace seemed to have formed such a consuming passion. This preference for two women of such opposite appearances may be taken, I presume, as an instance of the happy impartiality of Mr. Peace in his loves. Possibly Mrs. Thompson may owe some of her present uncomeliness to her experience whilst under the protection of the burglar. That she has undergone much suffering I think certain, from the hard and leather-looking hue of her shrunken face. There is an abiding distrust lurking in her cold, restless eyes, which is confirmed by the twitching of her fingers as she speaks to you. There are moments when Mrs. Thompson thaws, as it were, when the curiously Mephistophelian mouth, the corners of which curl upwards instead of downwards with a sharp precision of ominous intent, loses something of its rigidity. That is when Mrs. Thompson is face to face with the whiskey bottle. It is then that the lady becomes communicative. She croons over her connection with 'Charley' referring to the criminal in terms of admiration and horror. It is quite erroneous to say, as some papers have done, that she was educated at a boarding school and is a woman of culture.

Needless to say, none of these details are discernible in the illustration — all three of Peace's known paramours look remarkably similar in the hands of the *News* artists. The encounter must have taken place before the execution as the account ends: 'She appears to be oppressed by a dread that 'Charley' Peace will escape and cut her throat.'

But the story is taken forward with the real MONUMENT TO THE POLICEMAN COCK standing in stark contrast to Charlie's imagined mausoleum. It is becoming increasingly probable that a grave miscarriage of justice has been perpetrated upon the innocent young Irish lad, William Habron. This editorial, reprinted from the *Sheffield Independent*, is not afraid of pointing the finger at the Manchester Constabulary who are accused of 'manipulation of the case — they constructed a theory and then made the facts conform to it.' Habron's trial is revealed as a travesty of justice. Dr. Wade, the surgeon who tended the dying bobby, swore to Cock's dying words when asked if the Habron brothers were responsible: 'Mistake, mistake!' His fellow officers purported not to hear this exoneration and Wade '*was not called as a witness.*'
(italics in the original.)

> This further exposure of the manner in which the case against Habron was patched up by exaggerating the trivial points against the prisoner, and by altogether ignoring vital facts in his favour makes it one of the most glaring examples we ever knew of official zeal degenerating into a most lamentable forgetfulness of fair play... A petition for the release of William Habron was presented at the Home Office on Wednesday.

What really happened at Whalley Range would be the subject of next week's edition.

March 22, 1879. No. 788

This is the last time Peace will occupy an entire front page.

SCENES & INCIDENTS IN THE WHALLEY RANGE MURDER shows at the top left PEACE'S PLAN OF THE WHALLEY RANGE MURDER and at bottom centre the plan itself is reproduced. The small illustrations are of PEACE SCALING THE WALL; POLICE STATION; THE HOUSE AT WEST CLIFFE; MR DEACON'S HOUSE WHERE HABRON WORKED; VIEW OF THE NORTHUMBERLAND ARMS; THE ARREST OF THE HABRONS and POLICEMAN COCK MORTALLY WOUNDED. The centre is reserved for the dynamic rendering of POLICEMAN COCK, SHOT BY PEACE who wears a top hat and long black coat as if he's returning from a night at the opera.

As censure of the police mounts, this provides an opportunity to report, continuing the following week, the inquest on Cock and the trial of Habron. But the breaking news is of the imminent release of the wrongly imprisoned victim.

March 29, 1879. No. 789

THE WHALLEY RANGE MURDER — RELEASE OF WILLIAM HABRON is the subject of two-thirds of the front page The incidents depicted are: HABRON'S ARRIVAL AT MILLBANK; HABRON WORKING AT PORTLAND; HABRON'S ARRIVAL AT MANCHESTER; I SAW MR DEAKIN AND KNEW THAT I WAS FREE; MR DEAKIN HELPS HABRON TO UNDRESS; HABRON HANDCUFFED ON THE JOURNEY; THE ARRIVAL AT MR DEAKIN'S HOUSE and HABRON'S INTERVIEW WITH HIS BROTHERS. This is a story with a happy ending, which, of course, results in some pretty limp illustrations.

I have only been able to trace one ballad about Habron which is in the John Johnson collection of Printed Ephemera in the Bodleian Library, Oxford. It's on a one-sheet which contains two other Peace verses and a crude woodcut of a generic female face labelled 'Mrs. Dyson.' Perhaps significantly it was produced in Liverpool, a city with a large Irish population, by John White, Printer, Rose Place.

THE RELEASE OF WM. HABRON

It's of the cruel fate of innocent William Habron
Who was condemned to die for a deed he never done;
For the murder of a Policeman at Whalley Range near Manchester
He was tried and convicted though not the guilty man.
Upon the day that he was tried he stood by his two brothers' side:

'Altho' I have been wild' he cried 'I did no-one annoy'
But still he was condemned and to penal servitude did send
Innocent William Habron, the poor Irish boy.

The Government they did agree to set young William Habron free
His freedom and his liberty once more he will enjoy
And with a kind and welcome hand when he goes to his native land
They will receive poor Habron, the innocent Irish boy.

They ought to be more careful before they swear men's lives away
Or take from us our liberty which we so dearly prize.
They do not care or feel the smart of breaking his poor father's heart
Who went back to old Ireland in death to close his eyes.
If Charles Peace had not confessed to relieve his guilty breast
Poor Habron by his sorrow opress'd his hard Fate would bewail
A dreary life of servitude in misery and solitude
Poor William Habron would have lived and died in a gaol.

We know he fervently did pray that he might live to see the day
When this dark cloud would pass away and the murderer be found.
He's had to suffer years of pain, although he never did complain
He only wanted to clear his name to all his friends around.
The evidence it was not clear but it nearly cost him life so dear.
The gallows to him seem'd so near he was prepared to die.
Was it not a dreadful shame to brand him with a murderer's name
And send him away from home and friends in a convict gaol to die.

No one knows but those who feel the pressure of the tyrant's heel
Which every day and hour reveals in Penal Servitude.
Charles Peace, as you know, would rather die than he would go
The gallows did no terrors show like that fearful Solitude.
Many a man is suffering there, in misery and dark despair
Who perhaps had never a share in what he's sent there for.
Tis hard to be in such a place & to have the name of such disgrace
Like innocent William Habron, whose troubles now are o'er.

Charles Peace the burglar done his best to relieve poor Habron so opprest,
The wrong he done he has redress'd and got him free once more.
But the troubles that he has gone through and the slavery work he's had to do
The confinement he's been subject to, who's to pay him for.

Sent away on this pretence, of comfort robbed to a very sense
He ought to have some recompense to fill his heart with joy;
A hundred pounds they should pay down, the people say in every town
For the cruel false imprisonment of a poor Irish boy.

THE RELEASE OF WM. HABRON.

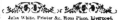

It's of the cruel fate of innocent William Habron,
Who was condemned to die for a deed he never done;
For the murder of a Policeman at Whalley Range near
Manchester,
He was tried and convicted though not the guilty one,
Upon the day that he was tried he stood by his two
brother side:
Altho' I have been wild he cried, I no one did annoy
Yet alas he was condemned, and to penal servitude did

Innocent William Habron, the poor young Irish boy,
The Government they did agree, to set young William
Habron free,
His freedom and his liberty, once more he will enjoy,
And with a kind and welcome hand, when he goes to
his native land,
They will receive poor Habron, the innocent Irish boy

They ought to be more careful ho'ere they swear mens
lives away,
Or take from us our liberty which we so dear a prize,
They do not care or feel the smart of breaking the poor
fathers heart,
Who went back to old Ireland in death to close his
eyes:
If Chas as I escaped had not confess'd to relic his guilty
breast,
Poor Habron by his sorrow oppress'd his hard fate
would bewail.

A dreary life of servitude, in misery and solitude,
Poor William Habron would have lived and died in a
gaol.

We know he fervently did pray that he might live to
see the day,
When this dark cloud would pass away and the murderer be found.
He's had to suffer years of pain, although he never did
complain,
He only wanted to clear his name to all his friends a-
round.
The evidence it was not clear, but it nearly cost him
dear,
The gallows to him it seem'd so near he was prepared
to die;
Was it not a dreadful shame to brand him with a
murderers name,
And sent him away from home and friends, to a convict
gaol to lie.

No one knows but those who feel the pressure of the
tyrants heel,
Which every day and hour reveals in Penal Servitude;
Charles Peace, as you do know, would rather die than
he would go,
The gallows did no terrors show, like that fearful
Solitude.

Many a man is suffering there, in misery and dark
despair,
Who perhaps had never had a share, in what he's sent
there for,
Tis' hard to lie in such a place, & to have the name of
such disgrace,
Like innocent William Habron, whose troubles now
are o'er.

Charles Peace the burglar done his best, to release poor
Habron so opprest,
The wrong he done he has redress'd and got him free
once more,
But the troubles that he has gone through, and the
slavery work he's had to do,
The confinement he a been subject to, who's to pay
him for,
Sent away on this pretence, of comfort robbed to a very
sense,
He ought to have some recompense, to fill his heart
with joy,
A hundred pounds they should pay down, the people
say in every town:
For the cruel false imprisonment, of a poor Irish boy.

John White, Printer &c, Ross Place, Liverpool.

LINES ON THE SAD FATE OF CHARLES PEACE.

The scaffold now has done its duty,
And sent a murderer from this world,
Cha les Peace he has been executed,
And to eternity his soul.
On the 25th of February,
Upon the drop Charles Peace did stand
To be sent before his heavenly Maker,
For breaking of the Lord's command.

For the murder of Mr. Dyson,
Charles Peace has met an awful doom

And his career at length has ended,
He sleeps for ever in a felons tomb.

He made a full and free confession,
When he found his guilt was known,
That his crime so sad and cruel
Upon his trial was clearly shown.
He had no mercy for his victim,
And none to him the judge could give
He had disgraced the name of man,
And was no longer fit to live.

Day and night he has been guarded,
By the wardens in his cell,
As each lonely day departed,
With fear of death his courage fell.

He's been a burglar and a murd'rer,
But his career it now is run,
At Armley he was executed
And suffered for the deeds he's done.

From his cell out to the scaffold,
Thro' the chilly morning air,
The Bannercross murderer was con
ducted,
And looked a picture of sad despair,
His sad career was quickly ended,
As the fatal bolt was drawn,
Beneath his feet the drop descended,
And Charles Peace died a death of
scorn.

What deeds of daring we must tell the like was never
seen
The Banner-cross murder brings to light;
In every town in England such commotion there has
been.
When they read the murderers fierce determin'd
Charles Peace you'll understand, has been a terror to
the land,
Dick Turpin and Jack Sheppard of renown
He was the Prince of robbers, he never join d no band
But his guilty deeds at last have brought him
down.

Charles Peace has suffered death, and with his latest
breath,
He acknowledged that he well deserved his
doom.
He's been a villain all his life, and caused trouble, pain
and strife,
But now he moulders in a murderers tomb

There's never been his equal in defying of the law,
The detectives he used to laugh to scorn,
His wild career is over he can not rob no more,
It were better that he never had been born,
A bold ingenious man, to always was his plan,
To plunder people for ill-gotten gain,
Had he used the gifts God gave him like an honest man
His character would never had a stain.

The murder of Mr. Dyson, there is no one can defend,
Life is sweet to every one we know;
He had no cause to bring his victims life unto an end,
We have no laws for Mrs Dyson he would show.
no right to judge, but every one must say
That perhaps the murderer was not all to blame
But he has had to suffer the fruits of being gay.
And on the gallows died a death of shame.

With courage so determined no man ever knew,
When travelling down to Sheffield on the line,
The window of the express train the convict he leap'd
through
Hoping that his life he could resign.
His time it had not come, his race it was not run,
Tho' bleeding from the wounds upon his head
On the line they saw him lying, Charles Peace was
nearly dying,
And in his heart he wished that he was dead.

On more than one occasion he has boldly fought for
life,
With his revolver fastened to his hand.
He commenced all his troubles when he forsook his
wife,
As all you married women understand,
'Neath adismal beam of wood, upon the drop he stood
A picture of death and misery,
Upon that Tuesday morn, the fatal bolt was drawn,
And Peace was launched into eternity.

MRS. DYSON.

April 5, 1879. No. 790

The following week there are only two more pictures relevant to the story:

WILLIAM HABRON INTERVIEWD by MARWOOD

WILLIAM HABRON
INTERVIEWED BY MARWOOD

and

MEETING OF HABRON WITH
HIS MOTHER AND BROTHER.

Purkess & Co. are running out of steam.

April 12, 1879. No. 791

The final transcription of the Habron trial indicates that the long-standing coverage of the case of Charles Peace is over... almost.

And finally... A letter, presented without comment, concludes the story. It is from A. F. O. Liddell, presumably some pen-pushing, salaried Home Office civil servant, to the Chief Constable of Lancashire. It remains capable of provoking outrage one hundred and thirty years after it was written — perhaps because we have witnessed other scandalous miscarriages of justice against innocent Irish accused.

MEETING of HABRON WITH HIS MOTHER and BROTHER

Sir,

With reference to the late inquiries in the case of William Habron and the confession of Charles Peace to the murder of the policeman Cock in 1876, the Secretary of State desires me to convey to you and the force under your command his thanks for the exertions you and they made to elicit the truth, and the assistance that you afforded him in forming a decision on a very difficult question. In doing this I am to add that the Secretary of State wishes it to be understood that he does not consider that his decision, under the altered circumstances of the case, can be treated as altering the views which were first presented to him by the learned judge, namely, that the evidence of the police was given with fairness and impartiality, and absence of zeal and eagerness; and the manner in which the duties of the police have been performed throughout meets with his approval.

Whitehall whitewash.

William Habron in a New Character

It has always been my contention that if Charlie's father had continued as a showman, exhibiting lions and tigers in a fairground menagerie, and that his son had followed in his showbiz footsteps, or that his billing as 'The Modern Paganini' had been financially successful, he would never have resorted to a life of crime. Though Charlie never became a convincing music hall turn, William Habron, strangely does appear to have had his board-treading moment, as this perplexing notice from the *Edinburgh Evening News* on Friday the 23rd of April 1880 seems to confirm:

> William Habron, who was sentenced to death for the murder of Police Constable Cock at Whalley Range, and afterwards released on the confession of Charles Peace, was exhibited on the stage of the Theatre Royal, Accrington, on Wednesday night. Habron appeared for the 'Benefit of the Two Macs' who were performing at the theatre and who, the bills announced, were friends of Habron. The building was crowded and Habron, on making his appearance, was warmly cheered. He wore evening dress and had four medals on his breast. He briefly referred to his trial, his conviction, and sentence, the confession of Peace and the receipt of the reprieve. He thought there was no one in that building had been so near death as he had. The grave intended for him was open for four days and he was measured for his coffin several days before the date fixed for his execution. Fortunately for him, Peace the notorious burglar, made a full confession and he was set at liberty just at the brink of death. Habron spoke for several minutes, and before retiring thanked the audience for the warm reception given him, remarking that he was not accustomed to public speaking.

No-one could begrudge William Habron making a few bob from his dreadful ordeal, but surely an audience in the North West would have been well aware that this Irish-born Manchester lad had his sentence of death over-turned more than two years before Peace confessed to Cock's murder. The scene of his last-minute reprieve on the brink of execution is pure melodrama, the true facts are quite startling enough.

If nothing else, this clipping demonstrates that reality shows are anything but a product of contemporary television.

***

These extracts from the *Illustrated Police News* are sufficient to confound the hatchet jobs of envious critics. The prose is generally measured, the presentation of facts is usually reliable, speculation is corrected when conflicting evidence emerges. This is no mere recycling from the dailies. There is genuine reportage here with journalists pounding the pavements, door-stepping, meeting the principals face to face, securing interviews that scoop the '*Times*es and the *Telegraph*s'. No other contemporary journal comes close as a repository of primary source material. True, the woodcuts might be criticised as frequently static and often generic, but it is in the layout of the blocks where true creativity resides; it is in the unexpected coincidence of clashing incidents for which they should be celebrated as valid instances of popular art. George Purkess had every reason to be proud as he banked his substantial takings and returned home each evening to his mansion in Regent's Park.

Here is a sample from the forty-two of Purkess's BOOKS FOR THE MILLION on offer which *The Adventures of a Notorious Burglar* would soon join:

G. PURKESS'S PUBLICATIONS.

Now Ready. Complete. Price 3s.

THE COOK AND HOUSEKEEPER: A Journal for Every Home. "The Cook and Housekeeper," as its title indicates, is a periodical devoted especially to subjects appertaining to domestic life and the management of the household.

BOOKS FOR THE MILLION. With Illustrations.— Price One Penny; by post, Threehalfpence, or the set, post free, Two Shillings.

1. Napoleon's Book of Fate.
2. Raphael's Chart of Destiny.
3. Egyptian Circle of Fortune.
4. Bird-Keeper's Companion.
5. Complete Angler.
6. Complete Toast Master.
7. Letter-Writer's Assistant.
8. Ladies' Letter Writer.
9. Swimmer's Handbook.
10. Card-Player's Handbook.
11. Poetry of Flowers.
12. Wishing Cards.
13. Modern Reciter.
14. Pretty Tales, containing Dick Whittington, Forty Thieves, Jack the Giant Killer, Children in the Wood, &c.
15. How to Obtain a Situation; or, Hints to the Unemployed.
16. Family Washing Book, containing a Complete List for each Week's Washing.
17. Ladies' Washing Book.
18. Gentlemen's Washing Book.
19. New County Court Act.
20. A New Game of Forfeits.
21. Rules of Every Day Life.
22 and 23. Christian Names—2d. the two Numbers.

Complete, Price 6d.; by post, 7d.

THE MYSTERIES OF THE EAST END; or, The Whitechapel Murders. —A Thrilling Romance.—This sensational story fully describes all the details connected with these diabolical crimes, and faithfully pictures the night horrors of this portion of the Great City.

Just Published, 1s.; post free, 1s. 1d. Or in cloth, 1s. 6d.; post free, 1s. 7d.

THE PHYSICIAN: A Family Medical Guide. Containing upwards of 250 receipts for the prevention, treatment, and cure of nearly all the ills incidental to the human frame, with advice to the healthy, rules for the sick, tables on digestion, &c. Also a treatise on consumption By Eminent Physicians. Carefully copied from the prescription book of a London Chemist of thirty years' experience.

Now Ready. Complete.

CHARLES PEACE; or, The Adventures of a Notorious Burglar. This exciting story, "The Life of Charles Peace," will be found a story of absorbing interest, in which are detailed the many thrilling episodes in which this notorious burglar sustained the principal character. With a hundred illustrations and Portrait of Charles Peace, bound in cloth, 10s., post free, 10s. 6d.

Now Ready.

THE LIFE OF CALCRAFT THE HANGMAN. This extraordinary romance forms a complete History of this most remarkable man. Partly compiled by Himself. It gives an authentic account of the various executions during his fifty years of office. Containing upwards of Thirty Illustrations, together with other interesting incidents never before published. Price 2s. 6d., bound in a handsome cover. By post, 2s. 8d.

Now Ready, the Complete Edition of

THE LIFE AND PROPHECIES OF MOTHER SHIPTON. Collated from contemporaneous Manuscripts and printed Pamphlets which have been placed in the hands of the Author. Beautifully illustrated. Price 1s., by post, 1s. 2d.

Bound in handsome red cloth, Price 7s. 6d.; by post, 8s.

BUFFALO BILL: His Stirring Adventures in the Wild West.— Contains a coloured picture, "The Attack on the Deadwood Coach," and upwards of seventy illustrations.

G. PURKESS, 286, STRAND, LONDON, W.C.

The publications of others who advertise in his columns seem far more scurrilous than those of the publisher, including:

The Forbidden Book. Illustrated 3s. 6d.

Adventures of a Woman 2s. 3d.

Priests, Women and Families or Tortures in Nunneries Exposed
and Appliances Illustrated 2s. 2d.

Matrimony made easy; How to win a sweetheart and Advice to the Single 1s

Confessions of a Lady's Maid, plates 1s 8d

Nervous Debility, its speedy alleviation and permanent cure, by a new and simple process with the necessary prescriptions and dietetic rules to be observed during the treatment. Address H. Bromley, Goldhawk-road, Ravenscourt, London W.

A sad postscript comes from *The Illustrated Police News* of December the 7th, 1892:

DEATH OF MR. G. PURKESS

We regret to announce that Mr. George Purkess, proprietor of the *Family Doctor* and this journal, died on Saturday morning at his residence in Avenue-road, Regent's Park, from tuberculosis. A few weeks ago he underwent an operation, and was thought to be going on well... Deceased was highly esteemed by a large circle of friends... Mr. Purkess was a Freemason and a liberal contributor to various funds.

His funeral took place in Highgate Cemetery. But his work lived on.

The Legend is Formed: the So-called 'Penny Dreadful'

Our granddads in past days enjoyed
The penny dreadfuls by E. Lloyd...
These books that once we used to read
Are like the Great Auk's Egg indeed.
Perhaps a copy you have got
Of Spring-Heeled Jack and all the lot...
The yarns we loved in days long past
And now I'll make this line the last.

That's a massively filleted version of *An Ode To Ye Penny Dreadful* written by Barry Ono — 'The Penny Dreadful King'– real name Fred Harrison. He is not remembered today as a comedian, an impersonator of his fellow music hall performers, a purveyor of doggerel or a councillor for Camberwell. Rather his name lives on because of his collection of nineteenth-century popular fiction, an El Dorado 'bigger than all the museums of the world combined'.

In 1937 Ono filmed a short piece for British Pathé News in which he displayed for the camera some of the gems he had collected. Few copies of these inherently ephemeral publications had survived into the twentieth century, as they were, in Ono's words 'ruthlessly stigmatised... confined to flames'. On his death, four years later, he bequeathed his priceless treasure trove of more than seven hundred items to the British Museum. Without this generosity little would be known about a species of popular fiction once far more widespread than any of the works found in the limited canon of scholastic curricula of 'English Literature'. The inventory of these wonders is catalogued in a British Library publication: *Penny Dreadfuls And Boys' Adventures — The Barry Ono Collection* (Elizabeth James and Helen R. Smith 1998). This is the stuff which folk had consumed in their hundreds of thousands. That doesn't necessarily make it good to read but, as Lévi-Strauss might have said, it does make it good to think with. For there existed a baleful influence even more insidious than the *Illustrated Police News*.

The *Pall Mall Gazette* (again!), in the edition of the 5th of April 5 1870, sixteen years before the article on the *IPN*, had vented conservative clubman's spleen on this species of periodical of which George Purkess was also a leading exponent.

THIEVES' LITERATURE
Some time ago the unlovely chronicles of the police-court recorded a case of particularly significant character. The theft of a pair of boots disclosed the existence of a robber band composed of five little boys, acting under the orders of a captain whose years of iniquity were not quite fourteen. Every member of the band bore an heroic name. There was a Blueskin of nine, a Jack Sheppard of twelve, a Jonathan Wild of eleven, a Dick Turpin of the same formidable age, and a Sixteen-String Jack, whose years were fewer by three than the garter-strings of his great predecessor.

The depredations of the confederacy were not of a serious character. Sometimes

Wild would sneak away with a pair of boots; Turpin sometimes would ravish a piece of beef from the butcher's open stall; but exploits more daring than these were not charged against either. Nevertheless, the robbers made it clear at the police-court where they were arraigned to answer for their crimes that they had done their best to attain to a heroic ideal, and, conscious of that merit, were enraged when the magistrate showed a disposition to treat them like mere pilferers. He would have sentenced them to a few weeks' imprisonment, but they spurned the degrading mercy, shouting, 'Give us three years! We want three years! We've a right to three years!'...

[S]ince that band of foolish boys was obviously inspired by the names which greatly illustrate the literature of crime, there must have been some revival of letters in the slums of London... Over and over again boys of various grades in life, from the lowest to that which is 'quite respectable,' have been arrested for committing crimes the provocation to which has been found in their pockets, in the shape of some spicy bit of gallows literature...

[S]ensational novelists have arisen in our day to move the heart with murder, to inflame it with arson, to tickle it with intrigue... The tastes they cultivate are not confined to the educated and the rich; they flower in the garret of the seamstress, and they are shared by the grocer's young man as well as by the guardsman. And as the demand is, so is the supply...

Among a filthy heap of 'penny numbers' now before us we find:

Claude Duval the Dashing Highwayman.
Wild Will, or the Pirate of the Thames.
Rose Mortimer, or the Ballet-Girl's Revenge; being the Account of a Virtuous Heroine in Humble Life, the Mystery of her Birth, her Struggles for Bread, her Firmness in Temptation, &c.
Red Ralph, or the Daughters of Night.
The Wild Boys of London.
The Wild Boys of Paris, or the Mysteries of the Vaults of Death.
The Work Girls of London.
The Dashing Girls of London.
Black Rollo the Pirate King, or the Dark Woman of the Deep.
Black Bess, or the Knight of the Road.
The Boy Detective, or the Crimes of London.
Red Wolf the Pirate.
The Dance of Death, or the Hangman's Plot.
Dare-Devil Dick.
The Boy King of the Smugglers.
The Shadowless Rider, or the League of the Cross of Blood, or the Mysteries of the King's Highway.
The True History of John Ketch.
Moonlight Jack, or the King of the Road; the Original Highwayman, afterwards Common Jack Ketch of London.

A catalogue to which we might add many more, and they are sold by tens of thousands.

In appearance these publications are all alike, and their price is the same, a penny. Each number consists of eight large octavo pages, the first page of every number being headed with a wood engraving illustrative of the performance of some crime, or the indulgence of some vice.

It is difficult in a newspaper to show what these publications are really like, because there are certain limits of decency beyond which we are not permitted to range even for the most beneficent purposes. But when the evil is of such magnitude as the regular culture of crime among boys and girls, and when this culture is carried on through the instrumentality of a press which distributes its abominable sheets by thousands every week, we hope we may be excused if we are not over-squeamish in exposing it.

There follows a lengthy analysis of *The Wild Boys of London*, the most notorious of the penny periodicals of the late 1860s, produced by the Newsagents Publishing Company (a neighbour of Purkess on Fleet Street). After its reissue as a bound volume, it was successfully prosecuted in 1879 under the Obscene Publications Act of 1852 in a suit inaugurated by the Society for the Prevention of Vice. The *Pall Mall Gazette* article concludes:

[T]hese publications for little boys and girls — these hideous romances of vice and crime designed to catch the halfpence of lads that run on errands or fag in workshops, and of girls scarce entered on their teens who unhappily fag in workshops too — these are the products of quite a new kind of literary enterprise. What can be done to suppress them? The mischief they do must be enormous. They are never seen by decent people, but they circulate by thousands in the lower districts of London and other great cities. Surely they come under the ban of the law, and it cannot be difficult to discover what scoundrel profits originally by their dissemination. It is a really grave matter.

Evidently the outraged 'gentleman' who penned this spluttering piece considered the spread of literacy among the lower orders, encouraged by the 1870 Education Act, a dangerous advance — the susceptible working classes refused to confine their reading to religious tracts.

But nowhere in this article is the term 'penny dreadful' evoked — maybe because it was not yet in common usage. In his catalogue for the exhibition *Penny Dreadfuls And Comics* at the Bethnal Green Museum Of Childhood in 1983 the collector and historian Kevin Carpenter states that the earliest recorded use he found was in 'the 1874 edition of Hotten's *Slang Dictionary* where it is defined as 'an expressive term for those penny publications which depend more upon sensationalism than upon merit, artistic or literary, for success.'

Christian moralists were fearful of the effects of such stuff upon the moral welfare of boys of all social classes, not just the poor. In *Penny Dreadfuls: Late Nineteenth-Century Boys' Literature and Crime.* (Victorian Studies, Vol. 22, No. 2, Winter, 1979.) Patrick Dunae quotes Lord Shaftesbury addressing a meeting of the Religious Tract Society in 1879:

'It is creeping not only into the houses of the poor, neglected and untaught but into the largest mansions, penetrating into religious families and astounding careful parents by its frightful issues.'

But not every true believer swallowed the conventional wisdom branding cheap periodicals as the scapegoat for juvenile crime. In *The Intellectual Life Of The British Working Classes* (Yale 2001) Jonathan Rose cites a more rational and measured memory of one voracious reader, reported in J.H. Howard's *Winding Lanes*, published in 1938 by the Caernarvon Calvinistic Methodist Printing Works:

> A South Wales miner [born 1875?] raised in an orphanage, acknowledged that 'Robin Hood was our patron saint or ideal. We sincerely believed in robbing the rich to help the poor... Our real heroes were robbers like Jack Sheppard, Dick Turpin and Charles Peace whose "penny-dreadful" biographies we knew by heart.' Yet in later life, as a Calvinistic Methodist minister, he did not condemn the genre: 'It introduced me to a romantic world when pennies were scarce, and libraries far beyond my reach. We read badly printed booklets in all sorts of places, even in church; they gave us glimpses of freedom, abandon and romance, heroism and defiance of fate, whilst we chafed at restrictions and shut doors. True, our heroes... were outlaws. But what boy is not a bandit, a rebel, a pirate at heart!'
>
> As a corrective to natural law-breaking propensities, the 'penny-dreadful' always ended with the punishment of crime.

And the penny papers had some illustrious supporters. The essay *Popular Authors* allowed Robert Louis Stevenson to meditate upon the fiction he had devoured in his boyhood, and to compare works which have crumbled into dust with his own popularity as a writer — which has proved to be not nearly as transient. For the author of *Treasure Island,* the 'effects' of fantasy upon the imagination might be far more complex than the condemnations of the magistrates court would prosecute: 'The tales were not true to what men see; they were true to what the readers dreamed. The reader... migrates into such characters for the time of reading: under their name escapes the narrow prison of the individual career, and sates his avidity for other lives.'

And that great contrarian G.K. Chesterton mounted an even more spirited attack upon the imitative fallacy of the crass 'cause-and-effect' merchants in *The Defendant* (squibs collected in 1901 but written earlier). Here he stands up for such common matter, anathema to haughty aesthetes and ultra-modern immoralists, as 'farce', 'slang' and 'detective stories.' For him, as for his creation Father Brown, higher truth resides in paradoxes to confound and bamboozle thought which is apparently rational. It is perhaps no surprise that, in this metaphorically legal guise, he accepts his first brief and steps up to the bar in *A Defence of Penny Dreadfuls*:

> It is the custom, particularly among magistrates, to attribute half the crimes of the Metropolis to cheap novelettes. If some grimy urchin runs away with an apple, the magistrate shrewdly points out that the child's knowledge that apples appease hunger is traceable to some curious literary researches. The boys themselves, when penitent, frequently accuse the novelettes with great bitterness, which is only to be expected from young people possessed of no little native humour... [I]t is firmly fixed in the minds of most people that gutter-boys, unlike everybody else in the community, find their principal motives for conduct in printed books.
>
> Now it is quite clear that this objection, the objection brought by magistrates, has nothing to do with literary merit... The objection rests upon the theory that the tone of

the mass of boys' novelettes is criminal and degraded, appealing to low cupidity and low cruelty. This is the magisterial theory, and this is rubbish...

Among these stories there are a certain number which deal sympathetically with the adventures of robbers, outlaws and pirates, which present in a dignified and romantic light thieves and murderers like Dick Turpin and Claude Duval. That is to say, they do precisely the same thing as Scott's *Ivanhoe*, Scott's *Rob Roy*, Scott's *Lady of the Lake*, Byron's *Corsair*, Wordsworth's *Rob Roy's Grave*, Stevenson's *Macaire*, Mr. Max Pemberton's *Iron Pirate*, and a thousand more works distributed systematically as prizes and Christmas presents. Nobody imagines that an admiration of Locksley in *Ivanhoe* will lead a boy to shoot Japanese arrows at the deer in Richmond Park; no one thinks that the incautious opening of Wordsworth at the poem on Rob Roy will set him up for life as a blackmailer. In the case of our own class, we recognise that this wild life is contemplated with pleasure by the young, not because it is like their own life, but because it is different from it...

It is the modern literature of the educated, not of the uneducated, which is avowedly and aggressively criminal. Books recommending profligacy and pessimism, at which the high-souled errand-boy would shudder, lie upon all our drawing-room tables. If the dirtiest old owner of the dirtiest old bookstall in Whitechapel dared to display works really recommending polygamy or suicide, his stock would be seized by the police. These things are our luxuries. And with a hypocrisy so ludicrous as to be almost unparalleled in history, we rate the gutter-boys for their immorality at the very time that we are discussing (with equivocal German Professors) whether morality is valid at all. At the very instant that we curse the Penny Dreadful for encouraging thefts upon property, we canvass the proposition that all property is theft. At the very instant we accuse it (quite unjustly) of lubricity and indecency, we are cheerfully reading philosophies which glory in lubricity and indecency. At the very instant that we charge it with encouraging the young to destroy life, we are placidly discussing whether life is worth preserving...

[Popular romance] will never be vitally immoral. It is always on the side of life. The poor — the slaves who really stoop under the burden of life — have often been mad, scatter-brained and cruel, but never hopeless. That is a class privilege, like cigars. Their drivelling literature will always be a 'blood and thunder' literature, as simple as the thunder of heaven and the blood of men.

So how does the Purkess weekly rate as a Penny Dreadful? Will consumption lead inevitably to a life of crime, culminating on the steps to the scaffold?

Charles Peace — or the Adventures of a Notorious Burglar

As soon as Charles Peace was arrested for the Banner Cross murder, George Purkess Jr. supplemented his coverage in the *Illustrated Police News* with a sixteen-page pamphlet titled *The Life and Examination of Charles Peace Charged with The Bannercross Murder Containing his Correct Portrait, with Eight other Illustrations* at the cost of one penny. But Purkess had more ambitious designs to keep the coppers rolling in — the story of Peace was far too promising a subject to be done and dusted with his own demise. The *Police News* was advertising the forthcoming serial work even before the execution. On March 1, 1879 the first issue hit the news-stands,

No. 1 was presented gratis with No. 2 in a beautifully coloured wrapper.

Beauty and the burglar

The popularity of this periodical is proved by the fact that it ran for nearly two years, one hundred issues, costing a penny each and, at the start of a new century, the publication could still be bought in a bound re-issued volume.

It is possibly the most extraordinarily digressive work of literature I have ever encountered. It is certainly the most expensive single tome I have ever purchased.

Though advertised as being written 'by a Popular Author' the dementedly divergent nature of the text makes one suspect it to have been the work of more than one writer — identity or identities completely unknown. Such anonymous toilers were designated 'penny-a-liners', defined as early as July 14th 1846 in the *North Wales Chronicle*:

> *Penny-a-liners* are a class of people so called because they are paid three-halfpence a line for what they write. Their meals are Accidents, their board and lodging Offences, and their clothes are generally got out of a Fire. These gentlemen have a phraseology exclusively their own.

The paucity of payment must have proved a great incentive to repetition and deviation, if not hesitation. Such diligence in the pursuit of word count can only be retrospectively applauded. Was the copy delivered straight to the printers ink-wet? Was it ever proofed by Purkess himself or one of his editorial staff?

Though it claimed to be 'Founded on Fact', much of the Purkess periodical was most certainly not. For the first few issues at least, most of the exploits of the titular hero were entirely fictional — establishing a precedent of the anything-but-seamless mixture of fact and fantasy when dealing with Peace's life. However, as the run proceeded this publication became an invaluable resource, a monumental work of inter-textuality, forming not only the most complete anthology of 'true facts' about Charlie Peace's life but also containing, between one cover, invaluable journalism which transcribes unedited texts of interviews with some of the main characters in the story, lengthy quotations from works about prison life and conditions, digressions upon the putative sciences of sociology and criminology... as well, of course, as conventional florid romances and even poems with scant relevance to the main spine of the story.

Does this hebdomadal periodical fit the definition of a 'Penny Dreadful'? It was certainly issued weekly, eight pages for one penny with a woodcut engraving on the first page, available for perusing in the windows of newsagents. But its intended readership could surely not have been juveniles — this is a weekly entirely devoid of boy heroes like Jack Harkaway, and the sordid details of the real Peace's life seem highly unlikely to appeal to the adventure-seeking young.

Long before I managed to lay hands upon a copy of my own, knowledge of this work had exerted a bizarre fascination. I had first read about it in one of the seminal books of my adolescence: *Boys Will Be Boys* by E.S. Turner (Michael Joseph 1948), a groundbreaking work of what would now be deemed 'cultural studies.'

I picked up my battered copy in a musty second hand bookshop — more of a shack by an old railroad track — where I would cycle on a Saturday to stock up on W.H. Johns and Richmal Crompton and, later, Wodehouse and Conan Doyle. But the Turner is the only one of these purchases still in my possession and it is much valued. I assume the book had been misfiled in the children's section because of its title and it was not until I began to read it back home that I realised it was a work of what might be dubbed literary analysis into a neglected genre — boys' fiction — not found on the syllabus at our school. The shop was presided over by a creepy proprietor with unsightly lumps on his face and always bedecked in a brown suit (which must have been brand-new because it was still shining). He had an unwholesome habit of rubbing his hands on his thighs, presumably to maintain the necessary polish, and standing inappropriately behind this young customer as I stretched to remove a Biggles from the top shelf — he was central casting's perfect Uriah Heep. I recall these reminiscences not because I have any great attachment to the personal memoir — my life has been as unremarkable as most others — but because I do feel that it is of some significance for bibliophiles to remember where, how, when and why they first encountered a treasured volume, whether in market-town charity shops or distant libraries where rare items must be opened with care and white-gloved hands. It could be that finding a book is more exciting than reading it.

Turner's description was magnetically attractive:

> One of the 'penny dreadfuls' which took Peace for hero... is a literary curiosity by virtue of the columns of staggering irrelevancies with which the author eked it out. For thousands of words on end Charles Peace was never mentioned then, in an effort to be disarming the author would say: 'We must now return to our hero, who probably many of our readers may think has been left too long unnoticed...' The author of *Charles Peace* was incapable of mentioning an inquest without discussing at length whether inquests served a useful purpose or not, and the behaviour of people who attended them. He could not mention a jail without describing the operation of a treadmill which 'must be terrible work for a fat man. It is possible for such a one to lose three stone in as many months.' At the end of such a digression he naively explained: 'Happily for Peace he was spared this dreadful infliction as the jail in which he was confined did not at that time contain a treadmill...'
>
> The hanging of the malefactor... inspired 1,100 words of discussion on the best

method of dispatching a condemned man; with notes on strangling as practised by 'our estimable ally, the Turk, and despotic Russia', the Spanish garrotte, the German sword, the French guillotine and the Jack Ketch technique in which the hangman perched astride the suspended victim's shoulders to ensure the breaking of the neck.

This sounded like an amazing work — surely the equal of anything in F.D. Leavis's canon of English Literature. It would take forty years before I held a copy in my hands and again saw the woodcut Turner's book had reproduced: *Charlie Peace in the tailor's shop.*

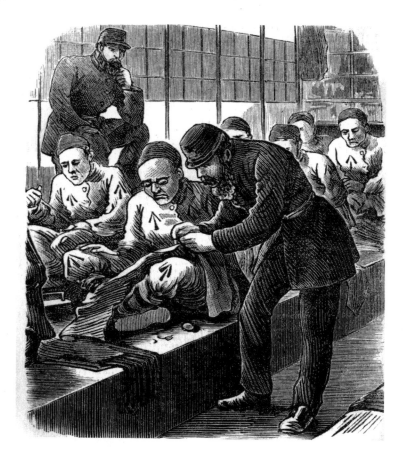

Now it is one of the most cherished occupants of my shelves, proving to be every bit as astounding as I had imagined. Though I obtained it from a book-dealer in Sussex my copy bears the stamp of E.B. SAMMONS of Revell Street, Hokita. Importer of Paper Hangings, Oils, Colors, Glass etc. A click on Google Maps reveals Hokita to be a small town in the South Island of New Zealand, with Revell Street the main road, one block away from the Tasman Sea.

When the hundred issues are collated the whole contains 798 large double-columned pages. The bound volume has a green cover with gold lettering *CHARLES PEACE THE*

BURGLAR The Illustrated Publication on the spine and a red motif of chains and manacles. There are about nine or ten words a line, roughly sixty-nine lines per column, giving something like one thousand three hundred and eighty words per page. As one hundred of those contain a woodcut which occupies nearly all the page, this adds up to a conservative estimate of over nine hundred and sixty three thousand words. Mind you, this is not a record. In that Pathé News clip Ono produces *Black Bess, Or The Knight Of The Road*, one of many thrice-told tales of Bold Turpin Hero, as 'the longest romance in the English language', which ran for an astounding 254 penny numbers, 1,136 chapters with a total of 2,028 pages. But Charlie does seem to have provided material for the longest of Purkess's publications, with only *Buffalo Bill*, a juvenile favourite equally mythologised, as the sole possible rival.

How to describe this extraordinary tome which intermingles fiction and fact in such a manner as to make the reader unsure of which is which? Was this the work of more than one author — one hand for the conventional, melodramatic yarn and another gathering together known facts about the real life of Peace, collecting precious journalistic material from widely diverse sources, performing a vital service for any later researcher who would never be able to trace the originals? To call the writer an 'author' seems unnecessarily high-flown; to call him a 'compiler' seems too dismissively passive. I prefer a term derived from nineteenth-century German Higher Biblical Criticism: the 'Redactor', presiding over a poly-semic *pot pourri*, producing kaleidoscopic postmodernism before there was modernism. Once you get the gist of how to peruse it — and how to skip — it's a truly remarkable read, saving hours in copyright libraries fruitlessly searching for primary sources. This task the Purkess redactor has performed for us, doing us the great favour of saving his own imaginative faculties by simply copying out the originals.

The volume has a title page which was doubtless inserted in an attempt to transform the individual bound issues into a unique volume.

The first woodcut of the first double issue is a portrait of Peace in his guise as 'a respectable gentleman', balding, high-collared, bespectacled with the grave expression of a non-conformist clergyman. He is flanked by iconographic elements such as chains, a key, a lantern, a revolver and a mask, denoting his nocturnal profession. This image bears scant resemblance either to the three known photographs or to the more grotesquely caricatured depictions of the following weekly numbers. Rather it more closely resembles some of the *Illustrated Police News* engravings and could possibly be by the same artist.

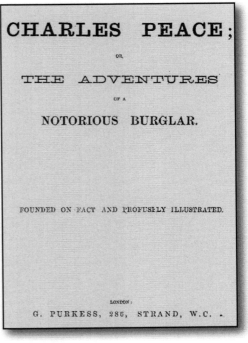

CHARLES PEACE;

OR,

THE ADVENTURES

OF A

NOTORIOUS BURGLAR.

FOUNDED ON FACT AND PROFUSELY ILLUSTRATED.

LONDON:

G. PURKESS, 286, STRAND, W.C. .

CHARLES PEACE

OR THE

ADVENTURES OF A NOTORIOUS BURGLAR

CHARLES PEACE.

The chain motif had long been used to border criminal portraits — as in the 1849 cover to *The Life and Adventures of Jack Sheppard*, the notorious thief and prison escapee from the early years of the previous century. In the Biographical Sketch which precedes Chapter I it is written that Peace was 'equal, if not superior, to the ruffians Jack Sheppard and Dick Turpin, and others of a similar class'.

In this short preliminary sketch the writer worries at the enigma of the man Peace:

> There appears to be a singular absence of motive, both for his general conduct and the murder which he is said to have committed.

An axiomatic mystery man, Peace is defined by a set of shifting binary oppositions: pious and religious/anarchistic and rebellious; supplicatory and charming/reckless and defiant; family man/lover with a magnetic attraction to the opposite sex; by day a citizen of credit/by night a thief and murderer.

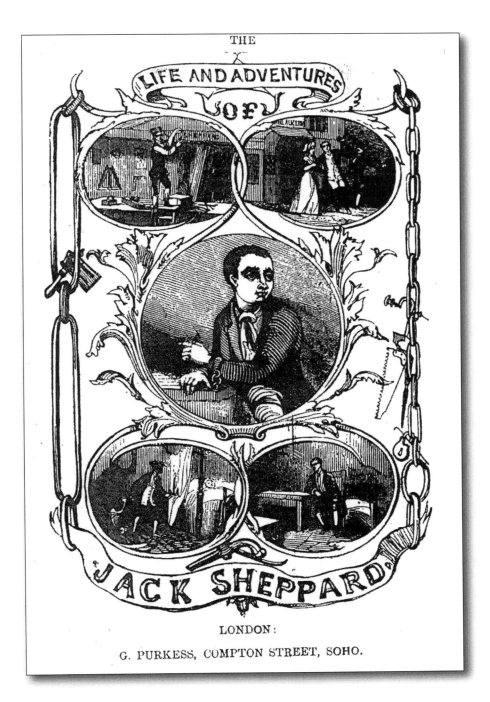

THE

LIFE AND ADVENTURES OF

JACK SHEPPARD.

LONDON:

G. PURKESS, COMPTON STREET, SOHO.

We are told that even dogs felt the influence of his power, and failed to give any alarm on his approach... The history of his life presents a combination of passion, craft, cruelty, great spite and audacity such as is rarely found in any single being... He trifled with Fate. She had made him rich in worldly goods, although they were not his own.

Stressing the veracity of his sources and even quoting verbatim from an apparent interview by himself with the eponymous not-exactly-hero, the author somewhat unconvincingly maintains this will be a work not of mere titillation but of high principle:

> The career of the notorious culprit whose doings are chronicled in this work furnishes the novelist with a moral. It will be clearly demonstrated to those who peruse these pages that, sooner or later, justice overtakes the guilty, and that it is impossible for the most astute and cunning scoundrel — such as Peace proved himself to be — to escape punishment. A life of crime is always a life of care, for the hearts of the guilty tremble for the past, present and future.

This might seem something of a hypocritical justification were it not so seriously expressed. From the outset the initiator of the sensational pages to follow separates this work from all previous instances in the well-ploughed field. Well aware of the condemnation of the moralists, he disarms criticism in advance. There is no way he wishes to be associated with any of those colleagues whose work leads juvenile readers into the dock of the magistrate court:

> The author of *The Life of Peace* reprobates in the strongest degree that species of literature whose graduates do their best to cast a dignity upon the gallows, and strive to shed the splendour of fascinating romance upon the paths of crime that lead to it — to make genius tributary to murder, and literature to theft, to dignify not the mean but the guilty. Let crime and its perpetrators be depicted as conscience sees them, as morality brands them; let them stand out in prominent but repulsive relief. There is yet wanted a picture of crime and its consequences true to nature and conscience, and it is hoped that the present serial will, in some measure, supply that want. The author proposes to present to his readers the felon as he really is — to describe facts as they were found — to present pure pictures of guilt and its accompaniments... It is our purpose in this work to throw a light on the actions and deeds of its lawless hero; not for the purposes of holding him up as an example, but rather as a warning.

Really? This character study in the prologue is very promising... But then, for the next one hundred and eighty pages, the first forty-nine chapters, the first twenty-two weekly parts, the patient reader is treated to a tale which has scant connection indeed with any of the known facts of the life of Charles Peace!

Was this conventional story, populated by such off-the-peg types as 'The Bristol Badger', 'Cunning Isaac the Jew Fence', 'Lord Ethalwood' and 'Bandy Legged Bill, the Gipsy', already written, with the criminal celebrity of the day occasionally shoe-horned in to justify the name above the title? Nevertheless, these haphazardly-numbered chapters have to be tiresomely pored over to mine the occasional nugget of fact. You have to dive deep to uncover the pearls. After a mind-numbing while it becomes apparent that digression and interpolation are not incompetent ravings but the over-riding stylistic principles of this volume. Right from page one the sub-text seems to be that there will never be a definitive version; fiction will always take its inspiration from fact, but fact will forever by structured by the demands of fiction.

> When... at rare intervals, some superior villain appears above the lawless crowd, we find the old tendencies to make the worst of him lingers not dead but sleeping. Our hero is an instance in point. We doubt, indeed, if any individual named in the long

black bead-roll of the criminal character has inspired more invention or figured in so much fancy as Charles Peace.

Quite! So in these early made-up chapters, before the actuality of Peace's life and crimes has settled down, sporadic realities, stranger than fiction, sometimes surface. So in Chapter V he appears, as in reality, as a 'public entertainer... The Modern Paganini':

> Little did those who purchased tickets for the concert imagine that they were about to listen to one of the greatest and most notorious burglars of modern times.

But in these early numbers his exploits are mainly generic.

He is shown robbing a safe.

Playing the violin.

Breaking into an upper window.

Stealing jewellery.

Filching a watch from a 'Sleeping Beauty'.

And making his escape.

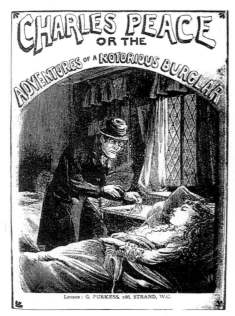

Delirious Digressive Delights

This monumental volume will never be republished, either in whole or even in part. So, having filleted some of the gold nuggets from the dross, I feel it a bounden duty to share some of the experience of actually encountering these pages. What follows is an anthology of extracts from some of the most deviating detours before selecting passages which provide illuminating information about the apparently eponymous hero not readily found in other sources.

CHAPTER L. A VISIT TO THE BLACK MUSEUM

The flimsiest of pretexts provides the justification for a fascinating contemporary account of this secret enclave, containing a bizarre inventory to rival Dickens at his most list-logging.

> This place is one of the sights of London, but it is rare indeed that any stranger is admitted into its sacred precincts. The uninitiated may possibly feel some interest in a description of this receptacle for criminal curiosities. We subjoin an account of the place, which the reader may rest assured is genuine.
> 'Take care how you step,' said a courteous official, who preceded the visitor up a staircase in one of the houses in Scotland-yard, and opened a door on an upper story. 'We are obliged to throw a great deal of this about;' the substance in question was a disinfecting powder... The room is that in which the articles of property taken from convicts are stowed away until they are claimed by their owners...

Overhead is the 'Black Museum,' in which during the last three years *pieces de conviction*, which until then had been kept indiscriminately with the other property of criminals, have been arranged and labelled, forming a ghastly, squalid, and suggestive show.

On entering the lower room the visitor is struck by its odd resemblance to a seed shop....

A motley collection... with a preponderance among them of grimy pocket-books and greasy purses. But there are valuable things in some of those parcels, and downstairs in the officials' room is a massive iron safe, fitted with sliding shelves, in which is kept a large collection of watches, rings, choice pins, scent bottles, pencil cases, and other jewellery, which are either the lawful property of prisoners or have been found in their unlawful possession and confiscated, but for whom no owners have been discovered. Among the watches are some beautiful specimens. One in particular, taken from a costermonger, of exquisite workmanship and ornamentation, is valued at fifty pounds...

Old books, a picture or two, some worthless table ornaments, innumerable articles which could not be described or classed except as odds and ends, form a portion of the collection which goes on accumulating, and which has no ultimate destination.

What is to become of all this? asks the visitor, and is answered to his surprise that nobody knows, that the things are nobody's property, and nobody has the power to do anything with them. A piece of information which makes them more ghastly and nightmare-like to the imagination than before. An ever-growing dust heap formed of thieves' clothing and unlawful possessions, which nobody can cart away to distribute or bury out of sight for evermore — an accumulating banquet spread for the moth, the rust, and the rat — the contents of these rooms are far from pleasant to think of. It seems supremely ridiculous, but it is a fact, that nothing but a legislative measure could rid the premises of these rotting garments, out of every fold of which one might shake with the dust an image of squalor, crime, and punishment.

Across the Threshold... into the Inner Sanctum:

The visitor... passes the heap carelessly, and enters the museum.

What are his first impressions of it?

They are various. That it is like a bit out of a game-keeper's room, with a bigger bit out of a smith's forge, a touch of a carpenter's workshop, a broad suggestion of a harness-room, something of a marine store complexion (and a good deal of its odour), a lump of an open-air stall in front of a pawnbroker's shop, a little of the barrack-room gun-rack, with no bright barrels, enforced a general air of a lumber-room, with just a dash of an anatomical museum; but above all, and increasing with every moment's prolonged observation, a likeness to the cutlery booth in a foreign fair, the articles being so rusty that the said booth might have been shut up for full half-a-century, and the salesman and his customers were all ghosts.

Opposite the door, and on the face of the wall to the right, are displayed on a wooden shelf with iron rings, which convey to the visitor a hint of the open-air stall in front of a pawn-shop in a very small way of business indeed, a common looking-glass in a wooden frame, four black glass buttons, two wisps of rope, a pair of trumpery ear-rings in card-box, two bullets, a pipe, a cluster of soft light brown hair wound round a pad, a comb, a pocket-knife, and a little wooden stand covered with glass, are the most noticeable articles. On the shelf to the right are a dirty Prayer-book, a pocket dictionary, a pair of boots, a gaudy bag worked in beads, and the crushed remains of a woman's bonnet, made of the commonest black lace, and flattened into shapelessness.

[O]ver the shelf fronting the door hung workmen's tools, hammer, and cleaver, and spade, and beside them to the right is just such a bundle as adorns the walls of a marine-store. It consists of a gown, a petticoat of cheap, poor stuff, bearing dreadful dim stains, and a tattered crinoline.

From the general to the specific, physical forensic evidences of known atrocities, perpetrated upon named victims with vicious tools by notorious villains:

> The visitor is in the presence of the objects which perpetuate the memory of peculiarly horrible crimes.
>
> The soft, brown hair is that of Harriet Lane, murdered by Wainwright; the buttons and the earrings are those which were found in the earth where her body had been buried. The bullets were taken out of her skull. The object under the glass case is the several pieces of her skin which completed the identification of her body. The wisps of rope dragged her out of the earth under the warehouse; the cleaver, the hammer, and spade are the implements with which the horrible deed, which led to Wainwright's detection, was done. The knife was Thomas Wainwright's... and when the visitor is leaving the museum he will be shown in the pack-cloth on the floor under the shelf outside the door the wrapper in which the dismembered body was packed, and one of the dirty coats — a horrid thing, with its hideous rents and smears — Wainwright's vesture on the occasion...
>
> Along the wall, on the right side of the room, is ranged a choice collection of guns, crowbars, and 'jemmies,' the latter implements of the housebreaking industry, which admit of great variety, and are susceptible of highly artistic handling; and among them is a pair of tongs unevenly rusted, and with a dirty paper book written all over with incoherent sentences attached to it.
>
> The tongs are those with which a man named Macdonald killed his wife some four or five years ago. He was hanged, as also were many of the proprietors of the horrid labelled assortment of hammers, knives, including the bread-carving and pocket varieties, razors and pistols which suggest a booth in a fair. There is dried blood on all the knives and razors, and some of the hammers also, and every one of them stands for a murder or suicide. In a terrible number of cases they record the murder of a wife by her husband. Several of the pistols, mostly beautiful weapons, are the instruments of suicide, and each is labelled with the name, date, and place...
>
> In a corner hang the clothes of the Rev. J. Watson, who murdered his wife at Stockwell, the horse-pistol with which he shot her, and the heavy hammer with which he knocked the nails into the chest, in which he proposed to hide her body. So carefully had the murderer washed his trousers and his coat-sleeves, that the blood stains could only be observed with difficulty at the time of the investigation. But since the coat and trousers have been hanging on the Black Museum's walls, the stains have come out close and thick...

Who was then allowed into the precincts of a grisly sanctuary, which until recently still existed in New Scotland Yard, and where vestiges of the notorious criminal Charles Peace continue to gather dust? For the past thirty years I have tried in vain to gain access to this hallowed space into which only serving police officers and sanctioned criminologists are permitted to tread. Would I have experienced the same ambiguous feelings of terror, disgust and gallows humour as the Purkess reporter who understood so well that this was a site of distorted pilgrimage, a 'dreary reliquary of crime'.

There can be no doubt that whoever wrote this account had really visited the Black Museum. Peace's own post-mortem memorabilia will soon have an honoured place within these 'sacred precincts.'

CHAPTER LI. FLASH LANGUAGE

I have no humiliation in admitting that I shamelessly plundered this invaluable repository 'of the phraseology made use of by thieves...the reader may rest assured that these are reprints from documents which have been found on the persons of criminals.'

Dear Dick,

I have seen the swag chovey bloke who christened the yacks quick. I gave him a double finnip. I am now on the shallow. I have got the yacks, so do not come it cocum. I am at the old padding ken, next door to puddling crib. I am gadding the hoof, but quick be a duffer, now on the square. I want a stalsman buttoner to nail prads. I last week worked the nulls. I have lost my joiner mun now.

TRANSLATION:

Dear Dick,

I have seen the person who bought the watches, and he altered the name in them immediately. I gave him a ten pound note for doing it. I am now going half naked to avoid suspicion. I have got the watches back again therefore do not turn informer. Be wary and sly. I am stopping at the old lodging house, next door to the boys' lodging-house. Do not say a word, but be very quiet. I am going about without shoes, but shall soon turn hawker. I am at present honest. I want a partner. Will you come and join me, and then we will commence stealing horses? I last week got through a great many bad five shilling pieces. I have left my fancy girl. Be sure you say nothing.

Another:

Dear Bill,

I have seen Cheeks. You must meet us at the old mushroom faker's at eleven; if not there go to the old padding ken — bring all your screws. The case of a bloak is planted, to be cracked, plenty of finnips, also some long tailed ones; be mum with your joiner, fight cocum, and be cocum with boozing kens, only a bloak and a shikster in the case, except a pig. Be cocum crabshells; a goun off was last week booked by a fly through crabs. I have seen a kidsman, who will fence two finnips three finnips. There are no flys about.

TRANSLATION.

Dear William,

I have seen 'Cheeks' (a flash name for an accomplice), and you must meet us at the old umbrella mender's at eleven o'clock, and if we are not there go to the old lodging house. Bring with you all your housebreaking instruments. We have arranged to break the house of a gentleman who has plenty of five pound notes, and also some large bank notes. Be sure you do not name this to your fancy girl. Be careful what you do, and keep from drinking shops. There is nothing in the house but a gentleman and a lady and another person. Do not put on your own shoes, a brother thief did last week and was taken by a policeman. I have seen a person who trains boys to thieve, who will take all the five pound notes at ten pounds for fifteen. There are no policemen in the neighbourhood.

I particularly relish the translation of 'Bill' to 'William'.

Can we imagine that the writer, or redactor, is barely able to suppress his irritation with the demands of made-up narrative and therefore misses no opportunity to shove in factual information at any possible opportunity? A criminologist *manqué*, he struggles to understand the mind of the felon, realising that merely spinning yet another conventional weekly yarn will get him nowhere. Frustrated with the task of writing for a multiplicity of audiences he himself becomes legion. It's as if he's longing for the time when he can quit being a penny-a-liner and become a proper dispassionate reporter, a conveyor of fact, an interpreter of motive, rather than being another tired old perpetrator of fiction whose tedious task is to get his puppets in through the window and out of the door. It's as if he is coming to an understanding that real characters are far more complex than fictional stereotypes — demanding to be explained even though such explanation may be beyond him.

Imaginary tales are, perforce, constrained by the teller's imagination. In stories motives must be clear, the invariable deep structure of narrative demands its *dramatis personae* behave in familiar ways. But the motives, quests and goals of real characters are far from simple and the tools available to the popular storyteller are not fitted to the task of interpretation.

At least, he provides us with facts — lots of facts.

Readers prepared to persevere to the bitter end would be able to pass an exam on the changing fashions in penal methodology in the gaols of the land during Peace's lifetime; they could rival Michel Foucault in their knowledge of outmoded practices of discipline and punishment. They would learn that Bentham's Panopticon, 'in which any number of persons may be kept in reach of being inspected during every moment of their lives', was abandoned as a failure for prisoner reform. They would find out about prison food: 'Sauces were, of course, not thought of, but there was a plentiful allowance of vegetables. Cabbages and parsnips were frequently served out, also rice, pease pudding, haricot beans and preserved potatoes'. They would shudder at the system of prison labour: mat making, rock smashing, oakum picking; about the useless toil of the treadmill or the crank — employed particularly viciously in Leicester where the convict would be refused food or even flogged if he didn't achieve fourteen thousand turns of the handle per day. They would read about 'wretched scrawls disfiguring the walls of the cells, many of which were blasphemous and profane'.

Unfortunately, only one example of such graffiti is transcribed:

> Whillem Meagram came here from the steel
> May 10ᵗʰ 1854 — 5 years for slinging his hook
> Him as prigs what isent hisen
> When has cotched vill go to prison — W.M.

To which is, rather sadly, added:

> Peace, however, has never evinced any predilection for indulging in this foolish propensity, and he professed to be greatly disgusted at the language on the walls. Many sentences were appended which were grossly indecent, and in some cases these were illustrated artistically.

What these were, alas, we will never know.

CHAPTER LXIII. A VAGRANT'S LODGING HOUSE

A scene set at a 'low-looking beer house' close to 'the glories of Bartholomew Fair, of Greenwich' allows for an invaluable detour to yet another of the dark by-ways of the underworld.

> The 'Travellers' Rest' was one of those houses which was known by all classes of mendicants, whether belonging to the *silver* class, or what are styled by all well-informed travellers *barkers*, to the *highflyers* or begging letterwriters to the *shallow coves* or impostors, who in various garbs obtain clothes from the compassionate and charitable to a great amount, and then sell them to the dealers as left-off garments — too often spending the produce in ardent spirits — to the shallow motts or females,

who, like shallow coves, go nearly naked through the world, begging ever for clothes, ever obtaining them, and yet never clothing themselves, but selling them for food, for lodging, for drink, and for the enjoyment of every conceivable vice, as well as to the separate race of beggars and match-sellers, who live by the ordinary tales, true or false, of real or supposed misery, and in which class is to be found much more of suffering than crime, and of destitution and heart-rending woe than we are either accustomed to believe or like to inquire into.

It has been well said that one-half of the world does not know how the other half lives, and the history of mendicants of every degree would furnish the outside public with strange revelations, many of which would appear almost incredible.

The mendicant poor are in every way a different race of beings to the working population of this country. They have signs of their own, a language of their own, plans and schemes of their own — or rather for their own class — homes of their own, or rather barns and out-buildings, reserved by compassionate farmers and landowners for them. They split society into fractions, calculate with tolerable accuracy all their chances, and could tell in many cases how much they should receive in a week. Generally speaking, they are distrustful of each other, living in a constant state of fear of arrest and imprisonment, concealing their own names even from their commonest associates, and changing their announced plans and movements in less than an hour, as they saw with a prophet's eye a lion in their path.

But then how different are their classes!

Once again the loyal readership must put aside their desire for news of the increasingly absent eponymous hero, Charles Peace, for a wonderfully digressive typology of beggary — whether they want it or not:

There's the systematic vagrant, whose life has been one of constant and unchanging mendacity. There is the occasional vagrant, who begs after pea-picking season is over and after hopping has terminated, in order to raise money to go back to London or to the county to which he belongs. There is another class of occasional vagrants, who migrate from a district where poverty and misery assail them, to the place of their nativity or of their former brighter fortunes, seeking for halfpence on their way to provide for their daily wants as they press onwards.

The vagrants in large towns and cities, and principally in the metropolis, are the very worst class. They are in eight cases out of ten rank impostors. They go about with clever concoctions of false documents: statements of losses by fire, shipwrecks, and accidents. They obtain precious attestations, counterfeit signatures of clergymen and magistrates to declarations of having lost their property by fire... Those who work with the *slum* and *delicate* (the statement and book of subscriptions) furnished them by the *smoucher*, often raise large sums of money, which they expend in vice and profligacy.

The shipwrecked mariner's lurk used to be one of the most frequent and lucrative. A person of this character, known by the nickname of Captain Johnstone, followed the lark of a shipwrecked captain for many years. He was an excellent writer, and had a respectable appearance, so the unwary were deceived, and he was enriched. It was said that he obtained some thousands of pounds by his mendacious statements. When any account of a shipwreck appeared in the newspaper which seemed likely to suit his purpose he would write out a new statement (slum), and provide a new book (delicate), and then set to work with the utmost zeal to obtain subscribers.

Polish counts, who had been driven from the land of their birth by Russian tyranny, used at one time to infest London, Liverpool, Manchester, and Bristol, but this form of begging has gone out of fashion.

'The victims of accidents,' wholly counterfeit, 'the sufferers from sickness,' quite unreal, 'the deaf and dumb lurkers,' who seem to be deprived of speech and hearing, 'the servant out of place,' who cajoles the domestics at gentlemen's houses, 'the

81

colliers who have suffered from water suddenly bursting into a coal pit,' and yet who never saw a coal pit, 'the starved-out weavers', who go about with printed papers or small hand-bills, representing that they are out of employ, although they have never seen a loom, 'the cotton-spinning lurk,' with that trick of leaving printed appeals and calling again for them and alms, though they know as much about diamond mounting as cotton-spinning, are a few of the dodges of active, cunning, and shameless mendicants...

'The calenderer's lurk' is another trick, and the doggerel poetry, in which their appeal is made to the 'kind and generous public,' contains amongst a variety of other verses the following record of their own virtues and charity when, as they pretend, they knew better days:

> Whene'er we saw one in distress
> We strove to help him through;
> But now we cannot help ourselves
> We have no work to do.

The final category of shabby-genteel grubbers must have been a perennial scourge of polite society as Dickens had earlier characterised such shysters when shadowing the Metropolitan Detective Inspector Field. Twenty years later the Purkess penny-a-liner gave a name to these confidence tricksters:

The systematic writers of begging letters are also much more common in London than in the country, and rejoice in the name of 'highflyers.' Year after year they invent new cases with different hands, and present their 'appeal,' and thus avoid detection, and collect an abundant revenue for the sins as well as the necessaries of life.

This is worthy to stand beside Mayhew in its proto-sociological categorisation of vagabonds.

CHAPTER LXIV. THE HIRING FAIR

As Charlie used to boast, his father was 'a tamer of wild beasts'. Later in this publication it is written that John Peace travelled with Kensett's Menagererie, rather than the better known Bostock and Wombwell's as is usually reported. So a fairground scene seems not inappropriate, giving rise to this splendid inventory of the marvellous entertainment on offer:

As to dwarfs and giants and giantesses they were innumerable, together with curiosities both natural and unnatural. An Irishman made up as a Red Indian, and called 'Yokoomana the celebrated fire-eater', undertook to put the end of a red-hot poker into his mouth, across his tongue, and on to the soles of his naked feet.

Then there were swings, roundabouts, gold gingerbread, gingerbread nuts, Wombwell's brass band playing their loudest tunes, a horse with two heads and six legs, a mermaid, a wild man caught in the Black Forest, a learned pig, waxwork exhibitions, performing dogs and monkeys, acrobats, Mademoiselle Clothilda Favirini, the celebrated tight-rope dancer who had performed before most of the crowned heads of Europe, a sword-swallower, a Chinaman (hailing from Dublin) who threw sharp-painted swords at another Chinaman (hailing from Cork), the Cork Chinaman standing all the while with arms outstretched against a board against which the swords were thrown within an eighth of an inch of his body.

There follows, naturally, several columns on the history of fairs. But there is also a useful description of the portable theatre shows, in which the tale of Peace was soon to feature so prominently:

> Now the whole company of the very minor theatre were assembled upon the outer platform, and the man with the leather-lunged voice was as vociferous as ever. He was a little hoarse with constant shouting, but this did not matter — he contrived to make himself heard.
> The company on the platform went through a wild pantomime, in which the clown was ill-treated by everybody. He was unmercifully whipped by a man in jackboots, but was heedless of the punishment which, to say the truth, did not appear to affect him in the slightest degree. He contented himself with making grimaces in revenge, at which the people laughed until they cried again. They had come to enjoy themselves, and it did not take much to move them to laughter.
> The external preliminaries having been concluded on the platform of Richardson's celebrated booth the *dramatis personae* retired behind the curtain, the man with the leathern lungs shouting at the top of his voice:
> 'Now's your time, good people; walk up — walk up! You'd better by half come in at once, if you means coming; we are just about to begin. Grand spectacular romantic drama as 'ud move the heart of stone. This way, gentlemen!'
> The harsh clang of unmusical instruments from within, the shaking of the tent, and the delighted shouts of the audience proved the interesting fact that there were still some spots in the world where theatrical announcements were not impostures.

***

Such digressive extracts (and many more could have been selected) show something of the wonder of this publication. But the work has much original material about the founder of the feast, Charles Peace himself.

> We must now return to our hero, who, probably, many of our readers may think has been left too long unnoticed.

Scenes from the Life of Charles Peace

As the weekly instalments progressed towards the second year the chapters containing the barely readable melodrama alternate with journalism which is well-researched and accurate. These sections might not be so gloriously bizarre as the above but as source material they remain unparalleled. This is a periodical which takes its readership seriously and parades its credentials by reproducing verbatim accounts from the main actors, which no other publication had managed, massively expanding upon material in the *Illustrated Police News*. From these chapters a picture of late nineteenth-century life never represented in respectable books emerges in all its quotidian detail.

CHAPTER LXXIV. PEACE RETURNS TO SHEFFIELD — HE TAKES UNTO HIMSELF A WIFE

In this chapter the reader is introduced to Peace's mother and told of a previous liaison before he met his wife, Hannah, which may or may not be invented.

> The first visit he paid was to his mother, who was overjoyed to see him. It has been alleged that he was her favourite child. Be this as it may she always demonstrated a great amount of affection for him. The poor old lady was not much to boast of as far as education or social position is concerned, but she was not credited with either refinement or gentility. Nevertheless, it is likely enough that she had occasion to deeply deplore the evil course some of her progeny fell into, more especially the ways of her son Charles...
>
> Upon his return to Sheffield he resumed his old practice of playing the violin at public-houses. Although this was not particularly remunerative it brought him in some little ready cash, and in the day time he hawked spectacles and other articles.

The actions, emotions, thoughts and motivations of the three women in the story, Hannah, Katherine and Susan, are mystifying. These people in no way resemble the heroines of Victorian literature, high or low. It is only in the pages of a publication looked down on as 'trash' by respectable and moralistic sections of society that some inkling might be gleaned of the real conditions of the real life of real women. So the back stories of all three of them — the loyal widow, the flighty Yankee lady and the Nottingham lass — are given at length as Appendices.

Almost a year into publication the Purkess author (or one of them) begins to express some anxiety about the character of a protagonist whose exploits, fictional and real, are proving so profitable to the company.

> It would be a great misfortune if the boldness and fearlessness of this bad man were to blind even the most thoughtless to the utter worthlessness and depravity of his character. In nothing does his baseness more transparently appear than in the miserable apologies and self-justifications with which his religious experiences are interlarded. Assuming, as we are anxious to do, that these pious utterances of his later days are not wilfully insincere, they none the less betray an utter moral blindness. He was very willing to call his past life base and wicked in general terms, but for his worst transgressions he had some extenuating plea which destroyed the validity of his assumed penitence. If he could have been turned loose upon society again, one can hardly venture to hope that his future life would have corresponded with his edifying conduct in gaol.

The curiosity of the public to know all about Peace and his life need not be regarded with too despondent an eye, provided it goes no further than curiosity.

But whilst qualities like his command so much reverence and win such high rewards in other fields of activity, it would be vain to hope that our full-blooded and high-spirited youth will not see something to admire in his career. If there are any such they will do well to remember that the grandest successes of a criminal course are at the best wretched failures.

Peace has probably had a far smoother life than most offenders of equal activity. Yet he has spent no inconsiderable part of his time in prison, and in the full noontide of his prosperity hardly reaped as much fruit from his misapplied talents as those talents would have yielded in any honest walk of life.

Can such concerns about the influence of Peace upon impressionable youth be dismissed as cake-and-eat-it hypocrisy? I think not, given this thoughtful and confident effort to take issue with none other than the Sage of Chelsea:

Thomas Carlyle, the philosopher of Chelsea, bewailing the degeneracy of the age, complains that we no longer, as in the old days, worship heroes. To us it seem there is no lack of hero-worshippers in the nineteenth century, but that our heroes are of the wrong sort — imperial tricksters like the Third Napoleon, garotters of liberty such as Bismarck, and super-cunning criminals of whom the man who suffered on the scaffold for the murder of Arthur Dyson, at Bannercross, on the 29th of November, 1876, was a shameful example.

How could Carlyle's theories of heroes and hero-worship be made to fit such a one as Charlie? How could respectable people feel admiration for such a celebrity malefactor?

There are thousands of kindly, well-nurtured folk, with a taste for the marvellous, who openly proclaim their sympathy for Peace. They tell us that every time he went out to rob, and, if necessity should arise, to murder, he carried his life in his hand: that he waged a daring and unequal war against the police and society; and that his courage, his resources, and his presence of mind in moments of the utmost danger, point him out as a man capable of greatness in a legitimate calling.

The argument is as worthless as it is specious, for those very qualities are shared in greater degree by predatory wild beasts of the jungle. If, however, sympathy for this sort of social outlaw were confined to ladies and ladylike men, very little harm to society would ensue.

The mischief lies on another and a lower level.

It is a notorious fact that the criminal classes are themselves unduly proud of this sort of superlative villain; and if by any chance he were, at the eleventh hour, to elude the hangman, there would be much joy in many thieves' kitchens.

Nor does the public danger arising from such a career as that of Peace end there. His evil example, in spite of its fatal ending, is calculated to debauch the wild imagination of foolish lads, and every atom of sympathy wasted upon him, every misguided attempt to cast the glamour of romance around his sordid, rapacious, and beastly life, is as a hand held out from the darkness to help the saplings of crime up the steps of the gallows.

Our sympathies are not for such as he.

Such ambiguities of response will in time transform Charles Peace into a folk-hero, but they continue to trouble the text. Who could doubt Peace's ingenuity — indeed artistry? But what law-abiding bourgeois could fail to fear an unwelcome nocturnal visitation from such an artist?

We are sorry for the respectable man whom he sent suddenly out of the world, the man whom he sought to rob of his honour, and did rob of his life, with as little compunction as he was wont to display in robbing his neighbours of their goods and chattels.

We wonder how sane men can feel, much less express, sympathy for the midnight burglar. A man leads an honest, laborious, and thrifty life, and after many years of self-denial surrounds himself with home luxuries, such as plate, jewellery, clocks, and what not. Suddenly a thief comes in the dark, and in a moment casts the shadow of irreparable loss over the decent citizen's existence. Admit that the robber does display a certain sort of brute courage; so does the fox when he steals the poultry; so does the tiger that lies crouching in the jungle and waits for the unsuspecting traveller.

But the farmer traps the fox, and the hunter shoots the tiger, and perhaps praises their courage — over their carcasses.

The origin of the famous false arm, made to conceal the missing fingers on his left hand, is recounted by his step-son, Hannah's lad Willie Ward:

'When father told us where he was stopping, we asked him if he was not afraid of the sergeant's seeing his hand. He said he could not see it, as he covered it up. We asked him how he did it, and he took from his pocket the guttapercha arm you have heard about. He told us he made it himself, and he certainly is very clever at making things. He had got a piece of fine guttapercha, and he made it into a tube large enough to allow his arm to pass down it. Secured to the bottom of the guttapercha was a thin steel plate, in the middle of which was a hole with screw thread. Into this hole he screwed a small hook, and at meal times he said that he took out the hook and screwed into the hole a fork which he had made for the purpose, and with it he used to eat his meals. At the top of the guttapercha was a strap, which he used to fasten over his shoulder, and in that way keep the thing in its place. No one who saw it could have told that it was not a false arm. He made his own tools, which were at once exceedingly simple and exceedingly effective, and once made a saw out of a piece of tin-plate.'

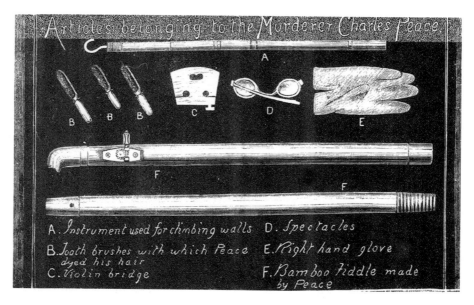

Articles belonging to the Murderer Charles Peace

A. Instrument used for climbing walls
B. Tooth brushes with which Peace dyed his hair
C. Violin bridge
D. Spectacles
E. Right hand glove
F. Bamboo fiddle made by Peace

The enumeration of his many cultural accomplishments only results in greater perplexity:

He had a goat (which he had taught to perform many tricks), a monkey, two dogs, some guinea pigs, and a cat or two — he had always displayed throughout his career a great partiality for animals — and he was an adept in taming them, and putting them through various performances for the amusement of himself, family, and friends.

Indeed he might have succeeded very well as a trainer of animals for performing purposes; as we have already signified he was clever in many ways, but his abilities, such as they were, went for nothing. They were overshadowed and submerged by his passion for criminal pursuits...

He played at this time in the evenings at various public-houses in Sheffield. He had taught his goat to stand on its hind legs and dance to the sound of his violin. This little animal is said to have been a most docile and amusing creature, and Peace made a considerable amount of money by its antics...

He had, moreover, very considerable histrionic faculty, acting all sorts of characters to the police, whom he specially liked to deceive, and 'changing his face' in a way which astonished those who knew him best, and made them declare that even they could not recognise him as he passed in the street. He certainly could effect remarkable change in a moment, and the one which most disguises dark faces, by bringing the blood into his face till he looked bloated, instead of thin, and this without holding his breath, or any preparation.

There can scarcely be any doubt that he could have lived, and lived well as a carver and gilder; while as an engineer, with his gift for invention, and his very peculiar daring, which was not so much courage as a force of will, enabling him to do exactly what he intended to do, he might, had he possessed any virtues, have risen to competence and credit...

Peace's daring never failed him by night or day, under any circumstances of danger or solitude, any more than it fails a ferret or an otter.

That such a man should have deliberately elected to lead a life of unsuccessful crime and violent crime can be explained only by an inborn propensity to evil...

The man, in fact, liked crime for crime's sake, and it was not possible for him to remain long without having recourse to his old practices — he was irreclaimable.

The writer continues to worry away at this enigma which even seasoned officers of law could not unravel:

To say the truth the life of this man is little more than a record of his escapades, troubles and trials, and a detail of the various robberies in which he was engaged. The scoundrel's hypocrisy forms a large element in his character. He was professedly a religious man; the neighbours thought him so, and possibly he thought so too; so he associated with the good folk who congregated in the sacred edifice, but never made himself conspicuous...

One of the inspectors who had been concerned in his capture, expressed his opinion of Peace's character in these words: 'There is not another demon in Europe like him, unless it's the Czar. What sort of scoundrels they have in Asia I don't know.' The words were graphic, but they were spoken with such vehemence as to show that even the London police were surprised at the revelations which were made.

The general opinion of the police was one rather of wonder mixed with surprise, but with a certain admiration for the fellow's cleverness in his profession.

The more inquiries that are made into the past history of Peace, the more does it appear that he was a head and shoulders above the ordinary criminal. He appears to have had ingrained in his nature a cruelty of mind and firmness of purpose which nothing could baffle.

He remains a riddle, his psychological profile inexplicable beyond recourse to a vague notion of 'innate criminality.'

CHAPTER LXXV. PEACE AND THE TRAVELLING SHOWMAN

The following magnificent fictional scene takes place in a tavern where Peace tells Macarty, a showman evidently from the Emerald Isle, a wonderful tale, a short story in its own right, from the unknown days of his childhood when he was travelling with his father's menagerie, casting a beam of light of how fairfolk are supposed to regard the credulity of their customers, who are all too eager to be fleeced.

'Ooh, but we niver draw a line in our business, divil a bit,' said the showman. 'I don't suppose any ovyez have the slightest idaya of the devices and fakements we have to resort to. Why a legitimate an' genuine article in many cases does not attract half as well as a 'fake.' Every exhibitor knows that. Faith, you may draw a line as much as yon plaze, but a man who underestands his business will soon jump over it, or else bedad he'll have to starve. It's the same in iverythin'.

'That's right enough,' said Peace. 'A fake will do more than a legitimate thing. I'll just give you a case in point. My father was a showman, or rather head man to one. He was a tamer of wild beasts.'

'Your father! Ochone, I thought you were a boy after my own heart when I first met you,' cried Macarty. 'Bedad, we mast have a friendly glass together at my expense.'

Glasses were ordered. Peace proceeded.

'When my father was travelling with Kensett's menagerie, and the proprietor was doing a good business in most of the provincial towns, business began to drop off in consequence of an opposition show visiting the same places as Kensett's. There was not room enough for both at the same time, and Mr. Kensett as a natural consequence was greatly annoyed. At one town the opposition shop (Barlow's menagerie, as it was termed), carried everything before them, the reason for this being that they had one of the largest orang-utangs that had ever been brought to this country. The creature was said to bear a remarkable resemblance to the human species, and crowds upon crowds were to be seen daily making their way to Barlow's establishment. Kensett shifted his quarters, and moved on to the next town, under cover of the night. He had not, however, been many hours there before Barlow made his appearance. Poor man, he was perfectly furious when he found that a similar course was adopted by his rival at other towns. Business fell off painfully, and the question was what was to be done under these perplexing circumstances. The orang-utang was the central point of attraction.

'One evening, after a wretched day's business, my father was smoking his pipe with Mr. Kensett, who was at this time down in the dumps, and, as you may imagine, my father was not in the best of spirits. He had been performing with his wild animals to comparatively empty benches.

"He's potted us — knocked us out of time, that's quite certain," said Mr. Kensett. "He carries all before him," returned my father, "and why? because he's got an ugly brute — the ugliest I ever saw — of the monkey tribe. One never knows how to deal with the public. They are so capricious and uncertain."

"Uncertain be d—d !" shouted Kensett, "there's no mistake about the matter! They are pretty certain to desert me for my rival — that is, as far as we can see at present."

"Luck may change, sir," says my father.

"It may and it may not... more of the latter than the former. Ah, it's a bad look-out for the remainder of this tour."

'The two companions lapsed into silence for some little time after this, and puffed away at their pipes. Presently Kensett said, in a reflective manner: "How about Old Jemmy?" Mr. Kensett struck his knee in a self-satisfactory manner. "I have it, old man," he exclaimed. "A bright idea has occurred to me. I have it. We will be down upon this Barlow, and take the wind out of his sails, please the pigs... Listen, you must transmogrify old Jemmy. He'll do well enough for a Pongo, or Wild Man of the Woods, just arrived from Africa... Shave his haunches, then colour them, encase the upper portion of his body with long hair, shave his face and colour it in the most hideous manner it is possible to conceive. I will get out large bills announcing the arrival of a savage monster in this country, which is exhibited now for the first time. 'The Missing Link.' Don't you see? Now I've given you the hint, and it only remains for you to carry it out. No one so well adapted to manipulate a case of this sort. You'll be able to make something of him. Do your best, old man, and upset the opposition shop."

'My father tumbled to the proposition at once... On the following day he set to work. Poor old Jemmy was a venerable specimen of the ape species, he had been in the show for years, and was as tame and harmless as a kitten, and would let you do anything with him. The hair was shaved off his posteriors, a long, shaggy coat of dark-brown hair was sewn round the upper portion of his body, the hair on the lower portion of his face was clipped quite close, then his face was coloured, and he was so completely metamorphosed that his own mother would not have known him. Taken altogether his appearance was at once extraordinary, and like nothing that had ever been seen before or since, I think I may add. A collar was put round his neck, to which a strong chain was attached, and the end of the chain was attached to an iron bar running across the back of the cage. By this means poor old Jemmy was kept in an upright position and compelled to walk on his hind legs. It was, no doubt, a sad trial to the poor brute, who, however, bore it complacently enough.

'When all was in readiness Mr. Kensett shifted his quarters to the next town, having previously beplastered its walls with gigantic posters announcing the arrival of a large Pongo or wild man of the woods, who was so fierce that visitors were cautioned not to approach too near the bars of the cage. Such a monster was surely never seen before. Jemmy was the very personification of ugliness and ferocity.

'Kensett's show was thronged with visitors all day long, and there was a perfect furore with the populace, who expressed themselves immensely pleased with the great natural zoological curiosity. A history of the animal, how it was caught, the nature of its food and general habits was given in a hand-bill presented to each visitor as they entered the menagerie.

'It was related how, in a visit of a British man-o-war to the island of Borneo, a party of the sailors were permitted on shore, and entered one of the dense forests which abound in that island. After some time spent in the search for fruit the party came upon an open glade, and right opposite them, where the forest again commenced, they saw a tree violently shaken. They rushed forward to ascertain the cause, and saw what they thought was a native woman leap lightly from the tree and disappear in the forest. But a hairy monster remained in the tree, and seemed in a furious passion, which was redoubled when he saw the sailors. Breaking a branch from the tree, the wild man (for this was what he was) bounded to the earth, faced the strangers, and then turned to run. But the tars had been too smart for him, and having surrounded him, he was brought to bay and captured, after a sturdy use of the branch of the tree. The "history" went down very well with the women folks, for the writer averred that when the wild man was first seen he was busy belabouring his wife, and thus suffered capture.

'Barlow came upon the scene of action and advertised his orang utang, which was really a fine specimen, but the creature paled before the effulgence of his painted rival, and Kensett's counterfoil brute fairly eclipsed the one in the opposition shop. Barlow was furious. He denounced Kensett as an impostor, and the rival showman had a set-to in the market-place to the infinite diversion of the town's folk; but all was of no use. The Wild Man of the Woods, the Missing Link, as Kensett termed him, carried everything before him, and Barlow's show was comparatively deserted.'

'Is it possible that people could be so silly as to be taken in with such a barefaced imposture?' said one of the company.

89

'My dear sir,' returned Peace, 'in this world are found people silly enough for anything. But it was a barefaced imposture, I admit, seeing that old Jemmy's face had been shorn of its hair.'

'Och, by the powers!' cried Macarty, 'people like to be humbugged and imposed upon. Bedad it was a mighty clane thrick, and desarved to sucsade.'

The good folks in the parlour of the Blue Dolphin had perhaps never in their whole lives learned so much about the doings of showmen, and, as a natural consequence, the evening passed away pleasantly enough.

Though this may not be true it is only too plausible.

***

There follows a useful summary of Peace's previous convictions and the sentences served in prisons in Old Trafford, Preston, Dartmoor, Millbank, Chatham (where he was flogged) and the penal colony at Gibraltar. His final conviction before the momentous events of 1876-9 was in Manchester where he received seven years for breaking into a house at Victoria Park. It was for this offence that he served time at Wakefield, and this chapter gives the fullest account of his daring attempted gaol break, as exciting as it is farcical.

CHAPTER LXXXIV. PEACE'S LAWLESS CAREER — CAPTURE, TRIAL AND CONVICTION — HIS ATTEMPTED ESCAPE FROM WAKEFIELD

The daring attempted escape from Wakefield Prison is one of the most exciting incidents in Peace's life of crime, but it rarely finds a place in the mythos as it predates the events of the crucial years 1876-9. How the Purkess writers got hold of such a racy account must remain beyond speculation.

Peace, as we have observed, was a handy man enough, and this was soon found out by the authorities of Wakefield prison. For the first few weeks after his introduction he was set to work at oakum-picking; but as time went on, and the warders and deputy-governor became better acquainted with his habits, he was set to work at whitewashing, painting, and doing other odd jobs in the prison. He contrived to make himself generally useful, and in addition to this he succeeded in impressing the chaplain with the fact that he was a very devout person, who had seen the error of his ways, and who was moreover duly impressed with the necessity there was for him to reform.

He had been convicted thrice; this fact he could not conceal; but when once he had another chance given him he said he would avail himself of it, and that nothing in the world should ever induce him to stray again from the path of rectitude. He talked so plausibly, entering into elaborate disquisitions upon certain portions of the Scriptures, that the chaplain was fairly imposed upon by the hypocritical prisoner.

Some repairs were being done in the prison, and Peace was one of the gang employed for this purpose. He worked industriously with his mates for some days. Although he was a cunning, clever rascal, and was unscrupulous and daring to boot, he does not appear to have rivalled the celebrated Jack Sheppard, as far as attempts at escaping from prison are concerned.

Once again the great escapologist of the 1720s is evoked, tying a contemporary criminal to a perennial protagonist of the popular prints.

As he was at work the thought crossed his mind that he might succeed in effecting his escape, and when once this idea entered his head he did not rest till he laid out his plan of operation.

The repairs he was executing gave him an opportunity of smuggling a short ladder into his cell. No one for a moment suspected what he was meditating, and, indeed, it would appear that much more latitude was allowed him than usually falls to the share of a convict. He managed to secure a piece of zinc, and took an opportunity of nicking it so that it would answer the purpose of a saw. When shut up for the night he set industriously to work.

The cell in which he was confined was not of a modern structure, with stone walls and an arched stone roof, such as are now invariably used in all our convict prisons. The roof was plaster; in the centre of it ran a beam. Peace had ascertained this before he began his operations. It did not take him long to make a hole in the ceiling. When this had been done he set to work with his zinc saw to cut through the beam.

The cell was one of the top ones; it was in close proximity to the roof. This he had also ascertained — if he could once get on the roof, he felt the rest would be an easy matter.

The chances are that he would not have succeeded in any case, but he was bent on his project, and was in a state of nervous excitement until it was carried out.

This is fine writing, taking the reader into Peace's very thought processes as the wheels of his mind begin to turn.

'I'll do them yet,' he murmured. 'If I gain the roof I shall be able to give them the slip, and there will be one prisoner less in Wakefield gaol, that's all. Ha, ha!' he laughed, at the prospect of doing his janitors.

For the greater part of the night he was at work, but the progress he made was so slow, in consequence of the clumsy instrument with which he worked, that daylight came before he had made a hole sufficiently large for him to pass through.

'The warders will be round presently,' he ejaculated 'and if I am not clean off before they make their appearance I am lost.'

He set to work with renewed vigour; the perspiration fell in thick beads from his forehead and temples. An exclamation of delight escaped him: the aperture was sufficiently large for his purpose.

Proto-cinematic in its breakdown of events, a real sense of suspense is created by the 'inter-cutting' between the escapee and his would-be captors.

He crept through the hole, and then seemed to breathe more freely. He laid hold of the top rail of the ladder, which he was in the act of drawing up after him, when the cell door was opened, and an official exclaimed in a voice of alarm: 'Halloa there, what's this? Come down!'

Peace made no reply. The moments were now precious to him. The officer advanced and endeavoured to seize the ladder. Peace gave him a blow with it in the chest, and knocked him down.

The man uttered an exclamation of rage and pain. But Peace did not wait for further parley: he drew up the ladder and ran along the roof in the greatest state of excitement.

After running over the roof he got onto the prison wall, and he was making his way along there when a terrible misfortune befell him: the bricks were loose, and it was impossible for him to keep his balance or maintain his foothold. He fell. It was supposed that he had fallen outside.

There was by this time a hue and cry after him. Consternation sat on the visages of the warders, and the whole place was soon in an uproar.

The deputy-governor asked what was the matter. The warders said that a prisoner had escaped... Davis, the warder who had been pushed down by Peace, not choosing to stop and explain matters, hastened at once into the governor's presence, and made him acquainted with the facts which had come under his knowledge. After this he ran round the outside of the prison in search of Peace, whom he did not succeed in finding.

Now the story descends into farce as Peace finds himself in the very last place he needs to be. Even his well-known reputation as a Master of Disguise will prove to be of no avail.

Peace had really fallen inside the prison wall, not far from where some servants were looking out from the door of the governor's house; but, notwithstanding their close proximity to him, they had not seen him either before or after his fall, the reason for this being that their attention was directed away from him.

The general impression was at this time that our hero had succeeded in making his escape, and the governor and deputy-governor were greatly incensed at what they termed the carelessness of the men in charge of the convicts. The prison officials were in no enviable frame of mind; they expected to be hauled over the coals, and were ransacking their brains for excuses to offer.

Peace, finding that the governor's servants had not observed him, determined upon a bold stroke. With the cunning of a hunted fox he slipped past the room in which they were at this time, entered the governor's house, and ran upstairs. No one for a moment supposed that he was loitering about the premises. Indeed, every one was fairly puzzled, and could not in any way account for his sudden and mysterious disappearance. People were started off at once in quest of the fugitive.

Upon Peace reaching one of the upstairs rooms of the house, he stripped off his prison clothes and dressed himself in a suit of the governor's. This done, he watched patiently for an opportunity of escape, but none came.

A throng of persons were in the lower rooms of the habitation, and, for the present at least, escape was impossible. Even if he had the temerity to drop from the window, he would be sure to be recaptured, for there were numbers of persons — policemen and warders — gathered round the walls of the gaol.

Peace was wild with fury. He was within sight of liberty, which was, however, denied him. He thought it best to remain concealed in his hiding-place till the aspect of affaire changed. But no change appeared likely to take place.

An hour passed. Then another half hour, at the expiration of which the room door was suddenly opened, and several piercing screams proceeded from a maid-servant, in whose room Peace was secreted.

The plot is thickened by the introduction of another character — for once his silver tongue will let him down. The comedic possibility of the scene is compounded by outrageous punning, yet the known characteristics of the criminal remain intact.

He strove in vain to silence the girl by placing his hand over her mouth for the purpose of stifling her cries. But the attempt proved futile. She was too much alarmed, and her voice was so shrill that it would have awakened one of the seven sleepers.

'Hold your deuced tongue, you little fool!' exclaimed Peace. 'Nobody will hurt you.'

But the mischief was already done. It is just possible that the maid might have connived at his escape if she had considered twice about the matter; as it was, he was lost. He knew and felt this, as the noise of ascending footsteps fell upon his ears.

The governor, with a cohort of prison officials, now entered the apartment. Peace cut such a rueful figure, and presented altogether such a comical appearance in the governor's clothes, which were a world too wide for him, in addition to being too long, in this respect resembling two towns on the Continent, namely Toulouse and Toulon, that more than one of the party could not refrain from laughing, the governor first setting the example himself.

'So, sir,' said he, 'this is how you repay the kindness shown to you, is it?'

'Oh, I am very sorry for what I've done,' said Peace, in a whining tone of voice, 'but liberty is sweet, and penal servitude is a sore trial. I hope you will take a merciful view of the matter, for I don't suppose it would have made much difference to anybody if I had got clean away. As it is I am to be pitied.'

'You are a hypocritical, worthless fellow,' observed the governor; 'and the sooner we are rid of you the better. You are not worthy of consideration, and as to kindness, it's thrown away upon you. But whose clothes is the rascal wearing?' he observed, as it suddenly occurred to him that the garments looked very much like his own.

'He's got on your clothes, sir,' said one of the warders. 'Upon my word, his impudence exceeds all bounds,' cried the governor in a fury. 'I couldn't find any others to put on,' whined Peace. 'I'll take them off at once.' He began to undress, slipped out of the garments in question, and put on his prison attire... 'I have a great mind to recommend a sound flogging.' 'Oh, pray don't, sir; I ask your pardon. Pray have pity on me, if you please. I declare most positively that I intended to lead a new life, to reform, if I had got back into the world, and I intend to do so, under any circumstances. I pledge my word as to this.' 'Your word!' exclaimed the governor, in ineffable disgust. 'Your word, indeed! There, take him away; place him in one of the refractory cells.'

Upon hearing these words Peace made a most piteous appeal to the governor, who, in reply, told him that he might think himself fortunate at being spared a flogging.

There follows an entirely convincing scene which imagines what must feel go through the mind of a prisoner banged up in solitary.

The refractory or punishment cells, as they are termed, have double doors, which are kept locked to effectually prevent any communication from without. The prisoner, on entering one of these dark cells, which do not admit a single beam of light when the doors are closed upon him, finds everything as silent as the grave. The furniture of these wretched places consists of an iron bedstead, securely fixed in the floor, and a water closet. There is also a bell to communicate with the officers of the prison, and a trap in the door to convey food, as in the other cells. When under confinement in these places the prisoners are kept upon bread and water. The bedding at night consists of a straw mattress and a rug, handed in at nine o'clock in the evening and taken away in the morning, when a tub of water is given to the prisoners for the purpose of performing their ablutions.

Peace was conducted back to the gaol by the warders, one of whom unlocked the door of one of the refractory cells, and the wretched prisoner was thrust into the dark and cheerless receptacle.

Without doubt even a temporary or short imprisonment in a dark cell is a terrible punishment to most men. When Peace heard the door slammed to his heart sank within him. A cold shudder passed through his frame as he breathed the mephitic black air, which seemed to be more like a fluid than an atmosphere. His allowance of bread and water had been given him as he made the acquaintance for the first time of his dark prison-house.

'Oh!' he exclaimed; 'and to think it should come to this! Had it not been for those loose bricks I should be breathing the fresh air now — be at liberty. But this is, indeed, most horrible. Ugh! this wretched darkness, this appalling gloom!'

He sat down on the side of his bed and pressed his hands to his temples, which were throbbing painfully. He remained for some time lost in thought.

'I am but a poor, silly fool after all,' he presently ejaculated. 'Why should a man like me shudder at the darkness? What does it matter when one's asleep whether there be light or not? How long am I to remain here, I wonder, and what will be their next move?'

He endeavoured in vain to penetrate the gloom — endeavoured to make out the objects in his cell, but all to no purpose. It was the first time in his life that he had been immured in a refractory cell — he had heard the horrors of the place described by those who had suffered confinement in such places. Now he had to learn them by his own bitter experience.

'After all it is better than being bashed (flogged),' said he, 'but it is bad enough, and a little of it goes a long way. If I keep still I shall be benumbed with cold. I must endeavour to get some exercise.'

Humour is abandoned as this terrific scene ends in existential isolation. How could the readership not be moved by the plight of Peace in the depths of his despair?

He groped to the wall, and keeping his hand on it, went round and round like a caged wolf. This exercise seemed to afford him some temporary relief, which, however, was but of a transient nature. He groaned and gnashed his teeth — the silence and gloom seemed almost insupportable. He sat himself once more on the side of his bed... He sat rocking himself to and fro — trying not to think of anything, for now the miserable nature of his position seemed to fall upon him with additional force.

'If they would only let me have one ray of light, however feeble, I would not complain. Nay, I would be satisfied, but this impenetrable gloom is more than mortal man can bear. I shall go mad. In a short time they will let me out of this place a howling maniac.'

He stretched himself on his bed, and endeavoured to sleep, but every now and then he started as if an adder had stung him; he started and groaned, then he turned round, covered his face with his handkerchief and remained quiet for awhile. If he could only sleep he would be satisfied, but he found this impossible. The place was cold, damp, and cheerless. He arose and crept towards the door of the cell. What would he give to see it opened and have free passage accorded him ? He listened at the door for some time; he could not detect the faintest sound, save the beatings of his own heart. He shouted out as loudly as he could, and his voice reverberated through the cell, making strange and uncouth echoes. He beat his fist violently against the door, the only effect of which was to bruise his hands; no one answered — there was nothing for him but darkness, silence, and solitude.

'They have no compassion, no feeling, and have left me here to die! Oh, the merciless wretches!' he ejaculated.

A thousand fugitive thoughts flitted through his brain; the incidents of his life were pictured before him with inconceivable rapidity. He had some feelings of remorse, and made good resolutions for his future conduct, which were afterwards broken, like others he had made when in trial and suffering, and now remorse and memory contracted themselves on one dark spot in Charles Peace's history. Fear came upon him, an icy tremor crept through his frame, and a feeling of faintness came over him. Once more the past rushed by with tenfold force. All this was bad enough, but worse followed.

He fancied something supernatural passed him like a cold blast.

His limbs shook as with palsy, and his teeth chattered. Thick beads of perspiration oozed from his forehead and temples, and coursed down his cheeks. He cried most piteously for help. He said the cell was full of evil spirits — uncouth forms were flitting about him — horrible faces were grinning hideously at him. He screamed and cursed, and prayed, and dashed himself frantically against the door, and ran round his cell like a mad person. But no one came to his assistance. He flung himself once more on his bed, and uttered a plaintive moan.

How long a time he had passed in his miserable prison house he could not possibly tell — to him it appeared an age...

After two days' confinement in the refractory cell he was taken out and placed in an ordinary prison cell, and in a few days after this he left the gaol with a batch of convicts who were bound for Millbank. The officials at Wakefield were but too glad to be rid of him.

***

Is there anything new to be said about the circumstances surrounding the Banner Cross murder, given that the writer himself acknowledges that 'everybody will agree with us when we declare that Peace's acquaintance with the Dysons is altogether incomprehensible'? Well, there are emerging facts about background of the unfortunate victim.

CHAPTER LXXXIX. CHARLES PEACE AND THE DYSONS

Mr. Dyson, the ill-fated gentleman who was murdered in 1876 by the miscreant Peace, was married in 1866 at Cleveland, Ohio, and took a house at Pinsbury. From thence he removed to Highfield, afterwards to Heeley, and again to Darnall, and from Darnall they moved to Banner-cross-terrace.

There is just a short period of the history and phase in the existence of Mr. Arthur Dyson after his arrival in this country from America, says a fellow country-man of his, which may not be uninteresting. Soon after his arrival he made application to the resident engineer of the North-Eastern Railway Company at York for employment as a civil engineer and surveyor, and his credentials were of such a character that an engagement was entered into with him. The character of his occupation in America led to the anticipation that he would be able to find 'his way about here,' and that in fact his services might prove to be of a most useful character.

On presenting himself for the purpose of commencing his duties, his personal appearance was the source of considerable curiosity and surprise amongst the remainder of the officials in the engineer's office. He was extremely thin and singularly tall, measuring over six feet; and he wore a low felt hat, as he afterwards explained to one of the staff, for the purpose of abstracting from his great height and from the observation which it had led to amongst those with whom he had to associate.

He cut a singular figure when engaged in his occasional duties as a draughtsman at the table which was general to the rest of the staff, and to mitigate the inconvenience which must have attended his tallness in the performance of this part of his duties, some special arrangements were made by which he might be able to keep a more upright position. Despite his great height, he is described as being as 'straight as a poplar.'

The general bearing of Mr. Dyson was that of a gentleman, and whether in conversation or written communication with those around him, he never bent from this position, and, as a consequence, commanded general respect. When he took his engagement in York, he dated from the Firs, near Rotherham, where he said that his wife was residing; and whilst he remained in the ancient city he lodged with a Mr. Waddington, of Holgate-lane. He was engaged there for only about two months, much of the time being occupied in surveying various stations on the York and Whitby line. He had at last been sent for this purpose to Grosmont Station, and as after his departure, as it was expected, for that place, nothing was heard of him for a fortnight, inquiry was made at Grosmont, and it was found that he had not been there. This led to an intimation being sent to him at the address near Rotherham that his return to duty was not required, and to the termination of his engagement with the North-Eastern Railway Company.

Peculiarity was noticed about the unfortunate gentleman, which gave rise at the time to the impression that something preyed upon his mind, and he on more than one occasion, in intimating to one of his superiors a desire that he should be allowed weekly to visit his wife, hinted that he suffered from some domestic trouble.

What the nature of this domestic trouble was it is not easy to say. Possibly it might be in some way connected with the mischievous, tormenting little rascal, Peace.

This is the only publication which gives the whole story of the life of Katherine Dyson, the second woman in Peace's life and the object of his obsession, in her own words. It will be found in full in Appendix B.

CHAPTER XC. PEACE'S ADVENTURES AFTER THE DEATH OF MR. DYSON

Amazingly, Charlie's own words are now quoted. This interview could only have been obtained after his trial for the murder of Dyson. There is no indication how the Purkess publication got hold of it.

> 'I want it to be properly understood that, from the moment I left Bannercross... I felt sure of making my escape. I felt I had no cause to do so, for I knew that I had done nothing wrong; for in the first place when it happened, I came down the passage and stood in the middle of the road not knowing what had happened. I did not know whether to run away or walk away, till I heard Kate (Mrs. Dyson) scream; and then not knowing what had happened, I took across the road and fields to Hentcleff (Endcliffe) crescent. I then walked to Broomhill Tavern, and took a cab into Church-street.
>
> I then went to see my mother, and remained with her for more than half an hour. I then went down to the Attercliffe railway station, and took the train for Rotherham. I then booked from Masborough for Hull, but having got into the York part of the train... when the Hull part of the train was liberated from the York part at Normanton I was taken forward to York.
>
> I remained at York in the Railway Hotel in the station yard all night. I took the first train next morning for Beverley. I took the next train for Cottingham. I went from Cottingham to Hull.

Though Charlie remains unrepetentant there does seem to be a shade of regret expressed about the effect of his violent actions upon his innocent family.

> I went to see my wife and family at 27, Collier-street; this would be about ten o'clock in the morning. I had been away from my family a fortnight, and was talking to them in the kitchen when I heard two [detectives] talking to my wife in the shop, asking if a young man of the name of Peace lived there. My wife said 'Yes; but he has gone to Sheffield to see his grandmother,' thinking that they meant my son.
>
> But I in the kitchen, hearing this, felt that it must be me they meant, went upstairs into my son's bedroom, put the window up, and went between the two roofs of the building, and remained there till the detectives had searched the house, and when they had gone out I came back again into the kitchen of my own house, and took my things and began to wash myself; but before I could finish washing myself I heard them in the shop again, so I went upstairs through the windows between the roof till they had searched the house and gone out again. So I then went down again into the kitchen.
>
> My wife and daughter were sobbing fit to break their heart, for they did not know what was the matter and I could not tell them. So I washed me, and put on my clothes, and bid them all good-bye, and went out through the window again between the roofs. I remained there again for some hours, till just before dusk.
>
> I then went down the spout at the further end of the building, which brought me into the next yard but one, and went to a woman's house that dealt at our shop, and told the woman I had to get away out of the shop over a warrant, or something of that, and asked her if she would go into our house and ask my wife to send me something to eat out, but mind the detectives did not hear and see her, and I had my tea in this woman's house. I then asked the woman to let me go through her kitchen window in her back yard and also go ask the woman in the next yard if she would let me go through her kitchen window, and pass through the house into another yard. She went

and asked and got consent, so that I went through the window and house into the other yard. This was three clear yards away from my house. It was then just dark.

I walked out of the passage end, and turned to the left down Collier-street, towards the fair ground, and went away — but not out of the town — and got lodgings; and I remained in Hull for nearly three weeks, and done some places for money.

I then left Hull and booked for Doncaster. I then booked from Doncaster to London. I then took the underground railway to Paddington, and booked from Paddington for Bristol. Bristol was the first place I saw a reward out for my apprehension. I remained in Bristol till January. I booked from Bristol to Bath. I stopped at Bath all night. I booked from Bath to Oxford, and in the carriage with me there was a police sergeant on his way to Stafford Assizes. We rode and talked together to Dickcot Junction (Didcott Junction), and arrived there in the middle of the night. We slept together in the waiting-room for four hours, and then went forward to Oxford by first train. We then shook hands and parted; he went forward to Stafford and I remained at Oxford all day. I then booked for Birmingham. I remained at Birmingham four or five days. I then went on to Derby. I stopped at Derby at an eating-house oppersite the railway, and there was a young man there just joining the police force, and the police-station was not more than 150 yards from there. I remained at Derby for something more than a week.

At last he arrives in my home town where his exploits, under the *non-de-plume* of Jack Thompson, will become the stuff of legend.

I then went to Nottingham, and took lodging at a little shop three or four doors from the police-station on the Burton-road right oppersite a timber-yard where I was stopping, and the police-station is at the corner of Leanside. I remained with them till they left there and went to live with them in a yard a bit lower down, that led out of Leanside into Narrow Marsh, but not more than fifty yards from the police-station.

I remained with them some time, working Nottingham and the towns round about. I then went to live with Mrs. Adamson, a buyer, next door to the 'Woodman Inn,' in Narrow Marsh. It was there I became acquainted with Mrs. Thompson.

Upon one occasion I booked from Nottingham to Sheffield, but got out of the train at Ely (Heeley) station, and walking past the police-station at Highfield. Inspector Bradbury was stood at the police-station door, at about seven o'clock at night, and I passed close by him, and he did not know me...

At Nottingham I done a big tailor and draper establishment and took a lot of overcoats.

How could he have practised his career before the invention of the railway?

While they have added to convenience and luxury, railways have to a great extent also increased the demand for skilled thieves — so much may be done by them on trains, in stations and in the attendent omnibuses.

***

The chronology becomes increasingly haphazard and repetitive around this point. The Peace material proceeds in anything but a straightforward direction and is abandoned for dozens of chapters at a time for the tiresome continuation of the penny dreadful romance.

But there is still much to be discovered about life at Evelina Road, Peckham, site of that well-furnished abode where that curious *ménage à trois* held their soirées. For instance, this account of the only creature with which Charlie had a 'stable' relationship:

CHAPTER XCI. PEACE'S DOINGS IN LONDON AND THE SUBURBS — HIS HOME LIFE AT EVELINA-ROAD, PECKHAM

The large menagerie of pets that he formed at Peckham was certainly extraordinary for so unpretentious an establishment, but he was a gentleman devoted to science, and might be allowed to indulge a hobby for zoology... The collection embraced thirty-two guinea pigs, some goats, cats, dogs, canaries, fowls, pigeons... He could manage his two cats, his three dogs, his billygoat, his Russian rabbits, his seven Guinea pigs, his young thrushes, his collection of canaries, his parrots, and his cockatoo — to say nothing of his pony — for which he had an inordinate affection.

He had studied dogs; and it is said that, stranger as he must have been in his burglarious prowls about mansions, he never had any difficulty in silencing the most ferocious mastiff or impudent terrier. It was a sight to see him on a Sunday walking through Peckham, followed by the six dogs that owned him as master.

Some of these pets he had trained to execute tricks wonderful enough to earn a showman his living. His pony, Tommy, especially had a marvellous obedience to command. At a word he would rear up and remain standing, and at another word he would lie down and remain as if dead... In short, Tommy had been trained to be a silent partner in burglary.

The custom of Peace was to go out during the day, with Mrs. Peace and Mrs. Thompson and the son in his trap, himself driving, and take a survey of the mansions he intended to rob during the night, and the precise spots to which he would carry the booty for subsequent recovery...

He went out early in the evening when the family were downstairs, and robbed the house upstairs, and later in the evening, or far on in the morning, when the family were upstairs, he roamed through the lower regions and abstracted the heavy articles of plate and gems, of pictures, and all valuables that were portable and transmutable into money. He went out alone on these expeditions.

The son, Willie Ward, was seen by the greengrocer at Forest Hill one morning at six, driving rapidly, as if he had business; and the greengrocer's man saw the son on two occasions out early in the morning. It is surmised that the son took these early rides in the vehicle, by arrangement with the father, for the purpose of collecting the plunder of the night, and conveying it in an unsuspicious way to the town...

The pony went out from Peace's stables at most unearthly hours, and sometimes the neighbours woke up when it returned... His pony apparently was much beloved, and he wept with tears of regret when Tommy died.

Faithful readers would have to wait another eight weeks before they can weep along with a fuller, more fanciful and less dispassionate portrayal of the death of the faithful steed — surely penned by another, more florid hand?

CHAPTER CXII. A PAINFUL SCENE — THE DEATH OF TOMMY — PEACE'S GRIEF

Peace arose, and said he must go into the stable. 'I don't like the look of Tommy — he's very queer...'

'He cares a deal more for Tommy than be does for either of us — you may rest assured of that,' said Mrs. Thompson. 'But then, you see, the faithful little animal don't cross him;

so there is, after all, good reason for his attachment.'

The two women went on bandying words for some time. There was nothing new in this; it was their custom, and had been so ever since they had become acquainted with each other. It was, as we have before indicated, not altogether perfect harmony in the house in the Evalina-road, and wrangles were of frequent occurrence. It was perhaps in the nature and order of things that this should be so.

Meanwhile Peace and Willie were busily engaged in the stables. The pony seemed to be in great pain. He would not take his food for all Peace's coaxing. He was restless and fidgety; nevertheless he pricked up his ears, and strove to put a better face on matters when spoken to and caressed by his master, but with all this it was easy to perceive that he was not in his usual health. As a rule our hero was not accustomed to give way to despair — his naturally sanguine temperament led him to look difficulties or troubles in the face. Had this not been so, he never could possibly have gone through what he had throughout his guilty and chequered career.

Perfect opportunity for one thousand, one hundred and seventy words of barely comprehensible psychological speculation on the subject of sanguinity, coming to the conclusion:

The sanguine temperament and self-reliant nature of Peace caused him to surmount difficulties which other men would have sunk under. And had he turned his thoughts and mind more in a proper direction, he had sufficient qualities to have caused him to have cut a respectable figure in the world; but it was not in his nature to abstain from wrong-doing. He was guided by no moral principle, but had been radically wrong from his earliest childhood.

But we must return to the stable to which Peace and Willie Ward had betaken themselves.

Why ever not?

The former was much concerned at beholding the pony rear on its hind legs as if in pain; then the faithful animal dropped on all fours again and looked inquiringly at his master. In a minute or so after this a sudden shivering seemed to seize the pony, who trembled in every limb, at the same time snorting like a war charger.

'Poor little fellow! He is bad,' cried Willie, in a tone of alarm. 'I never saw him like this before. What can be the matter with him?' 'That's not easy to say. He's dreadfully bad at present, but he'll get better after a bit.'

Peace, despite the symptoms, which were of a serious character, was still sanguine. He strove to put the best face on the matter, and proceeded at once to prepare a bran mash. In this he was assisted by his step-son. Tommy was the most docile, tractable little animal it was well possible to conceive, and took his mash without hesitation.

'Will that do him good?' said the lad. 'I hope so' returned Peace. 'It is a simple remedy, and can't do him any harm.'

Peace endeavoured to get the pony to take his food; he led him to the manger, and strove by every means in his power to persuade him to eat. Tommy swallowed a few mouthfuls of oats, but this was evidently an effort. Presently he turned away from the manger and lay down upon the clean straw which his master had previously prepared for him.

'We will leave him now,' said Peace. 'Quiet and rest will do more than we can do for him. Come along.'

The two passed out of the stable and returned to the parlour of No. 4.

Not even the fictional veterinary ministrations of Bandy-legged Bill the Gipsy have any effect. Reader, Tommy died. And for the first time in 470 pages Charlie expresses something akin to a common human emotion:

Peace sat himself down on an inverted pail, covered his face with his hands, and burst into tears.

'I've lost my best friend — my faithful companion... I would have given anything to have saved him... I can't help grieving. He was my pet, was to me as faithful and docile as a dog. There never was such a faithful creature...'

Peace could not readily get over the poignant sorrow he felt at the loss of his pony. This may appear strange with one of his callous temperament. But the fact remains the same, and many persons could testify to the great grief he demonstrated on this occasion.

It passed over, however, in the course of a few days, and Charles Peace was then himself again.

That's that, then. Time to leave Evelina Road again for an interpolated tale about Matt Murdock, the pirate, and his map of hidden treasure!

***

During Peace's months living incognito in London the capital was rocked by the arrest of four detectives who were put on trial for 'conspiracy to obstruct, defeat and pervert the course of public justice.' This would not be the last time high-ranking officers of the Metropolitan Police would be accused of consorting with criminals for their own pecuniary advantage, but the establishment of the detective force in 1842 was relatively recent and they were championed, at least by middle-class Londoners.

Dickens had helped secure their reputation in the 1850s with a series of articles about these resourceful and incorruptible thief-takers in his magazine *Household Words*. But now four members of that force were on trial for, among other instances of severe misconduct, accepting bribes from the swindlers William Kurr and Harry Benson to tip them off so they could avoid arrest. A full account is given in *The Victorian Underworld* by Donald Thomas (John Murray 1998) but the Purkess writer could not resist putting Peace into this picture, allowing an opportunity for an attack on the police. So Peace attends the hearing at Bow Street in disguise. Of course, this may well be based on truth as 'our hero' was known to take an interest in judicial proceedings other than his own. This account is, however, not a little anticlimactic.

CHAPTER XXCII. (*sic*, it should be CXXII).
THE TRIAL OF THE DETECTIVES — PEACE'S VISIT TO BOW-STREET

Charles Peace had read in the papers the report of the first inquiry into the charge made against the four detectives. He was greatly interested in the case, for, said he, with a sort of chuckle:

'I think I ought to know something about chaps of that kidney. I've dodged 'em a good many times, and when it answered my purpose I've bribed them; but this I only did when my dodgery failed. I'll go and have a squint at these beauties when they come up for their next examination.'

Presently the four detectives — Meiklejohn, Druscovich, Palmer and Clarke — were brought in.... It will be needless for us to give a detailed account of the proceedings, as the result has long since been patent to everybody.

What a shame. And what a departure from normal custom — other trials with no bearing upon the life of Peace are recounted in full and an account of this one would have made interesting reading. One of the detectives, Clarke, was acquitted with the other three being sentenced to two years hard labour. It was widely assumed that the web of corruption spread far further in the Yard. No wonder, we might conclude, law-breakers became heroes in the popular prints when the forces of law and order, whose wages we pay, were not to be trusted.

***

The next extract might be considered another digression except that it bears directly on the reality of Peace's profession. How he got rid of his ill-gotten gains remains a mystery. It seems likely that in Nottingham Ma Adamson disposed of the goods but what his practice was when conducting his one-man crime wave in London is still unknown. He must have had recourse to that 'set of blood-suckers' — the receivers of stolen goods. So in this story an 'Israelite' fence' in Whitechapel, 'Cunning Isaac Simmonds' has to be created, endowed with all the setreotypical characteristics that might be expected in such a son of Fagin. His statement 'Yesh, yesh, my tear friend, business is bad and money tight' is, unfortunately only too representative. But this fictional scene provides the impetus for a well-researched chapter.

CHAPTER CXXXI. THIEVES AND RECEIVERS

There are hundreds, and, indeed it may be said, thousands of persons of this description in the metropolis and the suburbs. It has been remarked by many who have a pretty good knowledge of characters of this description that without receivers there would be no thieves, but we do not quite agree with this hypothesis. Thieves it is not possible to eradicate, but certainly the receivers offer every inducement for men to pursue dishonest courses, and it is most remarkable how few are ever brought to justice.

Though he always preferred to work alone Peace must have had some contact with the criminal fraternity of the metropolis, though none of them came forward to to profit from any such association after his arrest.

When the name of Charles Peace was in every human mouth public interest was awakened by the spoils of a receiver of stolen property falling into the hands of the police. The following paragraph, from a newspaper of the period, will, perhaps, interest the curious and inquisitive reader. It runs as follows:

'There is at present, at the Bethnal-green Police-station, under the charge of Inspector Wildey, of the Criminal Investigation Department, attached to the K Division, and Detective-sergeants Rolfe and Wallis, about one of the most extraordinary collections of stolen property ever seen in this metropolis. The goods are laid out in the library and reserve-room of the station, and consist of articles of almost every conceivable kind — at least as far as things of a portable nature are concerned.

First come some dozen or so of gold watches, from the ordinary Geneva to the highly-finished and expensive article from the shop of some first-class London maker; then come silver watches, gold bracelets, lockets, chains, and guards, rings set with precious stones, silver spoons, forks, and fruit-knives. On another table is a quantity of really good electro-plate — one set of forks, spoons, ladles, &c., being marked with the letter B, and are supposed to have been the proceeds of some burglary committed a year or two back. On a table in the middle of the room are strewn cigar-cases, meerschaum pipes, small fancy thermometers, mantel ornaments of a superior kind, opera glasses, books, photograph cases and albums, some with portraits and some without, a large family Bible, a silver snuff-box ('presented to Sergeant Tierney by Mr. and Mrs. Maitland'), Crimean medal, with the Balaclava and Sebastopol clasps, the property of Private Wilson of the Royal Marines; and three boxes, each containing: a dozen silver thimbles.

On the mantelpiece are some half-a-dozen clocks, some of them of a very expensive kind, and evidently taken from the house of well-to-do people. Around the room are scattered coats, jackets, capes, shawls, rolls of flannel, cloth, and linen, about fifty or sixty pairs of new boots, and any number of umbrellas. Piled up against the wall are some sixty or seventy workboxes of various sizes and kinds, from the humble article costing only a few shillings to the more expensive article, which probably cost five or ten guineas. Cases of claret, champagne, and brandy, railway and carriage rugs, and a host of other things much too numerous to mention, but which do not form a tithe of the bulk of property originally seized — the whole lot, indeed, filling three large vans...

It is stated that seventeen years ago this modern Fagin was a poor labouring man, but he now owns some thirty houses in and about the district where he has been residing.'

There follows a masterpiece of ironic understatement:

Within the last few weeks another case has come under the notice of the police. It would appear that, a great number of robberies having lately been committed in the western suburbs of London, the attention of the police was called to the flourishing establishment of a marine-store dealer of Pimlico. We have no desire to prejudice the case of the person at present under remand. Marine store dealers are not supposed to traffic in jewels and gold, in the settings of personal ornaments made of the precious metals, from which the gems seem to have been ruthlessly severed, or in household plate from which the crests appear to have been recently erased.

All the same, the marine-store man may have come by such objects of art and luxury in a perfectly lawful manner; and inasmuch as he stands remanded, without bail, on a charge of receiving a stolen silver medal it is only fair to assume him innocent. Unfortunately for him his recollection of certain late commercial transactions did not tally with the information of Inspector White and Sergeant Day, of the 3 Division of police.

It happened that these agents of the law, having occasion to call at the shop to inquire whether its owner purchased any plate that day, the marine-store keeper was so ill-advised, or of such uncertain memory, as to deny the soft impeachment. Mr. White, however, proved too pressing for him, and, accompanied by his fellow officer, followed him and his wife upstairs, where they came upon a store of treasure of more than Oriental splendour and variety.

There, upon tables and under beds, and strewn about in confusion, the police found gold coins, travelling bags, bank notes, blue serge, watches, chains, tablecloths, brooches, lockets, studs, silver plate, pieces of alpaca, cutlery, artificial teeth, slippers, shawls, lead, and brass, and articles of almost every description — among other things, certain stolen property trade directly from the prosecuting owner.

It is, of course, within the bounds of possibility that the marine-store dealer may have purchased the articles catalogued in the regular way of business; and he may rest assured that every opportunity will be afforded him to make his title clear, not only to the silver medal, but to every item so opportunely discovered on his premises.

The broken jewellery found at Pimlico may have been accidentally damaged by the manufacturers themselves. It is possible that the late proprietor of the silver drinking-cup, in the shape of a thimble, with 'Just a thimbleful' in blue round the rim, shocked at the temptation to dram-drinking which its possession hourly put in his way, may have adopted a peculiar form of local option and chosen to dispose of the bauble to the shopkeeper for value received. The pair of gold solitaires engraved with 'a cock in the act of crowing' may have offended the aesthetic tastes of their former holder; the gilt whistle may have been found too noisy by its late custodian, and the lockets fitted with hair and the portraits of children need not necessarily have been stolen to have passed into the hands of respectable tradesmen.

We sincerely trust that the accused may be able to prove his innocence to the satisfaction of a British jury.

Once again this publication, of a class despised and rejected, has delivered the goods.

But it's not all gold. The patient reader must wait another fourteen weeks before finding the woodcut of a familiar, nay obligatory, scene on the cover of No. 78.

***

The next seven issues are all pure journalism — much of it culled from the *Illustrated Police News* reports, of course. No deviation is possible from the well-known sequence of events: the capture by P.C. Robinson, the imprisonment, the discovery of the true identity. The cover illustrations now become less fanciful and founded on documentary fact: the meeting with Hannah at Newgate and scenes from prison life before the trial leading to the inevitable climax on the scaffold at Armley Gaol in Leeds.

Before we join Charlie on the journey back north there is still unfinished business in Peckham.

CHAPTER CXLVII. A VISIT TO PECKHAM

Forsey Brion is a bit player in this drama, unwittingly caught up in his neighbour's machinations. Truth being stranger than fiction, he it was who became involved in Mr. Thompson's scheme to patent a device to raise ships from the sea bed in order to retrieve sunken treasure and his plan to divert the ocean to flood the Sahara! Such devices and designs caused Brion to believe that the gentleman from Number 5, so lavish with his hospitality, was a brilliant, if unrecognised, inventor whose entre-preneurial endeavours would make his fortune.

Should any contemporary reader imagine that door-stepping is a deplorably modern journalistic practice, this extract in which 'a writer for the press gives the following faithful account of his visit to Mr. Peace's 'friend' at Peckham, should forever disabuse them of such a delusion. Reporters then were as reporters are now.

How Peace came to live at Peckham is a story which has not yet been told, and, I suspect, will not be known unless it is told by Peace himself or by another party whom I called upon yesterday, and who, I suspect, could say a great deal if he could be induced to say it. This gentleman, who occupies a good house in leading road, was a great friend of Peace's. The people say that he and Peace were always together. Considering Peace's manner of life, that is more than I can receive as gospel; but it is certainly a fact that this gentleman was more in Peace's company than any other person in Peckham. My interview with him was not very encouraging.

A sharp-witted Peckham boy, who acted as my guide in showing me the residences of the people whose names I had on a card to visit, pointed to the street in which the house was situated, and said, 'You will easily find it; it is the only house on that side where the lower windows are frosted, to prevent people looking in' The boy added that the windows were frosted after this gentleman began to be seen a good deal in Peace's company. Sometimes he went and visited Peace at 5, East-terrace, and sometimes Peace came and visited him.

With the exception of Mr. S. Smith, who let the house to Peace, the latter kept himself very 'reserved' as far as his neighbours were concerned, and as the neighbours thought that the Thompsons — as they called themselves — were well-to-do people, considerably above their station, they did not like to intrude themselves upon the newcomers' notice.

The house of this gentleman is a better one than that occupied by Peace, and is in a more pretentious road. There is an apartment underneath the level of the roadway, with a large open window, and it was this window which was 'frosted.' I saw no other window on the road treated in that fashion. Of course it may have been done simply to prevent prying people from looking in, though none of the neighbours seem to have thought it necessary to take similar precautions.

Three knocks with the knocker failed to elicit any answer, and I was leaving to try my luck elsewhere, when a comely-looking lady put her head out. Happening to look back at the time, I noticed her, and returned. She kept me standing at the door for some time, but eventually, on my telling her as much of my business as I thought it prudent to mention, she asked me in, adding, as she showed me into a parlour. 'I don't think he will tell you anything about that.'

She closed the door, and left me to myself. The parlour, I had been told, was mainly furnished with articles from Peace's house. I sat down in one of the chairs belonging to the walnut suite which had adorned Peace's parlour, and here I may say that if the walnut suite is a fair sample of the 'luxurious furnishings' at 5, East-terrace, you must not suppose that there was anything very palatial about the place. In fact, the longer I inquire into this man's establishment the glory of it seemeth to fade away. The suite is a fairly good one, covered with rep [?], in green and gold stripes, considerably faded by wear — such a suite as the esteemed auctioneer over the way from our office would knock down any day for fifteen or sixteen guineas, and think he had done fairly well for the seller, and not badly for the buyer.   In the room was also a harmonium, on which 'Mr. Thompson' [and] 'Mrs. Thompson'... used to play sacred and other music. It is a fair-looking instrument, worth perhaps a ten-pound note. There are other nick-nacks which had also been obtained from Peace's establishment.

The life of the *ménage à trois* in South London seems anything but riotous.

While I had been using my eyes in this way a conversation had been conducted in undertones in another room. The wife was evidently telling the husband who I was. Then the door opened and there came close up to me a little man, wearing spectacles, through which he peered at me, with his small keen eyes, rather curiously, and 'took me in' from head to foot. After he had finished his examination he retired to a chair in the corner. The wife stood by his side, and he pointed me to a seat near the window.

Having established his credentials Brion tries to give the reporter the brush off.

'I knew Mr. Thompson; but before I say any more let me tell you that I have been before the authorities, and expressly cautioned not to say anything to anybody. They have heard my story, and if I am wanted they know where to find me.... The Greenwich police have asked me what I know, and I may tell you have warned me against saying any more. I must decline to give any information which may be used...'

Here the wife interrupted, 'You have said quite enough. Don't say any more." The husband drew up abruptly. I told him he had quite mistaken my mission... I simply wanted to know what kind of people they were, and how they lived, and was not anxious to know anything about the Blackheath business. 'Before I say any more,' he answered, 'I must ask you to promise me as a particular favour that you will not mention my name in any way.' 'Well,' I said, 'your name has been hinted at already. You have been spoken of as Mr. B, and I expect the Peckham people know very well now who Mr. B is.' He did not seem pleased at this information, and was about to tell me something more, when his wife again put the drag on, and kept it on all the time I was in the room.

'You were working with Mr. Thompson on a patent for raising sunken ships, were you not?' 'I must decline to answer any questions about that.'

Well, but that is a matter about which there is nothing to be gained by reticence. In fact, I know you have got that model in your house now, and that it is enclosed in a box like a plate-chest. I should really, as a mere matter of curiosity, like to have a look at it.'

It was no use. He entrenched himself behind his spectacles, the wife assisted him to hold the fort of his lips, and nothing further could I obtain from him.

The Ballad of Susan Bailey

After many long years of obsession with the Peace process — which I've rationalised for its significance in casting a exceptional light upon the way life was really lived in the dear dead days beyond recall — I have come to suppose that it is not Peace himself but the women in his life who are the most mysterious characters. And of the three it is Susan I find especially intriguing. Is this because she was a lass from my own home town, working, like both of my grandmothers, in the textile trade? My early attempts to discover anything about her background came to naught, until I got hold of *Charles Peace, Or The Adventures Of A Notorious Burglar.* The compilers of the Purkess publication also up to this point seemed somewhat dumbfounded by what might have driven this unlikely heroine — or should that be victim?

Mrs. Thompson played a most conspicuous part throughout the latter part of Peace's career. How she and Mrs. Peace could have consented to live under the same roof with the burglar Peace is altogether unaccountable... Mrs. Thompson had frequently a black eye, and indeed was rarely without one, and shrieking and cursing were not uncommonly heard proceeding from the house in the midnight hours and in the afternoon.

Mrs. Ward acted as a kind of working housekeeper. She is described to me as having usually the appearance of a cross between a washerwoman and a monthly nurse, wearing an apron, her arms akimbo, and altogether a slatternly, unlovable, unclean-looking personage.

Mrs. Thompson, on the other hand, was a likely lady for a companion. She was much taller than Peace, walked in a firm manner, carrying her head with a somewhat jaunty air, until latterly, when Peace's cruelties 'took it out of her,' as a neighbour put it to me. She was a good figure, inclined to full habit, had pleasing brown hair, which she sometimes wore in curls; a good, fresh complexion, dark eyes, Grecian nose (but no snub), and altogether, as I have said, a person of a rather attractive appearance. She dressed well, and never appeared to want for anything, Mrs. Long and other neighbours telling me that her wardrobe must have been very rich, and extensive, as she never wanted for changes of dresses, appearing sometimes in tightly-fitting costumes, and at others in richly trimmed and fashionably-cut jackets, donning for the afternoon drives a superb sealskin paletot.

The neighbours say that Mrs. Thompson's weakness was drink. The boy who piloted me about Peckham told me that the first week they came he fetched 4s. worth of whiskey for Mrs. Thompson, 'who,' he added, 'was a very nice person when she was herself,' meaning when she was sober. Mrs. Long, to whom Mrs. Thompson seems to have confided her troubles, believes that she would not have 'gone to the drink' if it had not been for the cruelty to which she was latterly subjected.

But that she did drink is beyond dispute.

'She could swim in gold if she liked,' said Mrs. Ward, on another occasion. 'He does not mind what he gives her, he is so fond of her, if she would only keep off the drink.' That was good Mr. Peace's greatest trouble, 'and that,' added the old lady, carefully removing a tear from the corner of her eye, 'frequently puts him out, and makes him angry, till the neighbours hear him.'

And the neighbours did hear him. Frequently, there were sounds of quarrelling succeeded shortly after by the shriek of a woman.

Mrs. Thompson found too late what sort of a man she had so imprudently taken up with. About this time the real character of Peace was presented to her in all its hideous deformity. But she found it difficult and next to impossible to detach herself from the cunning and cruel rascal who held her in bondage. It was not possible for her to be an inmate of the house in the Evlina-road, without having some inkling of the goings on in that delectable establishment. Numberless boxes were coming and going. 'Thompson' or Peace was absent at strange times. On the evenings he was absent he returned at all hours, nobody knew when or how, but with his return was associated an accession of worldly goods. How these were obtained those around him could make a shrewd guess, but neither of his housekeepers had the temerity to ask any question.

So Mrs. Thompson had her 'drops' at home. She had a weakness for strong drinks, and was an inordinate snuff taker, and, according to Peace's own account, she cost him a pretty penny... His weakness in respect to women is perhaps the most remarkable feature in his character.

Mrs. Peace became duly impressed with the fact 'that the game was up' and she was not disposed to remain any longer in her old quarters at Peckham. The consequence was, that Mrs. Thompson was left to fight her own battles in the best way she could.

And then — as the serial is only one hundred pages from its conclusion — comes, in Chapter CL, nothing less than her own autobiography. Tracked down by some tenacious reporter, Susan's testimony was transcribed, we must accept, as verbatim. Covering six double-columned pages and running to about six thousand words, it deserves to be reproduced for the first time at some length, for nowhere else can such an insight into how an ordinary working woman became so deeply embroiled in one of the most scurrilous stories of her age be gained. Susan's story is given in full in Appendix C.

***

Just when the true story is hotting up:

We must leave Charles Peace for a while to gather up the tangled threads of our story, and follow the fortunes of other characters who have figured in this strange eventful history.

Why? Readers have to wait for the definitive version of the incident which, perhaps more than any other, ensured Peace a permanent position in the penal pantheon. Considerable detail is added to the account previously given in the *Police News*.

It appears that when the warders brought Peace from Pentonville on the previous week he was exceedingly troublesome throughout the whole journey, and wanted to leave the train whenever it stopped; and indeed when it was travelling. At Peterborough he was allowed to get out, and the warders had considerable difficulty in getting him back into the train.

The chief warder adopted a plan of his own... and he provided himself with a number of little bags, and whenever Peace required it one of them was handed to him, and was afterwards thrown out of the window.

From the moment of their leaving Pentonville he appeared to set himself deliberately to work to annoy and irritate and vex the officers to the utmost of his power. And no one unacquainted with him can form any conception of his matchless powers in that direction. Having been in prison so many times, he is as well acquainted with the rules which guide the warders as they are themselves; and any infringement of those rules on their part he would quickly detect and make a noise about. His set purpose seemed to be to provoke them to a breach of the rules, and to serve him as he too richly deserved to be served.

He behaved more like a beast than a human being, until the carriage became almost unbearable.

The train had passed Worksop, and a part of the country was reached which Peace knew too well. All the way down on this, as in his previous journey, he had been adopting the most ingenious and cunning devices to put the warders off their guard, but without success.

Now was his last chance of eluding them, and if he could but escape from the carriage, he could follow, perhaps, well remembered 'cuts,' steal into Darnall or some other place of refuge, and, profiting by past experience, be no more discovered.

The train was whirling along at express speed; but what of that? To such a man to regain freedom was worth a supreme effort — though he died in the attempt. He had used several of the bags referred to on the journey, and he asked for another. The chief warder gave him one, and he stood up with his face to the window to use it, the under warder being close behind him.

Suddenly, with all the agility of a cat, Peace took a 'header,' and threw himself out of the window. The under warder sprang forward, and was just in time to catch him by the left foot. There he held Peace, head downwards, dangling out of the window — an extraordinary sight to those who happened to be passing at the time. Peace with his other foot kicked the warder's hands, and struggled most determinedly to get free from the warder's grasp.

The chief warder, finding the space too narrow to help his associate in the struggle, seized the rope communicating with the guard's van, and endeavoured to stop the train. Peace, knowing that the window was too narrow to let the other get forward, became more savage and ferocious still, and kicked and wriggled about with great violence.

Still the warder clung to him, and, for a distance of two miles, Peace was hanging head downwards by the carriage side. At last, by supreme effort, he managed to wriggle off his boot, which was left in the warder's hand, and the convict fell on the stepboard of the carriage, from which he bounded upon the ends of the sleepers.

The train was still travelling very rapidly. The communication cord having failed to work until a gentleman in the next compartment, hearing a noise, and suspecting something was wrong, managed to pull the rope, and the warders had the satisfaction of hearing the deep 'boom' of the gong.

The train slackened speed and the warders got out and ran back up the line for nearly a mile, where they found Peace lying as he had fallen, having evidently received injuries sufficient to prevent his getting away. He was conscious, however, and gave the warders a smile of satisfaction as they came up to him. They found him in the act of trying to wriggle the handcuffs off his wrists. Blood was flowing from a wound in his head. They picked him up, and, as the slow train which arrives at Sheffield at 9.20 a.m. was coming up, they signalled it to stop. The convict was put into the guard's van, where for the rest of the journey the warders kept a sharp look-out.

Now everything hinges on Katherine Dyson:

Without her Peace might be kept outside the law he had so long defied... There was a general belief that Mrs. Dyson knew a great deal more than she had divulged at the inquest, not, indeed, about the actual facts of the murder, but with reference to her previous knowledge of our hero, and her communications and transcations with him.

When she is finally tracked down and brought back to Sheffield her present condition can be described:

She was a person of considerable muscular development, and not without personal attractions of face and figure. Her countenance was round and ruddy, and neatly and fashionably tied up in coils.

The interest in her appearance was phenomenal:

The Bannercross murder led to the performance of extraordinary feats in telegraphing. On the day Mrs. Dyson was under examination in the corridor at the Sheffield police-offices press messages numbering 180,000 words were telegraphed away. The number of words actually sent from Leeds in connection with Peace's trial was 200,000. The number of words delivered to all papers was 300,000. With respect to Sheffield two special wires were used solely for the local papers. Ten men were specially employed at that end in writing up the news, and at no time throughout the day were they above twenty words behind hand. The news was delivered almost sheet by sheet by special messengers.

***

CHAPTER CLXII.
MRS. DYSON'S EVIDENCE

In the packed courtroom, where crowds have turned out to see her star performance Katherine passes her cross-examination by Frank Lockwood, Peace's counsel, with flying colours. She resists any implication that Peace might have acted in self-defence.

EXAMINATION OF MRS. DYSON.

Before going to the closet I put my little boy to bed. The bedroom is in the front. There was a light in the room. My husband at this time was downstairs reading, and when I went to the closet I left him still reading.

I said nothing to him before going to the closet. I had to pass through the room where he was. When I heard him coming I came out of the closet.

I was only four or five feet from the passage leading to the closet when my husband passed me to go down to the prisoner. I could see him plainly, and all that he did. He was going rather slowly. I am prepared to swear that my husband never touched the prisoner before the shots were fired. He could not get near enough to him... I distinctly swear that he never touched the prisoner... I noticed how my husband fell. He fell on his back. Nothing touched him before he fell. I will swear that after the first shot was fired my husband did not get hold of the prisoner. He did not catch hold of the prisoner's arm which held the revolver, and the prisoner did not strike my husband on the chin and nose. I will positively swear that my husband was never touched on the face except by the bullet which the prisoner fired.

Then Lockwood starts in to question her about their previous relationship:

FL: How long have you known Peace?
KD: Between three and four years. I never saw him before I saw him at Darnall. I cannot say whether I or my husband first made his acquaintance. He lived next

door but one to us. My husband began to dislike him in the spring of 1876.

FL: Was he jealous?

KD: No.

FL: Do you remember showing your husband a photo of yourself and the prisoner?

KD: Yes. It was taken at the Sheffield fair.

FL: How came you to be photographed together?

KD: We went to the fair together with some children. The children were photographed, but we were in a separate picture. I cannot say whether it was the summer or winter fair. It was summer fair, but I cannot say whether it was the summer of 1876. It certainly was not in 1875...

The nature of their relationship depends entirely on the authorship of the letters found when Peace fled the scene which are reproduced in their full glory in Appendix B:

FL: Look at that letter.

KD: *(after looking at it)* It's not mine, and I don't know whose it is.

Another letter was then handed to her, and she gave a similar answer. Mr. Lockwood next handed to the witness a scrap of paper on which she wrote some words when before the magistrates, and asked her to look at it...

FL: Did you ever write to the prisoner, telling him you were going to Mansfield by the nine o'clock train?

KD: No.

FL: Did you tell him he must not go by train, 'because he (Dyson) will go down with me,' and also say, 'Don't let him see anything if you meet me in the Wicker. Hope nothing will turn up to prevent it...' Did you write that?

KD: No.

FL: Just look at that *(handing up the note just read)*

KD: That is not my handwriting...

FL: At any rate, when you got to Mansfield he was there?

KD: Yes.

FL: And you told him you were going?

KD: No.

FL: Can you account for his being there?

KD: No, I can't. He was a constant source of annoyance to me, and was always following me.

FL: Do you remember the prisoner giving you a ring?

KD: Yes. He gave it to me in the winter; at least I cannot tell when it was, or the year.

FL: Was it before or after you were photographed together?

KD: That I cannot say. I cannot say, too, if I showed it to my husband. I know I threw it away. The ring did not fit me.

FL: Did you ever write this: 'I do not know what train we shall go by, for I have a great deal to do this morning? Will see as soon as I possibly can. I think it will be easier after you leave; he won't watch so. The ring fits the little finger. Many thanks. ... I will tell you what I think of, when I see you about arranging matters, if it will. Excuse the scribble.' Now, did you write that?

KD: No.

FL: Did you ever tell him that the ring would not fit?

KD: No.

FL: Are you now prepared to swear that you did not write to acknowledge the ring?

KD: I did not.

Mr. Lockwood then asked the witness whether she preferred a steel or a quill pen to write with, and Mrs. Dyson said it made no difference. A steel pen was given to her, and she wrote as follows from the dictation of the learned counsel: 'I write to you these few lines to thank you for all your kindness, which I will never forget. I will write you a note when I can.'

Mr. Lockwood asked: 'That is your best writing?' The witness answered: 'Yes.'

The cross-examination continued:

KD: On one occasion I went to a public-house with the prisoner, but I cannot remember the date. I cannot say where the public-house is. The prisoner told me that there was a picture gallery there. My husband became dissatisfied after that.

FL: Was it in consequence of your going to the public-house with the prisoner that he became dissatisfied?

KD: No.

FL: Are you sure of that?

KD: Yes.

Did you tell him you had been to a public-house with the prisoner?

KD: Yes.

Was it after that he became dissatisfied?

KD: I can't say exactly. I know a public-house in the same street as that in which the prisoner lived. I don't know it by name, nor do I know a man named Craig as the landlord. I have been to a public-house where there was a picture gallery, and there I had a bottle of 'pop.'

FL: Have you not been to the 'Marquis of Waterford' public-house, in Russell-street, Sheffield, on several occasions, with the prisoner?

KD: I may have been once or twice, but not more often.

FL: When you have been with Peace has he not paid for drink for you?

KD: I have only had 'pop' with him.

FL: How many times have you been with him?

KD: I am sure of once, but I don't know that I have been any more times.

FL: Do you remember when this was?

KD: No...

FL: Did you tell your husband that Peace had taken you to a public-house and paid for drink for you?

KD: Yes.

FL: And after that he became dissatisfied?

KD: Yes.

FL: Do you know the Norfolk Dining Rooms in Exchange-street?

KD: No.

FL: Have you ever been to some dining rooms, near the Market-place, with the prisoner?

KD: Yes.

FL: Alone, I mean?

KD: Never alone...

FL: Never alone, you say.

KD: I will swear I have been to some dining rooms with Peace on several occasions. I have been to some near the market once. Then we were not alone. There were two children with us. They were my own little boy, and a child of Mrs. Padmore's. I had refreshment there. That was at the time of the Sheffield fair — the same fair at which I was photographed — the same day that I had been photographed with Peace. And these children went to the dining-room.

FL: What had become of your husband?

KD: He was away from home.

FL: Was he not at the fair?

KD: Yes. I saw him there and met him in the evening after the photograph was taken. My husband did not come into the fair until evening.

FL: Do you know a music-hall in Spring-street, Sheffield? What is the name of it?

KD: The 'Star.'

FL: Is it a picture-gallery? Have you ever been to the 'Star' music-hall with Peace?

KD: I don't know it by that name.

FL: Have you been to any music-hall with Peace?

KD: I have been to a place where there is a picture-gallery, and where it looked as if singing went on. There was a small stage and tables and chairs...

FL: Have you not been three or four times to the music-hall in Spring-street?

KD: No; I have only been once. I know a public-house at Darnall, called the 'Halfway House.' To my knowledge, I have never had drink there which was put down to Peace.

FL: That won't do. Are you prepared to swear that you have not had drink there on Peace's credit?

KD: Never to my knowledge.

The Jury were evidently not impressed by Lockwood's cut and thrust and, after a mere fifteen minutes deliberation, the Guilty verdict was inevitable.

But doubts remained in the popular mind concerning the character of Katherine Dyson. Maybe she was not as innocent as she would like herself to be painted. An intriguing reference to her conduct when back on stateside soil remains, unfortunately, unglossed:

> After the trial and condemnation of Charles Peace, Mrs. Dyson left for the United States, and subsequently she conducted herself while in New York in anything but a creditable manner.

Perhaps the cops wanted to make certain they were rid of her for good and all.

> She left Sheffield for Liverpool on Thursday morning, Feb. 26th. 1879, and later in the day she embarked on board the White Star steamer *Britannic* (the vessel in which she returned to this country) en route for Cleveland, Ohio. She was accompanied by Police-constable Walsh as far as Queenstown.

CHAPTER CLXIII. PEACE AND MRS. THOMPSON

That's one of his women despatched. But what about the lover who shared his bed in Nottingham and South London? On February 7th, Susan wrote to the authorities:

> Gentlemen, I beg to be allowed to see the condemned man, Charles Peace, Thompson, or Ward, now in Armley Gaol, Leeds. He has been my reputed husband for years, and he has no other legal wife. He has earnestly desired to see me, and for reasons that can easily be understood. I deeply hope and pray, gentlemen, that you will furnish me with the authority to see him before the end. I will not disturb his mind, but try to sooth him. Imploring you will speedily grant my prayer,
>   I am your obedient servant, S. Thompson.
>   P.S. Please address to me 'Post Office, Leeds', to be left till called for.

Poor Sue, cold-shouldered by the family presumably because she was suspected of being responsible for his identification, was denied this request. She makes her final appearance pathetically trying to make a visit to the condemned cell.

MRS. THOMPSON REFUSED ADMISSION TO SEE PEACE UNDER SENTENCE.

The following is the letter that Mrs. Thompson received from Peace, the envelope being addressed, 'On Her Majesty's Service, Thompson, letter box General Post-office, Leeds, to be called for.'

'From Charles Peace, H.M. Prison, Leeds, Feb. 9, 1879.
My poor Sue, I receive (sic) your letter to-day and I have my kind governor's permission for you to come and see me at once so come up to the prison and bring this letter with you and you will get to see me I do wish particular to see you it is my wish that you will obey me in this one thing for you have obeyed me in many things but do obey me in this one Do not let this letter fall into the hands of the press.
Hoping to see you at once I Remane (sic) your ever well wisher Charles Peace.'

But this visit was never to take place, and Sue wrote a final letter:

'Tuesday, Feb. 10, 1879.
Dear Charley, Why is it, after all my anxiety and trouble to come to see you after your especial desire to see me, and your letter asking me to come at once, and now you don't see me? What have I done to not merit to see you? You have turned to me in all your troubles since I have known you. Is it because your relations have been? They had the first chance. Or were your feelings too much overcome? I pity you much. I sincerely thank you for your second letter you sent by the governor... I do forgive you all as you ask me, as I hope to be forgiven... As you blame me for all that is being done, in regard to letters and in the papers, let me tell you I am not to blame... You cannot leave this world without seeing me again. You know I have been faithful and true to you if I have other faults. Now one word — clear your conscience of everything before it is too late.'

And so Susan Grey/Bailey/Thompson disappears from history.

Peaceiana

As soon as he is imprisoned the traffic in Peaceiana begins. The sale of his violins led to scores of interested parties crowding into Harvey's Auction Rooms. His 'Duke' fiddle fetched twenty and a half guineas, knocked down to one Mr G. C. Millward, provision merchant of York. The 'Kit' fiddle was sold to Mr Lofthouse, of the George Hotel, Bridlington for £9/10s. His 'Short Grand' piano made twenty-four and a half guineas, 'the purchaser being a gentleman from Hull, who desired that his name should not be published.' The provenance of a violin Peace had made himself, twenty years before, was assured by its current owner, a person named Hewitt, better known by the name of 'Little Teddy,' who told the bidders that he and 'Charley' had played upon the instrument many a time. To enhance the reputation of Peace as a music hall turn it was bought for a mere £6/10s. by Mr John Stansfield, of the Music Hall of Varieties, Leeds.

This item was in *The Era* on February 16th 1879, nine days before the execution:

Charles Peace's Pianoforte. To let on hire the semi-grand pianoforte purchased at the sale of the notorious burglar Charles Peace, February 4th, at Sheffield. A great attraction and novelty to Concert Hall, Free-and-Easy, &c. Terms £10 per week, including all Railway expenses. Will sell for a favourable offer. Apply W. Waites, Hornsea-parade, Hull.

Could this instrument, which evidently escaped Harvey's salerooms, have been purchased from Hannah? A month before she had been acquitted at the Old Bailey, on January 14th, accused of 'feloniously receiving seven pocket handkerchiefs and a quantity of other articles, the proceeds of different burglaries committed in the neighbourhood of Blackheath last year by a man named Peace, who she alleged was her husband, well knowing them to be stolen.' The charge was dismissed as, even though there was no conclusive proof that the pair had ever been lawfully wed, 'it was a principle of law that a married woman was supposed to act under the direction of her husband.'

Whether the piano was ever hired or sold, how it was exhibited and what tunes were played upon it must remain matters of speculation.

Such unholy relics are, it goes without saying, incapable of performing intercessory miracles. Nevertheless, pilgrims must have experienced some deformed frisson of transcendence in the presence of metonymic objects which, if not venerated, were at least absorbed visually. A part stands in for the whole, but of what?

Charlie himself was well aware of the monetary value of his memorabilia. It is to be hoped that his legacy allowed Hannah — surely the most maltreated of all Victorian wives — to live out her remaining years in comparative and anonymous prosperity. Her man always was, if nothing else, a good provider.

CHAPTER CLXIII.
PEACE'S CYPHER CODE

Could there be any more peculiar particulars to be uncovered before Marwood makes his entrance and Charlie makes his exit? Well...

The Central News special reporter, wrote: As doubt has been expressed respecting the existence of Peace's cypher code, the following is furnished as an accurate copy of it, the original having been for some time in the hands of the police authorities.

Where did this come from? Was it ever employed? And if so, how? What recipients were in on the key? The only possible comment is: 18 14, 48. 2 19 20 142 143 1 87 13 84 72. 2 19 20 55. 73, 46 46 46.

1 one	2 I	3 is
4 oh	5 be	6 to
7 me	8 my	9 in
10 as	11 it	12 at
13 of	14 up	15 on
16 or	18 a	18 aye
19 am	20 so	21 we
22 us	23 but	24 you
25 nap	26 hope	27 they
28 thy	29 was	20 will
31 she	32 well	83 went
34 who	35 has	36 let
37 and	38 can	39 call
40 time	41 still	42 her
43 out	44 four	45 give
46 kiss	47 dear	48 pet
49 there	50 some	51 that
52 had	53 life	54 are
55 poor	56 course	57 come
58 coming	59 where	60 but
61 from	62 much	63 many
64 what	65 this	66 mean
67 when	68 must	69 may
70 read	71 uneasy	72 money
73 love	74 loving	75 every
76 then	77 old	78 how
79 never	80 name	81 Ben
82 sent	83 say	84 —
85 almost	86 friends	87 sum
88 pull	89 post	90 happy
91 wish	92 pain	93 until
94 bear	95 word	96 shall
97 used	98 house	99 back
100 pounds	101 night	102 right
103 write	104 mind	105 oblige
106 cannot	107 sold	108 things
109 said	110 know	111 just
112 railway	113 yes	114 believe
115 about	116 owes	117 told
118 fact	119 belong	120 word
121 since	122 away	123 early
124 such	125 finish	126 best
127 first	128 whose	129 early
130 Monday	131 Tuesday	132 Wednesday
135 Thursday	134 Friday	135 Saturday
136 Sunday	127 home	138 have
139 fancy	140 face	141 washed
142 ready	143 for	144 Johnny

Johnny being of course himself.

PEACE AFTER HIS INTERVIEW WITH THE REV. MR. LITTLEWOOD.

***

By the standards of his age Charlie fully deserved to pay the ultimate penalty for the crime to which he confessed to the Reverend Mister Littlewood shortly before he swung — the murder of P.C. Cock and his callous indifference to the cruel fate of William Habron. But it would seem that he went to his death continuing to maintain that the shooting of Arthur Dyson was self-defence to protect himself from the rage of a jealous husband — what across the Channel would be exonerated as *une crime passionelle*. Certainly it was the cuckolding of an elderly man unable to satisfy and corral a beautiful young wife half his age which sparked the popular imagination, rather than the cold-blooded killing of an unarmed constable.

OFFERS TO HANG PEACE

After Peace had been tried and condemned, the authorities had several applications to fill the grim office of executioner. These were from amateurs, one of whom, from the neighbourhood of Sheffield, wrote to say that he would undertake the duty gratuitously; whilst another asked the modest sum of only £3/10s. for his services, should they be accepted. It is scarcely necessary to say that no notice was taken of them, and Marwood was engaged to carry out the sentence.

CHAPTER CLXXI. SCENES OUTSIDE THE GAOL

The atmosphere on the dawn of execution produces some really fine penmanship:

It was a fearful morning. The air was raw, and a searching wind pierced through one almost to the bone, yet the fields dividing the gaol from the houses near seemed to be covered with people almost immediately. They ran eagerly to get the best places that could be obtained. Everybody ran and everybody was anxious to get the best places. The peculiar coign of vantage, known only to the experienced, was said to be behind the prison, near the hospital. This was where the scaffold had been erected, and it was said that outside the walls, at that point, the falling of the trap and the thud caused by the jerk to the rope could be distinctly heard.

It is no exaggeration to say that at least five hundred people assembled at this spot, and that until the hoisting of the flag the most careful silence was preserved. Indeed, some of the people who were standing there declared that they heard Peace speaking, but could not make out his words.

A large knot of people, numbering several hundred, appeared at the outer gates, without any warning, and undisturbed took up positions commanding a view of the flag-pole on the high tower. About ten minutes to eight snow began to fall slightly, but it soon discontinued, and at five minutes to eight the weather was fine again.

CHAPTER CLXXII. THE EXECUTION OF PEACE

The obligatory scaffold scene is an expansion of the coverage in the *Police News*, though the woodcut is somewhat less frontal and more naturalistic in form and the gruesome events following judicial murder are yet to be delineated:

Marwood had done his work most effectively. The victim never quivered.

The bystanders looked down into the space beneath the scaffold, and then only a few officials were left on duty. At nine o'clock he was cut down, very little altered in appearance so far as the bloodless face was concerned. The mark of the rope was clearly shown. The body was then conveyed to the deadhouse. After the inquiry the lid was adjusted to the coffin, and without mourners, without others than officials to bear the burden, the body was taken into the burial-yard of the prison, and lowered into the grave reserved for murderers. Others are in company in the dust adjacent, who have suffered the same dread penalty and been borne to the same ignominious repose. Like others also, he had a stone erected, with his initials and date of the execution.

VISIT TO THE CONDEMNED CELL AFTER THE EXECUTION.
The prison chaplain was deeply affected on returning from the execution of Peace on Tuesday morning. Dr. Price, the gaol physician, escorted him to his official residence. Under-sheriff Gray, his clerk, Mr. Waite, and the governor, together with the representatives of the press, in leaving the fatal spot passed into the wing of the gaol from which Peace had so recently emerged. The cell which the condemned man had occupied was also passed. The gas was still burning in it, and the door was open. On the bed was a closed bible and a prayer-book, whilst the convict's shoes, slippers, wide-awake hat, and other articles of apparel were placed on the benches in the inner cell. On the little table were a number of books and several sheets of paper, on which the convict had apparently been scribbling.
A tin quart measure, nearly full of milk, also stood on the table.

What more to be said?

Come on, our redactor still has lines to scribble and pennies to earn. The imminent prospect of narrative closure beckons. This time next month it might well be a session on *The Complete Toast Master*, or, worse still, no gig at all.

Keep the wheel turning. Keep the pot boiling.

CHAPTER CLXXI. THE MORAL OF PEACE'S CAREER

So now comes a last hurrah which is anything but a let-down from the perspective of high-flown prose style, particularly in the specious justification for having recorded every last enthralling detail. That's what the insatiable readership demands to satisfy their gluttonous appetites. Every stop will be pulled out, including citations from the Bard and the founder of the Christian faith.

The last days, the confession, the letters, the will, the dying speech, and the execution of Charles Peace will make a sensational history of the most dangerous description. The large place which his villainy marked for him in the public attention for several weeks proved a stimulant to many a depraved appetite for notoriety. All persons, in short, who have had occasion to watch the effect upon the public at the noisy passage of a great malefactor from the day of sentence to the morning of doom, must have remarked the extraordinary copiousness of the record of the sayings, doings, and writings of Charles Peace with positive alarm...

[T]here is a fascination in the horrible as well as in the beautiful, and the people who were dismayed while they contemplated the brutal jaw, presently craved details of the crimes its owner had committed; of the manner in which he wrote and talked of the human creatures who had associated with him — nay, loved him; of his appetite for the fare of the condemned cell, and his capacity for sleep, with Marwood for the subject of his dreams. The poisonous food was forthcoming in large doses, and be it observed, its production is the inevitable, the forced, result of the demand.

The blame lies, not with the newspapers, but with the system of turning upon the murderer's cell a light as fierce as that which the poet tells us beats upon a throne. The journalist is the servant of the public, and the appetite for news about the murderer's daily habits being strong, he has no choice but to provide all he can obtain. He may condemn the publication of a rogue's correspondence with his wife, his mistress, and his pals; but he cannot prevent it.

It has often been our duty to comment with severity upon such a parade of crime as the career of the man who was hanged in Armley gaol-yard on that Tuesday

118

afforded to the British public. In Peace's instance, however, the abuse was carried to the wildest excess. The public were with the Bannercross murderer night and day, from the hour when he was condemned, to the gallows. The comings and goings of the unfortunate people connected with him were chronicled as methodically as the 'Court Newsman' imparts to the public the airings and the dinners of the Royal family.

That on the fatal morning bacon and eggs were provided for him before his long journey; and that, albeit livid white, he ate with some relish before he sat down to write a parting letter to his wife, are facts in the biography of Charles Peace which the world that dotes on Newgate records would not willingly let die. We have chronicled them accordingly.

The culprit was even allowed to address a homily to the reporters, in the character of a man who had done with the wickedness of this world, and would be, in a few moments, among the angels. He gave friends and foes his blessing, and wished they might follow him to Heaven.

There are still people who, as the author of 'The Fable for Critics' remarks: '*think it looks odd to choke a poor scamp for the glory of God.*' These old-fashioned folk may be also of the opinion that there is something very monstrous in this spectacle of a malefactor, speaking, with the rope round his neck, to 'you reporters.' And they may go on their way pondering on the strangeness of a society, in which the honest and heroic poor die by the hundred unsolaced by the priest, while a holy man stands at the elbow of the murderer on the gallows, and as the hangman draws the bolt, cries 'Lord Jesus receive his soul!'

[It is a] curious fact that great scoundrels apparently shuffle off the mortal coil more comfortably than honest people. Possibly it is that long inurement to crime has so blunted their sensibilities that even conscience no longer makes cowards of them, and Hamlet's great query, 'To die, to sleep, perchance to dream!' troubles them not. But, in whatever way the phenomenon is to be accounted for, the fact remains that condemned culprits, as a rule, mount the scaffold with a firm step, and, while consenting to death, apparently conquer agony.

Charles Peace proved no exception to the rule. He slept well up to within an hour and a half of his execution, and on awaking partook of a hearty breakfast. On emerging from the condemned cell to the courtyard in which the scaffold was erected, he heard the bell tolling for his own funeral without giving signs of terror. Upon the scaffold he appeared to be in a contented frame of mind...

It must be confessed that it somewhat detracts from Peace's piety that he did not take refuge in the consolations of religion until he found there was no chance of his regaining his liberty. We fear it would have been a dangerous experiment to have let him loose again upon society, even as a 'converted man!'

There seems to be something repulsive in the idea of such a consummate rascal making sure of Heaven with so little effort, after having spent his whole life in the shameless violation of every law of God and man!

The wretch was so steeped in vice and crime that his death seems to remove him beyond the liberality of the old *de mortuis* injunction. Had he been really repentant of his atrocious crimes rather than of the fearful consequences to which they had brought him, it would surely have been more becoming on his part had he humbled himself in the profoundest silence, and not run the risk of intensifying the enormity of his hypocrisy by palming himself off as a local preacher upon the scaffold.

When Christ converted people He told them to go home and keep quiet: 'See thou sayest nothing to any man.' But nowadays converts seem to be encouraged to advertise themselves as much as possible.

Charles Peace's demeanour in the presence of the hangman is, to our thinking, far from being edifying.

We may search in vain through the annals of crime to find the record of a more infamous life than his... The sooner all memory of the career of this cunning, cruel, and abject criminal is obliterated, the better it will be for society.

And this after nearly a million words which sought to accomplish anything but obliteration!

On the penultimate page the writer has the gall to attack his rival journalists for their coverage — doubtless prompted by envy at not being one of the four pressmen allowed to witness 'the sickening ceremony', unlike the man from the *Daily Telegraph*.

> [T]he story was nasty enough to suit the palate of an epicure in Topsyturvydom. Every step, every pause on that vulgar *via dolorosa* that leads from the prison door to the scaffold was counted, criticised, described. Little scraps of the beautiful Burial Service were desecrated by being quoted beside the doomed man's call for drink. The demeanour and voice of the hangman, the culprit's dress, his tremors, his appetite, his letters, his speeches, the scaffold itself, with its draping of black sacking or black glazed calico (authorities differ), all this forms as pretty a page of contemporary history as confirmed *Daily Telegraph* writers will ever care to dwell upon.

But there is a fortuitous conclusion for one character caught up in this unhappy drama:

> It is pleasant to record that the unfortunate young Irishman Habron has received Her Majesty's pardon, and is at present in Ireland, a small yearly stipend having been settled upon him sufficient to support him in comparative comfort for the remainder of his life. This is as it should be. A great wrong was done to the ill-fated young man, but every possible means has been taken to place him in a respectable position, for which it is understood he is duly grateful.

All that remains is the delivery of a final homily, ironically the very same truism which inaugurated this monumental tome in the very first chapter some seven hundred and ninety pages and two years previously:

> A life of crime is always a life of sorrow and care, for the hearts of the guilty tremble for the past, for the present, and the future.

Amen.

This is the mother-lode. Nothing else will ever come close to its detailed descriptions, its wild animadversions. There will be many other accounts.

Ned Kelly, the Ironclad Australian Bushranger

An index of the speed with which the aspects of a real life was transformed into the traits of a fictional character can be seen in the unlikely pages of a penny periodical which made its first appearance in July 1881, two years after Peace mounted the steps to the scaffold, and ran for thirty-four weeks before being re-released between hard covers. *Ned Kelly, the Ironclad Australian Bushranger* was variously published by Alfred J. Isaacs & Sons, 16, Camomile Street E.C., the General Publishing Company, 280, Strand W.C. or the London Novelette Company — all three companies seem to have been under the same management.

What could the King of the Lags possibly have to do with the celebrated antipodean outlaw who was hanged in Old Melbourne Jail only a year before — apart, of course, that they were both 'Victorians', in differing senses of the word?

Unlike *Charles Peace, or The Adventures of a Notorious Burglar*, this is clearly the production of a sole scribbler with a distinctive authorial voice, a 'real writer' whose identity is beyond dispute. For, though the first page states this is 'By One Of His Captors' this is the sole work of James Skipp Borlase. Through assiduous detective work by Lucy Sussex, an Australian chronicler of popular fiction down-under, the lineaments of a lacklustre literary life can, for once, be revealed. (*"Bobbing Around": James Skipp Borlase, Adam Lindsay Gordon, and Surviving in the Literary Market of Australia, 1860s* in *Victorian Periodical Review* (Winter 2004)). And what a fascinating biography this turns out to be.

He was born in Truro in 1839 and trained as a solicitor before emigrating to reside beneath the Southern Cross in 1864. After hanging up his shingle he soon found the gold-rush city unconducive to legal practice:

> There are 205 solicitors and 85 barristers now practising in Melbourne, a city possessed only of a population of 125,000... very many make a smaller income than the carpenter or stonemason.

Was this why he followed the advice of his middle name and skipped his wife, Rosanna? When he was eventually tracked down by the colonial authorities 'Borlase's reputation and consequently his legal career' were, as Sussex puts it, 'destroyed'.

Deprived of making an honest living, he was compelled, as so many a ne'er-do-well before and since, to write his way out of his difficulties. In this endeavour he proved not at all unsuccessful. No less than fifty-four works have been attributed to him in the *Australian Dictionary of Biography* and he is widely regarded as one of the earliest writers of crime fiction, in collections such as *Memoirs of an Australian Police Officer* and *Adventures of an Australian Mounted Trooper*. Despite lucrative accomplishments following this change of profession, however, he returned to the mother country some few years later. All his stuff thereafter was churned out for juvenile weeklies under the mask of anonymity and for which he received no nominated credit.

Was this subsequent subterfuge because he had been forced to leave an erstwhile penal colony as he was himself a criminal? Did he leave under a cloud following accusations of plagarism? Computer analysis by Lucy Sussex and her collaborator John Burrows seem to confirm that some of the tales he passed off as his own were, in fact, by Mary Fortune — certainly the first female author to embrace the embryonic genre of the police procedural, who wrote under the wonderful nom-de-plume 'Waif Wander', and whose prolific career ended in vagrancy and alcoholism... But, stop, for hers is another, though no less fascinating, story.

James Skipp Borlase died in 1902, scribbling to the last and now all but forgotten. In the immortal words of Ned Kelly as the noose was placed around his neck: 'Such is Life.'

Ned Kelly, the Ironclad Australian Bushranger is a fast-paced read with a fine ear for colloquial dialogue and action frequently conveyed in snappy one-sentence paragraphs. In Australia Kelly remains a hero of (Irish) resistance against (Anglo) colonial authority, protected by his home-forged armour which covered his head and body in his final shoot out at Glenrowan in 1880. Continually immortalised not only in the masterful paintings of Sidney Nolan but in many films from as early as 1906, his history is well-documented and his legend is a metonym for antipodean masculinity and mate-ship security. Not that there's much reference to the historical record in these pages. Each weekly part was preceded by quotations from the *Telegraph*, the *Times* and the *Press* asserting the factuality of the account — all of which were fabricated by the publisher.

Borlase only rarely resists the temptation to indulge in digressive sermonising, though the tendency does infrequently break through. As an instance, he abandons an account of a fixed card game in Paris to interject a judgement on the Sport of Kings:

> The Turf has become impossible since horse-racing has ceased to be a sport and has become, in nineteen out of twenty cases, sheer swindling... With the exception of Lord Portland, Fred Johnstone and others, all runners of horses are blacklegs — pure and simple.

Some personal motivation perhaps?

More characteristic of the Borlase-ian approach is a penchant to shovel in celebrities of the age into his fanciful narrative. In the second number 'the infernal rascal', wearing his metal helmet and riding his faithful steed, Marco Polo — equine analogue of Dick Turpin's Black Bess — holds up a Cobb & Co coach. His daring attempt at highway robbery is thwarted by one of the passengers: a 'beautiful veiled female with a slight foreign accent.' None other than Lola Montez!

It is geographically conceivable that these paths might have crossed. The infamous mistress of, among many others, Franz Liszt and King Leopold of Bavaria did indeed capitalise on her notoriety by performing her erotic dances in the theatres of the gold diggings of Australia. But this was in 1855 when Ned Kelly was but one year old!

More feasible is the possibility that the bushranger might well have become acquainted with another character who makes periodic appearances in this periodical and whose exploits had been the talk of the 1870s. Tom Castro, butcher of Wagga Wagga, achieved fame when he fetched up in England claiming to be the heir of a Hampshire baronetcy who had been lost in a shipwreck some years before: Sir Roger Tichborne. An enormously corpulent man who in no way resembled the svelte missing knight and who, when questioned, seemed to suffer from amnesia about his early life, he was nevertheless welcomed with open arms by a grieving mother. Only when Lady Tichborne died did the rest of the family mobilise against him and hire a detective to discover that he was, most likely, one Arthur Orton of Wapping. His court case for perjury divided the nation before, after the longest lasting trial in British legal history, he was convicted. Following his release from Dartmoor Orton/Castro/Tichborne, like Señora Lola Montez who was actually born in Ireland, made a precarious living on the halls variously proclaiming his imposture was true or false.

But how could the machinations of even the most ingenious of wordsmiths contrive a collaboration between Ned Kelly and Charles Peace?

In some months of young Edward Kelly's life hidden from history he, according to this account, escaped from Sydney Jail and, after further hitherto unreported adventures in the south seas, fetched up in the metropolitan centre of Empire where, naturally, he bumped into his old chum Tom Castro, now masquerading as Sir Roger Tichborne. Seeking 'a quiet suburban lodging... he fixed upon the district of Peckham.' The habits of his next door neighbour soon aroused suspicion. If there could be any doubts in readers' minds about the identity of 'the occupant of the house on his right' they might well have been answered by the heading of Chapter CLII on page 305: ALL HIS WAYS WERE "PEACE".

> This was a precise-looking man of about sixty, with a clean-shaven face and long white hair. He was usually dressed in a black frock-coat and very white shirt and collar, and presented the perfect type of the retired small tradesman with a dash of the dissenting minister... who went by the name of Smith.

This was, indeed, the notorious resident of Evelina Road.

Ned quickly surmises that, in spite of his pious demeanour as 'a respectable outwardly-religious man... devoting all his spare time to his music', his nocturnal wanderings mark him out as 'a rum 'un' and so he follows 'Smith' on one of his midnight adventures. What follows is an exciting scene in which the old reprobate, in the act of breaking into a villa, is rescued by the young rogue from being caught *in flagrante* by a patrolling bobby.

> Ned saw that he had before him a man even more dangerous to society than himself, even as the serpent's bite is more dangerous than the tiger's claw. In this cold, crafty, calculating villain he recognised a master hand.

In the next chapter, THE HOLY ALLIANCE, Kelly makes Peace an offer he can't refuse. What follows is a heavily abbreviated version of the thieves' colloquy:

> 'Look here, you are a leery one, but I've had my peepers on you... I want you as a pal.... For a job or two in your own line... But who the devil are you and what's your real name?'
>
> 'I haven't got one... I am just the opposite of you... I have been working for forty years in the quietest way possible... I have had twenty different names and twenty different identities, twenty separate existences.'
>
> 'And you haven't been caught?'
>
> 'Not often.'
>
> 'Hang it, man, the police must recognise your face.'
>
> 'Do you think so?'
>
> He turned away for a moment then faced Ned... By some marvellous power acquired over the facial muscles Smith had transformed every feature... If Kelly had not seen him before his eyes the whole time he would have sworn it was another man...
>
> 'I can knead my nose into any shape, like a piece of putty, screw up my eyes, bring wrinkles on any part of my face at will or smooth them away, alter the shape of my mouth and the slant of my eyebrows, and, what is the best trick of all, I can thrust out or

draw back my lower jaw a couple of inches... You haven't seen my Sunday School face... I always perform my Christian duties with regularity. I rest on the Sabbath; I never work on the seventh day. I'm too conscientious, I am. Now you see the advantage of a good character and thorough respectability. It gives one such a pull when a job's up.'

'By Jingo, you're a whole team and two bullocks to spare you are. You're the stuff I like to meet. Why, we could work together like a matched pair in the shafts.'

'I work alone and have no pals to betray me, purposely or accidentally.'

But there is one job which needs more than one pair of hands, 'a crib to be cracked in town... where the swag is too tempting to be neglected.' So Peace and Kelly join forces to rob a Hatton Garden diamond dealer.

No need here to recount the complicated methodology of entrance and theft, the nail-biting suspense of discovery and escape, nor even the obvious twist that the wily merchant had substituted false stones of paste in his safe until the real location is eventually discovered and the jewels finally appropriated.

What is significant is the fictional attempt to harness together two unlikely criminal associates. When the spoils have been divvied up and it is time for leave-taking a mutual respect has been grudgingly achieved:

'What a valuable assistant in the vineyard,' snuffled Peace, clasping his hands in veritable admiration.

'I'll tell you what it is, old pater-noster. I thought you'd grabbed the grapes from that vineyard and left none of the bunches for me; but now I see I was on the wrong track, and that you acted on the square.'

'Oh no, friend. Straight is the path and narrow is the way...' ejaculated the pious one, exposing the whites of his eyes.

'You're better nor a dozen parsons, you are.'

'I'll try and merit your favourable opinion,' responded Peace with a solemn twinkle in his eye.

For all its dash and bravura *Ned Kelly, the Ironclad Australian Bushranger* remains a generic production. The conventional narrative of the colonial invader is revealed in truly dreadful scenes of blood-thirsty genocide against the indigenous inhabitants of Australia ('savages'). Ultimately, a stereotypical Villain has been made into a pasteboard Hero, in spite of unconvincing protestations to the contrary in the closing pages:

We regret we cannot dignify [Ned Kelly] with the interesting qualities usually decorating the character of highwaymen such as Paul Clifford, Dick Turpin or Claude Duval, to say nothing of Robin ('Robbing') Hood; but our history is a true one, not like those alluded to, pure fiction. We 'show vice in its own feature', the authors of the other named works show vice the feature of virtue and make infamy romantic.

Small wonder that this publication came in for particular condemnation. In his indispensable website *Yesterday's Papers*, John Adcock quotes this all-too-familiar judgment from the *Saturday Review of Politics, Literature, Science and Art* from November, 1881:

We have no hesitation in saying that the life of Ned Kelly, the Ironclad Bushranger, is as disgraceful and disgusting a production as has ever been printed. Lord Campbell's Act recognized the moral mischief which might be done by publications which offend against common decency, and provided for the condign punishment of the scoundrels who write print and sell them. They are, as the annals of the police courts prove every day, direct incentives to murder and robbery.

James Skipp Borlase's apotheosis of Kelly serves only to reveal of the lasting socio-logical and criminological significance of the *Charles Peace* so-called Penny Dreadful.

***

Around the turn of the century the Daisy Bank Printing and Publishing Company of Gorton, Manchester issued a small book, *The Life and Trial of Charles Peace*, which, at a mere thirty-two pages, told the tale in fewer words than a single number from Purkess, puffing their products as 'BEST AND MOST RELIABLE EVER PUBLISHED — Each Publication is carefully compiled by an Expert'.

It was popular enough to be reissued with a new cover.

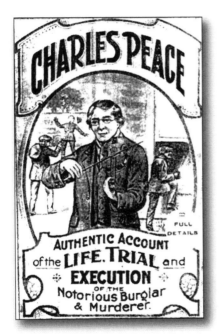 

Peace joined other villains in the Daisy Bank canon such as Sweeney Todd, Palmer the Poisoner and Burke and Hare, together with 'how to' volumes on conjuring, ventrilo-quism, fortune telling, magic and even *How To Become A Detective*.

Known as 'the last of the penny dreadful publishers' the Aldine Printing and Publishing Company managed somehow to hang on until the 1930s, largely by reprinting western titles from the US — *Buffalo Bill* among them. The New Aldine Half-Holiday Library (355,000 Readers Weekly) issued twelve titles, each featuring a complete story, of a fictional Charlie Peace by one Tristram K. Monck, clearly aimed at juvenile readers. In 1911 Aldine also put out a 128-page factual account, *The Master Criminal* (now republished in facsimile by Fredonia Books, Amsterdam.)

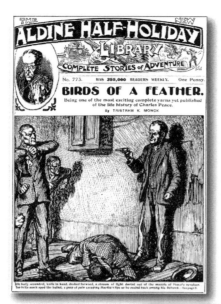

And 'Famous Crimes' issued a 'Police Budget Edition' with a dynamic cover illustration by Harold Furniss. But nothing comes close to the *Adventures*. The Purkess publication is less a book than a library. Once again the publisher of 'the worst newspaper in London' confounded high-minded critics.

From now on it will be the Legend not the Life, the Myth not the Man which will keep the memory green as Peace becomes transformed and immortalised in wax, on the stage, in the cinematograph and in kids' comics.

An untitled ballad on the same sheet as *The Release of William Habron*:

What deeds of daring we must tell, the like was never seen
The Banner-cross murder brings to light
In every town in England such commotion there has been
When they read the murderer's fierce determined flight.
Charles Peace, you'll understand, was a terror to the land
Like Dick Turpin and Jack Sheppard of renown
He was the Prince of Robbers, he never joined no band
But his guilty deeds at last have brought him home.

Charles Peace has suffered death and with his latest breath
He acknowledged that he well deserved his doom
He's been a villain all his life and caused trouble, pain and strife.
But now he moulders in a murderer's tomb.

There's never been his equal in the defying of the law
The detectives he used to laugh to scorn
His wild career is over, he cannot rob no more
It were better that he never had been born.
A bold ingenious man it always was his plan
To plunder people for ill-gotten gain
Had he used the gifts God gave him like an honest man
His character would never had a stain.

The murder of Mr. Dyson there is no man can defend
Life is sweet to everyone we know
He had no cause to his victim's life to an end
But his love for Mrs. Dyson he would show
We have no right to judge but every one must say
That perhaps the murderer was not all to blame
But he has had to suffer the fruits of being gay
And on the gallows died a life of shame.

With courage so determined no man ever knew
When travelling down to Sheffield on the line
The window of the express train the convict he jumped through
Hoping that his life he would resign.
His time it had not come, his race it was not run
Tho' bleeding from the wounds upon his head
On the line they saw him lying, Charles Peace was nearly dying
And in his heart he wished that he had died.

On more than one occasion he has boldly fought for life
With his revolver fastened to his hand
He commenced all his trouble when he forsook his wife
As all you married women understand.
'Neath a dismal beam of wood, upon the drop he stood
A picture of death and misery
Upon that Tuesday morn, the fatal bolt was born
And Peace was launched into eternity.

A more concise summation was conveyed by Edmund Clerihew Bentley in the four-line squib to which he gave his middle name:

'No,' said Charles Peace,
'I can't 'ardly blame the perlice.
They 'as their faults, it is true,
But I sees their point of view.'

Life After Death

Peace in Wax

Joe Smith's Waxworks, supposedly written by Bill Smith with the help of Mrs. Smith and Mr. Saunders with pictures by Mr. Pitcher, was published by Neville Beeman Limited, 6 Bell Buildings, London E.C. in 1896.

Everybody in the wax line knows that no show would go down without the last horrible murder. When a show comes to a fair every year the same visitors get familiar with the old figures after a time so that a new murderer is always an attractive novelty. There is always something that draws in a murder — everybody appears to like it so much. If we cannot see a murder modelled in waxworks, like it was in our show, we like to read about it in the papers. If there are not enough murders naturally as they occur we like to have them invented and put in our plays and tales. People must have them somehow or be disappointed and get low-spirited... I should say a little more about murderers, as these remarks may be useful to anybody entering the wax-line. Everybody knows waxworks and murderers are always associated together even in the greatest waxworks in London in agreement with the public taste. But as regards the wax line these are just convenience figures... They can wear almost any old togs and worn out boots.

JOE SMITH AND HIS WAXWORKS

The shoulders were padded up with hay and covered with canvas tacked down to the shoulder board. A few small brass-headed nails were driven into the edge of this board, the standing heads of which formed studs to hang the breast on. The breast was made of canvas, with cane ribs to the shape of the body, like a pair of stays, only stiffer. The stays had button-holes at the top to go over the nail-head studs, to hold them firmly. When

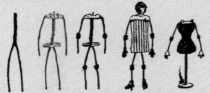

the show was struck, the stays were taken off and rolled up for portability.

The knees and elbows of the men were formed of hay-bands tied on with string. If the arm was to be placed horizontally, several hay-bands were tied upon it. Large holes were cut through the soles of the boots, so that the leg sticks could go through them into holes in the floor board, to hold the man up stiffly. As the boots were loose on the sticks, they could be set out as desired. If stockings were shown, the entire legs were moulded up with hay

MAKING UP THE NEW SHOW

and string, and covered with canvas. The figures show the different stages of a man in making.

Men made in the manner described were not all alike as with the moulded papier-mâché figures of the ordinary shows, or even of the best London

The Regular Style.

ones. They varied according to the bends of the sticks and were much more natural. If Joe tried to make them look stiff, he could not. As regards the hands, they are always a difficulty.

Joe Smith's Style.

Wax hands cost six shillings a pair, which is

The hair on the old figures was generally rusty, and the wax was brown, or green, or dirty. This had a neglected look, which was recognised to be very suitable for a murderer... Otherwise our murderers were originally figures of very respectable persons, as Lord Byron, Lord Brougham, Richard the Third, and George the Third, in the old show. If the figure desirable to convert into a murderer had originally a kind of smile or smirk upon his face, this did not come in so well for a murderer; but with a warm skewer you could easily bring the corners of the mouth down and colour the place over to make him look as savage as desirable.

The *Illustrated Police News* had reported how Charlie, awaiting death, had the good sense to secure a deal with Madame Tussaud's for the sale of memorabilia, including the fantastic edifice to his memory (consciously reminiscent of those memorials to Sir Walter Scott, in Edinburgh, or to Prince Albert of Saxe-Coburg Gotha, in Kensington) which he painstakingly constructed out of cardboard in the death cell. These relics were to be exhibited even before his execution. Peace made sure the small matter of his demise would not get in the way of his ability to pilfer.

He became synonymous with waxworks — not all of the high quality of Tussaud's — but, however unrealistic, crucial to the continuing circulation of his representation. Indeed, he has been honoured to be the only miscreant featured in the Chamber of Horrors with two figures: one shows him lurking in the shadows, whilst in the other he is seated under the noose with Marwood about to pinion him. Unique among criminals, two of his nemeses are depicted:

PC Robinson apprehended Charles Peace in 1878 while Peace was committing a burglary. Peace fired at and wounded the constable who nevertheless effected the arrest.

Marwood, William was Public Hangman from 1874-84 and introduced the 'long drop'. When not engaged in carrying out executions he followed the trade of cobbler. Among the many criminals hanged by him the most notable were Peace, Mapleton, Kate Webster and Wainwright.

Could there ever be a diversion more weird than waxwork shows? Life-size figures, moulded from a substance resembling human flesh, so like yet so unlike their living, breathing, moving originals, are the quintessence of the Uncanny (*unheimlich* in Freud's great study, the German word meaning literally 'unhomely', something other). Allowing the paying punter to approach static personalities usually stratospherically distant, time itself seems suspended as characters from every historical epoch, preserved from putrefaction, stand side by side immortalised by celebrity.

Beginning as devotional effigies then later to be deployed as medical simulacra in societies which considered post-mortem anatomical dissection sacrilegious (the *Museo La Specola* in Florence has a massive eerie collection of these), waxen bodies evolved from their religious and academic origins to become secularised as a species of popular entertainment.

Maria Tussaud survived the Terror of the French Revolution by making death-masks of those that didn't, keeping alive their expressions at the moment of death as a history lesson for those whose turn for a free ride in a tumbril to visit Madame Guillotine might yet be a future possibility. Stranded in England during the Napoleonic wars, she was obliged to tour the country with her collection, before finding a permanent location on Baker Street.

In 1846 'a magnificent display of Court Dresses of surpassing riches' was mounted. This, at a time of widespread famine and deprivation, provoked the outrage of Mark Lemon, the editor of *Punch*:

> The collection should include specimens of the Irish peasantry, the hand-loom weavers and other starving portions of the population all in their characteristic tatters; and also the inmates of the various workhouses in the ignominious garb presented for them by the Poor Law. But this department of the exhibition should be contained in a separate Chamber of Horrors and half a guinea should be charged for the benefit of the living originals.

(Quoted in *Madame Tussaud's Chamber of Horrors — Two Hundred Years of Crime*, Pauline Chapman, Constable 1984.)

The appellation 'Chamber of Horrors' stuck, applied not to victims of social oppression (for who would wish to be reminded of them?) but for gruesome characters with blood on their hands.

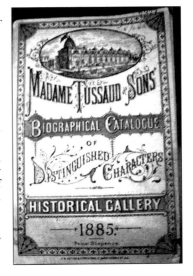

In John T. Tussaud's memoir *The Romance Of Madame Tussaud's*, published in 1919, the founder's grandson recounts three anecdotes about Peace's place in the family firm. The first concerns George Bernard Shaw when he was invited to 'join the company of the Immortals':

> I thought I detected a certain shyness about Mr. Shaw in the Chamber of Horrors. He was very reserved, and surveyed the faces of degenerate men and women without offering any criticism. I remember that the crafty, and yet not wholly repulsive, face of Charles Peace engaged Mr. Shaw's attention several minutes.

The second only serves to confirm Charlie's notoriety among the populace:

> In the Berlin Treaty Days a staunchly Conservative borough was celebrating the event, and among other decorations was a large transparency showing Lord Beaconsfield and Lord Salisbury standing together with the motto 'Peace With Honour' beneath them. An old woman went up to the borough M.P. and asked: 'If you please, sir, will you tell me which is Peace?' Charles Peace was the man of the moment just then.

And the third ruefully illustrates the transience of fame:

When Dr. Jackson was Bishop of London he gave a breakfast to several curates before they left to take up missionary work abroad and one of them, in the course of conversation at the repast, observed that he had just visited Madame Tussaud's where he had heard a figure of his Grace had been on view for many years. He said he much regretted that he could not find the figure anywhere in the Exhibition, although he had searched for it high and low. 'Oh,' said the Bishop, 'haven't you heard, my dear boy, that they've melted me down for Peace?' — a sally that was greeted with roars of laughter.

John Theodore also gives a mawkish personal account of his dealings with Marwood, indicative of the creepy aura which should forever surround a Public Executioner. His figure, unlike that of Charlie, was 'modelled from life' and, generously, he asked for no reimbursement for the sittings. This scion of the Tussaud clan came to know him personally:

The executioner would sometimes visit the studios when his spirits were low, and a pipe and a glass of gin and water — his favourite beverage — were always at his service. Then he would go down to the Chamber of Horrors to see some of his old acquaintances around whose necks he had so delicately adjusted the fatal noose. He would stop before each one with a grim look, whilst his lips moved tremulously. 'Put me there,' he once said after he had given a sitting. It was like a man choosing the site of his grave. His companion on these visits was a grizzled terrier. One day he came alone. 'Your dog, Mr. Marwood — where is it?' he was asked.

The old man was sad. 'My poor old dog is dying — my dog that knew the business like a Christian and the inside of every prison; that has played with my ropes; that has caught rats in my business bags.' 'Dying by inches,' was the unfeeling rejoinder of a bystander, followed by the cruel suggestion, 'Why don't you hang him?' Marwood gave him a reproachful glance. 'No, no. Hang a man, but my dear old dog — never!'

Poor Marwood had a good heart.

The Era reported on the 7th of June 1884, a year after his death:

FIRE AT THE EAST LONDON AQUARIUM
In this section were a number of articles which had formerly belonged to Marwood, the late hangman, including the rope and other apparatus used by him in his official functions. These were destroyed but his Gladstone bag, together with a presentation sword were saved.

Not only villains bequeath precious relics.

Another ditty in *Punch*, undated but from the late 1890s, is quoted in *Madame Tussaud* by Leonard Cottrell (The Non-Fiction Book Club 1951):

There's a refuge, if Cabinet duties cease,
Where Ministers anxious to rest — with Peace
May do so
Political stars who are on the wane
In a popular Chamber may wax again
Chez Tussaud.

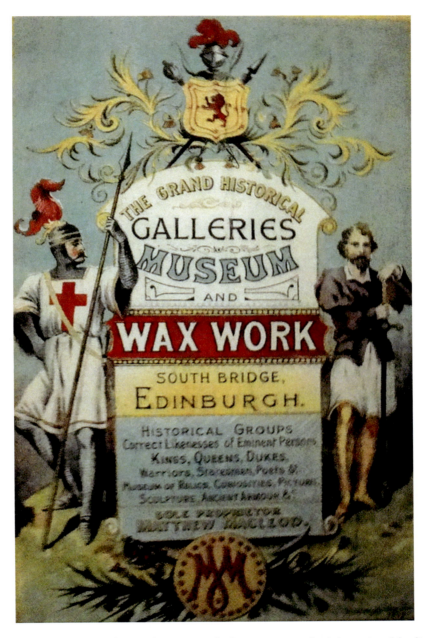

Catalogue descriptions from other waxwork shows express the inherent ambiguity of the character. This pitch comes from The Grand Historical Galleries Museum and Wax Work, on South Bridge, Edinburgh:

> The popular interest in this man is due, we imagine, mainly to his unusual courage, and the notion that he was a kind of criminal gladiator, always staking himself against society. He was a man of a type in some ways unusual among violent criminals — a

man with something of the artist organisation about him, which is usually accompanied by sensitiveness, and is often supposed to be inconsistent with the callousness which was the most marked characteristic of Peace. He was a very fair musician, a good carver and gilder. He was ingenious too, as well as artistic; he was a mechanician of some skill, having invented and made the false arm which he greatly relied [upon] to conceal his crimes. Taken altogether he must be considered to be an extraordinary man. He made burglary his business, neither drank nor wasted money, and it is one of the strange facts of his career, that he was, for the latter part of his life, a tolerably well-to-do man.

Louis Tussaud was another great-grandson who split with cousin John T. and set up in opposition in nearby Regent Street in 1892. In the first year of the new century he moved his operation to Blackpool, with a show specialising in exhibiting instruments of torture. His catalogue stresses Peace's double life whilst exaggerating the number of his homicides:

> The 'King of Burglars' is remarkable for having lived a life of apparent respectability, whilst planning and carrying out single-handed the most daring burglaries in all parts of the country. He possessed undoubted talents which, if properly applied, would have gained him a high position in the world. Several murders were traced to him which he had committed to escape capture.

His Blackpool collection also boasted exhibition of:

> The Revolver with which Peace shot Mr. Dyson. This was discovered in a field near Banner Cross some time after the crime was committed.

Strange... this firearm was neither mentioned nor exhibited in the trial!

Louis made the papers a few years later in a case which even Dickens could not have invented. It was news in the farthest flung colonies, as this report from the *New Zealand Herald* of the 27th of December 1902 confirms:

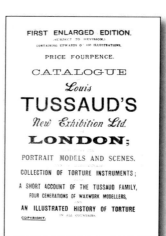

WRONG HEADS ON WRONG SHOULDERS
The humorous side of waxworks shows was revealed in an action brought by Mr. Louis Tussaud... for an injunction to restrain Mr. Walter Stiff, waxworks proprietor and modeller, from carrying on a business at Edgware Road, and exhibiting models there in such a way as to induce the public to believe that either the exhibition or the models were the plaintiff's work. The case was heard in the Chancery Division before Mr. Justice Buckley.

Mr. Ashbury K.C., for plaintiff, stated that for some time his client had a waxworks show in Regent-street, described as 'Louis Tussaud's New Exhibition', by which he made £4,000 profit in six months, and which was ultimately gutted by fire. He then started a show at Alexandra Palace, and in 1893 a company was formed under the style of 'Louis Tussaud's New Exhibition (Limited)' to whom all the models which the plaintiff himself had made were assigned. The company got into trouble in 1897, and the trustee for the debenture holders appointed receivers, who sold the models under a hire and purchase agreement to defendant. Defendant, who ran several exhibitions, divided the models amongst them, and added to them models which plaintiff alleged were much inferior. Plaintiff visited defendant's show in Edgware Road, and there found that a head of the Archbishop of Canterbury modelled by him had been placed upon the body of Charles Peace *(laughter)* while his model of Napoleon was taking part in the execution of Mary Queen of Scots *(laughter)*. Plaintiff was approached by some people in London, who offered to finance him to the extent of £30,000 for a new exhibition of his work, but the principal of them happened to see the show in Edgware Road and was so disgusted that it should be associated with plaintiff's name that he refused to go on with the matter until this action was settled...

Mister Tussaud, what was in front of defendant's premises in Edgware Road when you visited it?

Before the issue of the writ 'All of the exhibits from Louis Tussaud's New Exhibition, Regent-street.' After the writ was issued the word 'all' was altered to 'some'.

What did you find inside?

I found a few hands modelled by myself, but the greater part were put on wrong bodies *(laughter)*. This is doing me a terrible lot of harm. There is not one complete figure of mine in the exhibition. Tailor's dummies are not portraits, and the defendant's models are worse than tailor's dummies *(laughter)*. Still there was plenty to see for a penny...

The *Boston Evening Transcript* contained further verbatim protestations from the scion of the 'illustrious name' of Tussaud, as Louis defended the artistry of his profession:

'If you shift a head once you may get it tolerably right, but if you employ different people to do it repeatedly the thing goes from bad to worse... The hands and the bodies are detachable and it takes a man who knows the work to put them together again. If you paint and wash them down the wax melts and disfigures them. If that is done with my models the exhibition is no longer mine. I say you are making a fool of the exhibition by putting the wrong heads on... If you cut the nose and ears off and polish them no man could tell it for his own work...' The fact was brought out that, besides, mixing up the bodies and heads, Bismarck's robes were put on the figure of Charles Peace.

Surprisingly, His Lordship 'held that there had been no passing off in the name of plaintiff, and dismissed the action with costs.'

An even more bizarre court case from the early 1920s, concerned the Cardiff Continental Waxworks (source and date unknown, unearthed from Wales Online.)

CHAMBER OF HORRORS WAS TOO MUCH FOR CLEARED MAN
In March 1922 a unique libel action took place at the Cardiff Assizes when wax effigies were brought into the court to provide evidence. One of the effigies which had been exhibited at D'Arcs Waxworks, was that of Llanelly solicitor Mr Harold Greenwood who had been acquitted eighteen months earlier of murdering his wife by poison. Mr Greenwood had taken action for damages against the owner Mr John D'Arc claiming that the figure of himself labelled 'Harold Greenwood' had been exhibited in the Chamber of Horrors and had been placed between the notorious murderer Charles Peace and that of the Irish rebel Terence McSweeney.

Mr Greenwood, who had learned about his effigy being on show at the waxworks by a friend who had paid sixpence to visit the exhibition on a visit to Cardiff, said that he was an innocent man and that as he had been acquitted he did not deserve 'such questionable and distasteful publicity'.

He went on to say: 'I do not wish to be a celebrity and I don't want my name in the public eye.' Questioned by the defendant's solicitor, however, he admitted that he had written articles about his ordeal for the Sunday Herald and had received £3,000 for his efforts. He also admitted that his picture had appeared in the press some 13 times and that of his second wife 11 times.

When the wax effigies were brought into the court room, they caused some amusement as the one purporting to be Charlie Peace was that of Prime Minister Lloyd George!

As for the one depicting Mr Greenwood, he said it was rather clumsy and that they had given him deformed ears. Mr D'Arc denied that Mr Greenwood's effigy had been exhibited in room three which was the Chamber of Horrors. But the jury accepted the view that it had been exhibited there if only for a short period and Mr Greenwood was awarded £150 damages.

The original and greatest show, now relocated to the site where it continues to draw in the tourist hordes, was in the news again on March 18th 1925. This evocative account comes from Leonard Cottrell *op.cit*:

At ten o'clock people passing along the Marylebone Road saw a red glow coming from the windows. The wiring of an electrically driven organ in the main hall had fused and within a few minutes the flames had attacked the woodwork. Quickly the fire spread, in spite of the efforts of Messrs. Tussaud's firemen, who were soon joined by the main fire brigade. In a short time the floor of the main upper hall was a glutinous mass of blazing wax. The delicate dresses of queens and princesses, the silks and satins and kings and courtiers dissolved in flame. Iron girders bent like burning matches. Throbbing hoses snaked up Baron Grant's marble staircase, at the top of which crouched the sweating firemen, half-choked by the smoke and stench of burning wax. Above the hiss of the hoses and the crackle of burning timber rose a roar like a blast furnace, as flames poured from the upper windows and lit the sky. From all directions Londoners came running towards the glare, as the incredible news went round 'Madame Tussaud's is on fire!'

The flames quickly ate into the room containing the precious relics of Napoleon. The great coach which had borne him through the snows of Russia, his bed from St. Helena, his Coronation robes, jewels and orders crumbled into white ashes. Soon the upper floors were completely gutted, and while the Hall of Tableaux on the ground floor escaped the worst effects of the fire, water cascaded down from the floor above, drenching ruffs and doublets, farthingales and periwigs in a indiscriminate deluge. But the occupants of the Chamber of Horrors got away with a mere soaking, and among them, fortunately, were most of Madame Tussaud's own valuable death-masks. On the following morning, as policemen, firemen, and journalists followed John Tussaud and his sons through the foul-smelling debris, the faces of Robespierre and Marat, of Charles Peace, William Palmer and their companions, still stared at them, wet but triumphant among the ruins.

It seems morbidly ironic that the great and good should be liquefied whilst the base and the bad should survive. The day after the fire the *Manchester Guardian* added:

Members of the crowd inquired after the safety of Charlie Peace, Crippen, and other notorious criminals of the Chamber of Horrors... It is strange to think of the number of eminent, and highly respectable people being burned in effigy in London. Madame Tussaud's famous waxworks spread its net far and wide, and at least forty people of the present Parliament and scores of notabilities outside were represented in wax in these burning galleries. Criminals represented in the Chamber of Horrors, however, will have no feelings in the matter, as they are all dead.

Mark Twain evokes Charlie to have a dig at this public fascination with celebrity criminals in *Captain Stormfield's Visit to Heaven,* the last satirical squib he published in 1909, the year before his death:

'The finest thing that has happened (up in Heaven) in my day... was Charles Peace's reception — him they called "the Bannercross Murderer", an Englishman. There were four patriarchs and two prophets on the Grand Stand that time. There hasn't been anything like it since Captain Kidd came.'

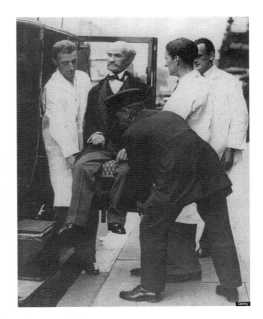

Charlie only left the Chamber on one further occasion when his figure was treated to a ride in a horseless carriage, a vehicle which post-dated his lifetime, to serve as honorary president at a meeting of the writers of the Crime Club in Grosvenor House.

His transformation into a comic character was complete.

In the Music Hall

THE ADVENTURES AND TRIAL OF CHARLEY PEACE was put out by W.S. Fortey, General Steam Printer and Publisher, 2&3 Monmouth Street, Bloomsbury. As it scans to *Villikins and His Dinah* this 'lay' might well have been sung in the halls.

Now listen to my lay, I have got a lot to say
And while I'm singing your join tackle cease.
The game is all up now, they've got me fast I vow,
So listen now to poor old Charley Peace.
For you know they have me lagged,
Now they want to have me scragged,
Mrs Dyson's trying hard, what a shame!
They'll believe what she'll relate
I'll get out some morn at eight.
And Marwood then will stop my little game.

CHORUS: Oh what a blooming shame,
They stopped my little game
And my funny little capers soon will cease.
So listen while I tell what things I've seen as well
As done to me — they call me Charley Peace.

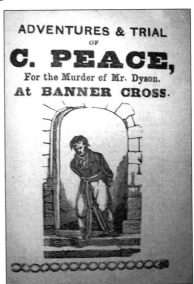

Oh wasn't it a lark the first time I made a start
I could crack a crib three hundred pounds a time.
I could roam and sport about, and they couldn't find me out.
And I could cheat them, boys, it was so fine.
If I thought they me could trace I would quickly change my face
Says I, my lads, you cannot nobble me.
But at last the game is done for me now they in have run
And I fancy now that Charley's all U.P.

Nothing me it was beneath so I visited Blackheath
And I reaped a pretty tidy harvest there,
But it makes me feel so ill for they say I Dyson killed
And my life away his wife she means to swear.
Thinks I, oh here's a frost! when I went to Banner Cross
At the inquest I heard all they had to say,
For I found it getting hot so I left the blooming lot.
Says I, you don't have Charley Peace today.

When the folks began to talk I went to Hull in York
And at Hull a pretty booty there did find
Mrs Thompson there I met, Charley Peace she won't forget
While I'm here, says I, I'll make some overtime.
On the Holborn Viaduct, just as if it was my luck
Bill Fisher saw me there as you must know.
Why that's Peace, I heard him say, thinks I, Charlie get away.
For they haven't got you yet so off you go.

Then they took me in the train to examine me again.
Thinks I, Oh dear what ever shall I do?
If for murder they me try Charley Peace is sure to die
Lor! I'll cheat the judge and jury Marwood too.
For the train it gave a bump out the window I did jump,
Thinks I, there's only once that I can die.
But, my boys, 'twas not to be, for again they captured me
And for murder in my cell now here I lie.

I can play upon the fiddle and the bobbies I did diddle
So a warning take, my boys, who e'er you be.
And don't you be too fast for be sure it cannot last
For when the game is done you're up a tree.
Charley Peace he tells you plain, no matter what your game,
That honesty is best you will agree.
For the game is up, I know, no white feather I will show,
So a lesson take from Charley Peace — That's me.

Should any further proof be required for the abiding connection between Peace and the waxworks then other songs of the Music Hall might well be mobilised.

In 1891 Albert Chevalier, 'the costers' laureate', best remembered today for his moving song of workhouse separation *My Old Dutch*, wheeled out *The Waxworks Show* in the guise of one such spruiker:

Just give the drum a good old bang and let the trumpet blow, sir,
Walk up! Walk up! you mustn't miss the monster wax-works show, sir,
I've figures representative of every blessed nation,
I tell you wot this show of mine's a lib'ral education.
    It's gospel true, I give you my word
    I ain't a man to 'blow'
    One 'D's' the price, and too absurd
    For sich a gorgeous show.

However, he never name-checked Charlie, referring only generically:

I've celebrated burglars too, and popular murderesses
In fashionable tourist suits and most expensive dresses.

This lost opportunity was soon rectified in 1898 by W.P. Dempsey in *They're All Like Life; or My Nobby Little Waxwork Show*, written and composed by Castling and Leigh. Verse Two goes:

Now the Kaiser's on the right — 'e's a German bloke he is!
He's notorious for having too much to say!
The little fat bloke watching him is Mister Johnny Bull,
'E's a blooming little terror in his way.
Further on is Charlie Peace, the man wot broke the bank,
Then there's Billy Griggs wot broke the copper's nose.
Just behind the screen is Venus, but we ain't showing 'er
Till the wife has finished making 'er some clothes.

The reference, of course, is to Charles Coburn's *The Man Who Broke the Bank at Monte Carlo* which Dempsey had already parodied as *The Bank That Broke the Man* at the same Riviera location. Music Hall fed upon itself.

Two years earlier Harry Champion ('Cockney Bill of London Town'), champion indeed of such metropolitan delicacies as *Boiled Beef and Carrots, A Basin of Soup, Home Made Sausages* and *A little Bit Of Cucumber* had already — albeit briefly — name-checked Charlie in a verse about, of course, a waxwork show in *It's A Pretty Little Place Inside*:

There's Adam and Eve and Charlie Peace
And Gladstone tearing up his Home Rule lease.
Don't grin, walk in, and see the fat man's bride
She's got no nose, and not many clothes
It's a pretty little place inside.

In 1910 the great songsmiths Fred Murray and Bert Weston took this waxworks visit further in another wonderfully exuberant song for Champion. Everybody of a certain age probably knows this ditty, but not this memorable verse, because the whole song was too long to fit on a wax recording:

Now at the Waxwork Exhibition not so long ago
I was sitting among the kings, I made a lovely show
To good old Queen Elizabeth I shouted "Wotcher Liz!"
While people poked my ribs and said 'I wonder who this is?'

One said 'It's Charley Peace' and then I got the spike
I shouted 'Show yer ignorance!' as waxy as you like.

I'm Enery the Eighth, I am
Enery the Eighth I am, I am
I got married to the widow next door
She's been married seven times before
Well every one was an Enery (Enery!)
She wouldn't have a Willie or a Sam (No Sam!)
I'm her eighth old man named Enery
Enery the Eighth, I am.

The celebrated monologist (and Dickensian character actor) Bransby Williams also kept Charlie's memory green in his guise as *The Waxworks Watchman* (penned by W. Frank and Frank S. Wilcock). This harnesses the figure of Peace to the unknown Whitechapel murderer, for whom his waxwork effigy was forever being mistaken:

Then Charlie Peace strolled in and said 'I've just left Jack the Ripper,
He's having quite a ripping time a-ripping up a kipper.
I'd like to murder someone too, it must be quite a time
Since last I had the pleasure of committing of a crime.'
His nasty eye then fell on me, my blood began to freeze,
My breath came in short pants and I was shaking at the knees
'It's time that you were dead,' said he, 'so someone fetch a chopper.'
But Joan of Arc then butted in, just like a female copper,
She said 'You'll hurt his feelings if you this crime commit,
If you must murder someone, murder me, I'm used to it!'
But just then Charlie saw my nose, and that made him see red,
With my wife's Christmas pudding then, he bangs me on the head.
Eight savage blows he struck me on my poor blinkin' pate,
And then I found 'twas daylight, and the clock was striking eight.
And when I found 'twas daylight, my courage rose once more,
I punched old Charlie on the nose, and knocked him on the floor.

Even George Formby got in on the act in 1933 when he was *Running Round The Fountains In Trafalgar Square*, though this verse, too, never made the well-known recorded version:

And then there's Madam Tussauds, that's a well-known waxworks show
Now that's the place where all the country trippers like to go
The figures that you heard about now they're no longer there
There's only one place you will find them, I will tell you where.
They're running round the fountains in Trafalgar Square
That's the thing that everybody's doing down there.
Henry the Eighth, chasing Anne Boleyn
Doctor Crippin looking haggard and thin.
And Charlie Peace with his old violin
Are running round the fountains in Trafalgar Square.

A vein of humour must always be conjured up as sublimated protection from the shivering terror provoked by 'life-like figures in wax'.

Literature?

In *The Ethics of the Detective Story from Raffles and Miss Blandish* (1944), George Orwell, drawing on a commonly held knowledge of Charlie's dress-up box, harrumphed:

> Charles Peace in his clergyman's dog-collar, seems somewhat less of a hypocrite than Raffles in his Zingari blazer.

The gentleman burglar, however, had a soft spot for his working-class colleague as E.W. Hornung's 1905 story, *The Raffles Relics*, attests. Raffles and Bunny pay a visit to Scotland Yard's Black Museum where some of his own burglary implements are being exhibited. Raffles is moved:

> 'Fame at last! It lifts one out of the ruck of robbers into the society of the big brass gods, whose little delinquencies are written in water by the finger of time.'

And Bunny Manders relates:

> We entered the forbidding precincts; we looked relentless officers in the face, and they almost yawned in ours as they directed us through swing doors and up stone stairs... (The clerk) carried a loose key, with which he unlocked a door a little way along the passage, and so ushered us into that dreadful repository which perhaps has fewer visitors than any other of equal interest in the world. The place was cold as the inviolate vault; blinds had to be drawn up, and glass cases uncovered, before we could see a thing except the row of murderers' death-masks — the placid faces with the swollen necks — that stood out on their shelves to give us ghostly greeting...
> In a moment I discovered that I knew far more about its contents than our pallid guide. He had some enthusiasm, but the most inaccurate smattering of his subject. He mixed up the first murderer with quite the wrong murder, and capped his mistake in the next breath with an intolerable libel on the very pearl of our particular tribe.
> 'This revawlver,' he began, 'belonged to the celebrated burgular, Chawles Peace. These are his spectacles, that's his jimmy, and this here knife's the one that Chawley killed the policeman with.'
> Now I like accuracy for its own sake, strive after it myself, and am sometimes guilty of forcing it upon others. So this was more than I could pass.
> 'That's not quite right,' I put in mildly. 'He never made use of the knife.'
> The young clerk twisted his head round in its vase of starch.
> 'Chawley Peace killed two policemen,' said he.
> 'No, he didn't; only one of them was a policeman; and he never killed anybody with a knife.'
> The clerk took the correction like a lamb. I could not have refrained from making it, to save my skin. But Raffles rewarded me with as vicious a little kick as he could administer unobserved. 'Who was Charles Peace?' he inquired, with the bland effrontery of any judge upon the bench.
> The clerk's reply came pat and unexpected. 'The greatest burgular we ever had,' said he, 'till good old Raffles knocked him out!'
> 'The greatest of the pre-Raffleites,' the master murmured.

This is far from the only literary reference. *The Lodger*, Mrs Belloc Lowndes' 1913 'Story of the London Fog', was inspired by the exploits of Jack the Ripper, but this didn't stop Charlie from ingratiating himself into the tale. In Chapter Nine the author allows herself a lengthy digression as her heroine, Daisy Bunting, and her father are given a privileged conducted tour:

A broad-shouldered, pleasant-looking young fellow... came forward suddenly, and, unlocking a common-place-looking door, ushered the little party... through into the Black Museum.

[T]he centre was taken up with plain glass cases fixed at a height from the floor which enabled their contents to be looked at closely. She walked forward and peered into the case nearest the door. The exhibits shown there were mostly small, shabby-looking little things, the sort of things one might turn out of an old rubbish cupboard in an untidy house — old medicine bottles, a soiled neckerchief, what looked like a child's broken lantern, even a box of pills. As for the walls, they were covered with the queerest-looking objects; bits of old iron, odd-looking things made of wood and leather, and so on. It was really rather disappointing.

Then Daisy Bunting gradually became aware that standing on a shelf just below the first of the broad, spacious windows which made the great room look so light and shadowless, was a row of life-size white plaster heads, each head slightly inclined to the right. There were about a dozen of these, not more — and they had such odd, staring, helpless, *real*-looking faces.

'Whatever's those?' asked Bunting in a low voice. Daisy clung a thought closer to her father's arm. Even she guessed that these strange, pathetic, staring faces were the death-masks of those men and women who had fulfilled the awful law which ordains that the murderer shall be, in his turn, done to death.

'All hanged!' said the guardian of the Black Museum briefly. 'Casts taken after death.' Bunting smiled nervously. 'They don't look dead somehow. They looks more as if they were listening,' he said... 'They looks foolish-like, rather than terrified, or — or hurt,' said Bunting wonderingly. He was extraordinarily moved and fascinated by those dumb, staring faces. But young Chandler exclaimed in a cheerful, matter-of-fact voice, 'Well, a man would look foolish at such a time as that, with all his plans brought to naught — and knowing he's only got a second to live — now wouldn't he?'

'Look here, in this here little case are the tools of Charles Peace. I expect you've heard of him.' 'I should think I have!' cried Bunting eagerly. 'Many gents as comes here thinks this case the most interesting of all. Peace was such a wonderful man! A great inventor they say he would have been, had he been put in the way of it. Here's his ladder; you see it folds up quite compactly, and makes a nice little bundle — just like a bundle of old sticks any man might have been seen carrying about London in those days without attracting any attention. Why, it probably helped him to look like an honest working man time and time again, for on being arrested he declared most solemnly he'd always carried that ladder openly under his arm.'

'The daring of that!' cried Bunting.

'Yes, and when the ladder was opened out it could reach from the ground to the second storey of any old house. And, oh! how clever he was!

Just open one section, and you see the other sections open automatically; so Peace could stand on the ground and force the thing quietly up to any window he wished to reach. Then he'd go away again, having done his job, with a mere bundle of old wood under his arm! My word, he was artful! I wonder if you've heard the tale of how Peace once lost a finger. Well, he guessed the constables were instructed to look out for a man missing a finger; so what did he do?'

'Put on a false finger,' suggested Bunting.

'No, indeed! Peace made up his mind just to do without a hand altogether. Here's his false stump: you see, it's made of wood — wood and black felt. Well, that just held his hand nicely. Why, we considers that one of the most ingenious contrivances in the whole museum.'

For years I have vainly tried to gain access to the Black Museum (recently more blandly re-branded as The Crime Museum), but entrance is strictly restricted to serving police officers, supposedly because the grisly objects would be far too destabilising for lay sensibilities. The nearest those of us not possessed of a warrant card could approach before the 2015/16 Museum of London show was via an extract from a 1990 documentary *Inside the Black Museum* (available on YouTube at the time of writing). This is fronted by Shaw Taylor, erstwhile presenter of *Police 5*, granting him the sanctioned role of early television's mediator between the Force and the public. It is impossible to watch without some envy as the camera casts a privileged pan over a violin case containing:

> The tools of his burglar's trade, the folding ladder, the drugged pieces of meat for possible watchdogs, the skeleton keys, the pick-locks, the jemmies and the chisels, the cosh to persuade waking victims back to sleep, the candles and matches, for there was no electric torch to light the way of the nineteenth century burglar... For who would suspect the dapper little man, supposedly hurrying home from a late night concert?

And if this has not been insufficient to lather up the aficionado:

> To disguise the missing finger he fashioned this steel tube, covered in cloth with a hook.

What will become of these precious relics when this collection might well be dispersed due to the imminent relocation of the HQ of the Metropolitan Police, as New Scotland Yard is about to be put up for sale to realise its real estate value given its lucrative central London address? And what has happened to the Tussaud reliquaries? I have luxuriated only in the presence of an apparent pair of his glasses, displayed in the Sheffield Fire and Police Museum. But the sentiment was short-lived, for the necessary aural emanation was completely absent given the lack of any convincing provenance — these could have been any old pair of specs. What I really want to see is his cardboard memorial, perhaps because this monument might give some insight into the demented, self-glorifying manner Peace thought of himself and expected to be remembered.

From the *Nottingham Guardian* September, 1936:

> **NOTORIOUS CRIMINAL**
> Concerning the demolition in the slums in the Sussex Street area of Nottingham... although there is no corroboration of the statement that Dick Turpin visited the neighbourhood, there is no doubt that Charles Peace frequently resorted there, one of his favourite hiding places was in a rock-hewn recess at the *Trip to Jerusalem* inn. The proprietor, Mr. George Ward, informs me that the King, when he was Prince of Wales, visited the inn on more than one occasion and displayed interest in the place where Peace concealed himself whilst being pursued for the murder of Constable Cock and a Mr. Dyson. It is an indication of his fortitude and vanity that whilst awaiting his fate he made a paper model of an elaborate monument in the style of the Albert Memorial, which he asked might be erected over his grave!

I felt some deep-felt need to rescue our theatrical model, constructed out of paper and clothes pegs, from the post-show skip to occupy a dubious place among my souvenirs.

Completists might welcome the inclusion of a throw-away allusion by Pelham Grenville Wodehouse (comic master 'Plum') from his 1923 Blandings Castle novel, *Leave It To Psmith*, which couples Charlie with equally mythologised U.S. robbers:

> Here, he told himself unhappily, was a job of work which would test the combined abilities of Charlie Peace and the James Brothers.

Even the prolific Edgar Wallace got in on the act in his coarse pot-boiler *The Devil Man*. Dictated in the course of a weekend in 1930, this book probably takes longer to read than it took the author to write. The writer certainly must have had more fun than the reader. Here Charlie has few redeeming features, the publisher's blurb thundering: 'He was a repulsive creature to look upon; a colossal braggart; a gifted musician; a murderer; a dwarf in stature and a Samson in strength; the perfect burglar...' not forgetting, of course, to stress that Peace was 'a man with an irresistible attraction for women.'

These 'literary' references prove Charlie's abiding fame and his skills other than criminal. How else can he be represented?

Lines on the Capture of Peace, the Sheffield Murderer

The higher literary ability displayed by the eponymous writer of the following poem is coupled with a vehemence towards its subject unparalleled in any other of the extant verses. Not a 'Chorus From The Gallows' nor a pitiable scaffold confession, this is an anti-paean of hatred from, as it were, an outraged 'Society'. A copy was displayed in the Museum of London exhibition, 'The Crime Museum Uncovered' — the first time memorabilia from Scotland Yard's notorious 'Black Museum' had been put on public display. Also on show were the tools of Peace's trade, including his celebrated folding ladder. These verses must have been penned after the arrest but before the execution and is on a one-sheet also reproducing the bearded picture circulated on the reward poster with a short account of the murder of Dyson and the apprehension of Peace. Sordid details of his deeds are deemed 'unspeakable' and, indeed, 'unprintable'. Nonetheless, the comparison with Turpin is again evoked as so often in the popular prints.

'Murder will out!' there is that in the crime
Which Justice must grapple tho' often she lingers,
'Tis a blackness which cannot grow whiter with time
And blood will not wash from the murderer's fingers.
Vainly he strives from his conscience to flee
Retribution comes on and is ever pursuing.
There's blood on his hand and on all he may see
There is blood in his dreams and in all he is doing.
But how shall this monster be painted by pen
The unspeakable eye and unprintable thing?
Adulterous Murderer — blackest of men,
Grey Hypocrite, viper of venomous sting.
Burglar, Betrayer and all that is vile
Compared to whom Turpin was saintly and pure
With a murderous heart and a hypocrite smile
Stern Justice has bound him — at last he's secure.

Society breathes a deep sigh of relief
For worse than wild beast was this devil let loose.
Of fiends the most perfect, of wretches the chief —
Of snivelling sentiment where is the use?
Mercy sickens to think of him — merciless brute!
The psalm-singing sneak, much religion professing
Whose work was to plunder, whose pastime to shoot,
The heart and the claw of the serpent professing.
Was anything ever that looked like a man
So hateful, abandoned, so vilely ferocious?
What shall we call him? Let call him who can
So long as the meaning is wholly atrocious.
We've finished and now let the law do the rest.
May he prove quite the last as the worst of his kind
And when he has gone, execrated, unblest
May his fate be a warning to villains behind.

145

Stage-Struck Charlie

This report comes from *The Era*, weekly for theatrical pros, of July 13th 1889:

AN UNLICENSED 'PLAY HOUSE'

At the Derby Police-court on Tuesday, Arthur Scottorn and William Morton were summoned by the Chief Constable for that on the 20th and 24th June last they did unlawfully cause, permit or suffer to be acted a certain play... in a certain place, to wit, a wooden structure in the Morledge, such place not being duly licensed. Some discussion took place as to whether the building, consisting as it did of wooden sides and stage and canvas top, came within the definition of the Act, but the Bench decided to hear the evidence. Detective-Sergeant Payne stated that on the 20th ult. he went to the show (which was a structure of about twenty yards by seven, having wooden sides and canvas top). On the front it was described as 'Theatre of Varieties, Scottorn and Morton.' A board outside contained the following announcement: 'Tonight at 7.45, that sensational drama *Charles Peace, the Bannercross Murderer*. Prices 1d, 2d and 3d.'

An undercover operation is mounted:

Witness went in at 8.30, having seen several people pay for admission. There were about two hundred people in the building. The stage was at the far end, and witness described the performance. Two girls, he said, came on selling newspapers about Peace, and a policeman entered to remove them, as they were quarrelling. He was attacked by the girls, his hat knocked well over his ears, and the girls escaped. Morton then came on dressed as an old man, being accompanied by a young woman, who addressed Morton as 'Peace' and he addressed her as 'Mrs Dyson.' They talked for some time, and quarrelled. He wanted her to accompany him to America, but she refused and expressed herself as sorry for ever having made his acquaintance. He threw her on the stage and produced a pistol, getting a promise from her, and that ended Act One. Act Two represented a cottage in a wood, and represented Peace finding Mrs Dyson at supper with her husband. After a scene between Peace and Mrs Dyson, a man (Mr Dyson) came out of the cottage, and Peace fired at him, and he fell on the stage apparently dead. In Act Three Peace was dressed as a clergyman, and was living with a Mrs Thompson. Peace went away, met Police Constable Robinson, and eventually wounded him in the arm after a lot of 'foolery', which was introduced to liven the piece up, as it was getting a bit dry. Peace was captured, however, and the next scene was his execution. Witness had known the show to be in the Morledge for weeks together... Both the defendants, who said they were natives of the town, pleaded that they were in ignorance as to the law.

The Bench had no doubt that the building and the play came under the Act. They thought the defendants were not aware they were doing wrong, and they would be fined 20s. and costs each.

Ten years after his execution and Charlie had evidently already become a stalwart of the popular stage. I was naturally determined to track down Peace's theatrical guises to see how earlier playwrights had tackled the character and the incidents of his life.

Setting out to dramatise Charlie raises immediate questions: Is he a hero? A villain? An anti-hero? A trickster? Surely one of the reasons playwrights might have a desire to dramatise this complex character is because he was himself, at least in the tales that were subsequently attached, a performer:

> Inconsiderably known to fame as 'The Modern Paganini' and 'The Great Ethiopian Musician' among his favourite melodies were *The Campbells Are Coming* and he is said to have composed a song he often sang *My Own Sweet Will.* He performed chiefly at public-house 'sing-songs', fairs and kindred entertainments and occasionally offered his services as a reciter at public schools. Of one such occasion Sir Archibald Bodkin has given me a brief account: 'It is a curious fact that in about 1873 or so, while I was a schoolboy in Highgate, this rascal came and, with permission of the headmaster, gave a recitation in the Big School to us boys, and chose the gravedigger's scene from 'Hamlet'. We had, in consequence, nearly a half-holiday, and much enjoyed it.'

(*Trials of Charles Frederick Peace* W. Teignmouth Shore, Notable British Trials Series, William Hodge & Co. 1926)

This letter which appeared in the first volume of *The Dickensian* in 1905 compounded the legend:

DICKENS'S FAT BOY

Sir,

The matter having aroused some local notice, I may be permitted to state the version for the interest of my fellow Dickensians. When lecturing before the Manchester branch recently on 'Dickens and his Friends'

I exhibited a letter of Gustavus Vaughn Brooke's, which I held as a mortgage for money lent to Charles Peace, the burglar and murderer, who was executed in February 1879. I had met him very shortly after his shooting P.C. Cox [*sic*]. He came to my school in order to give an elocutionary and whistling entertainment... He told me he had been proprietor of a theatre at Richmond, that he knew Dickens well...

Peace was a very entertaining (little, thin) fellow, and I look upon the incident as a curious sidelight of Dickensiana.

Yours faithfully,
E.J. Collings.

Whistling is a new contribution!

Peace remains an object of perennial fascination. In life he was undoubtedly possessed with charm, charisma, sexual attraction. But should a theatrical crowd relish his criminal presence, or should paying customers be repelled? This story has become a legend, yet the tale is rooted in actual fact in a real historical context. Always a problem with true-life drama: How to impose a structure upon the shapeless nature of reality? What to show and what to leave out? Where to end (on the gallows) is something of a given, but where to start? How to deal with explanatory back-story? What should be the most appropriate dramatic form? Is this tale a tragedy? A comedy? A farce? Though it has elements of all three, it's clear this could never conform to an Aristotelian narrative structure, observing the unities of time, space and character. Charlie's very nature is metamorphic, his chosen profession demands shape-shifting; at the very least the story demands a three-year time-span; geographically diversity is a necessity.

One dramatic form is entirely appropriate: Melodrama.

Rare enough to see any late nineteenth-century popular dramas on today's stages and even more exceptional to witness the form taken seriously. Such productions usually cannot resist shamelessly laying out a row of tents more camp even than the founder of the Scout movement could ever have envisaged.

There are precedents for this contempt of pre-Ibsen popular theatre. In *The Old Fashioned Way* the magnificent W.C. Fields, as the fly-blown Great McGonigle, leads his histrionic troupe of no-hopers in *The Drunkard* whilst avoiding the pursuit of sheriffs and debt collectors. Such parody achieves comic greatness.

Mostly, though, Today looks down on a style of writing and playing of Yesterday with barely-concealed disgust. But to read accounts of the production of those neglected plays is to realise that theatre in those days was literally spectacular — a night out must have been wonderful. 'Melodrama' has become an insult, implying a debased, psychologically simplistic genre with cack-handed tale-telling techniques and crude audience participation whose appeal can only be to the unsophisticated.

Of course, the term originally means 'drama with music', developed as a cunning way for producers to circumvent the restrictive theatre licensing acts. Charlie Peace was a musician and a master of disguise — his tale is inherently melodramatic.

There are also problems of motivation, not simply for the protagonist but for the characters who surround him. Was Charlie really a religious hypocrite, or could his assumed piety be turned on and off? What attracted Katherine to him? What was he expecting from her when he stalked her to Banner Cross? Why did Hannah stick with him? If Sue was indeed the one who revealed his identity (as seems more than likely given her attempt to get the reward) when and how did she find out who he really was? There is no strong historical or documentary evidence for Sue's discovery and her betrayal, so it has to be invented speculatively if it's going to be a feature of the narrative. How should the forces of Law and Order be presented? Comic coppers? Vengeful judiciary? Representatives of class warfare?

The earliest mention of a play about Charlie comes from the *Manchester Times* of October 18th 1879, eight months after his execution, and is yet another warning of the baleful influence of popular dramas about the notorious felon upon susceptible young mentalities:

MYSTERIOUS HANGING CASE AT TYLDESLEY
On Tuesday Mr. Edge, coroner, held an inquest at the George and Dragon, Tyldesley, on the body of a boy, Peter Mahon, who was found hanging to a cart shaft on Sunday evening. Several boys gave evidence to the effect that Mahon was one of five who went out to hide. When found his neck was in the noose of a rope, which was knotted behind. One of the boys lifted him up with the remark, 'Come on, thou art catched,' but finding the deceased made no answer, he allowed him to drop down again, and went for assistance. It was considered improbable that anybody would hang a lad for simply going to hide in a yard, and the Coroner said there was nothing to warrant the supposition that any violence had been used.

Dr. Trail gave evidence and said his theory was that the lad had voluntarily put his head in the noose and that he had fainted, which would account for the position of the body when found. At the close of the inquiry, it transpired that the deceased on Saturday evening attended a penny theatre in Tyldesley, at which the hanging of Peace was acted. A verdict was found that the deceased was accidentally strangled, but how or by what means there was not sufficient evidence to say.

Maybe sensational literature and drama really does have calamitous effects!

There must have been many other productions in the fairground theatres immediately following the trial. Another such gained a passing mention in the *Sheffield Independent* of 1934 in the course of an article about Alfred Peasnall, a member of Rayner's Portable Theatre. He recollected that they were playing Ilkeston in 1879 when Charles Peace was hanged, so he and Jimmy Rayner knocked off a play in which Peasnall played Dyson, doubling as PC Robinson and Jimmy Rayner played Charles Peace: 'Jimmy got too excited and fired [a stage gun] straight at me. The wadding from the revolver struck me straight between the eyes, and the powder blinded me for two days.'

Not the only casualty, as will be seen, associated with theatrical representations.

In the National Fairground Archive at the University of Sheffield there are two play-bills from the collection dating from the early years of the twentieth century, further proof of the popularity of earlier produc-tions.

Cecil Price provides some information on such a show in *Portable Theatres in Wales, 1843-1914* (from *The National Library of Wales Journal, Volume IX/1*, 1955).

Some of the largest portables could hold 2,000 spectators, and could put on quite as an elaborate spectacle as the smaller permanent theatres. Their overheads were low, as was the price of admission. They avoided towns where stock companies played and sought audiences in the villages and townships of the new indus-trial areas...
The Holloways had a circuit in Warwickshire and occasionally crossed the border. Eight members of the family (with five other actors) played Abersychan and Pontypool in 1865. The company included a brass band... They were at Blaina and Aberdare Workmen's Hall in the same year...
In 1876 T. Holloway advertised for extra staff: 'Wanted, for Holloway's Portable Theatre, Gent. for Heavies, Juvenile Gent., and Low Comedian to sing between the Pieces. Terms, shares or salaries, low. Letters to be addressed to Mr T. Holloway, Theatre, New Town, Montgomeryshire... Send lowest terms.' They were also at Newton and Knighton in 1876, Newton again in 1878. The latter venue saw the tragic death of Holloway's

children who were suffocated whilst asleep by the fumes from a coke fire. In 1909 they are again in the news when Horace Holloway's Portable Theatre was destroyed by fire at Flint.

Something of the flavour of their performances can be gleaned from this report from the *Brecon County Times* in May 1867, describing Abergavenny May Fair:

The general appearance of the fair is much the same as at other places; there is the usual confusion of tongues, gingerbread stalls, toy stalls, nut stalls, with the importunate invitations to 'taste and try before you buy'; there is a confused hubbub of sounds, comprising a very tempest of dissonance from neighbouring ballad singers, the customary squeaking of penny trumpets, ringing of bells... We pass on to the centre point of attraction — the show yard. There, in company with the pugilist's tent, is a strolling theatre, the aspiring *Rocci* of which are taking a preliminary promenade prior to retiring to satisfy the ardent cravings of the lovers of the drama. There they are in all the faded glory of trusseted grandeur strutting up and down their limited stage with all the pomp and circumstance of monarchs, princes, knights and gay cavaleros. They can treat you for a nominal charge of threepence, with a most exacting tragedy on the most approved 'blood and sawdust' principle; can beguile the tears of romantic young noodles...

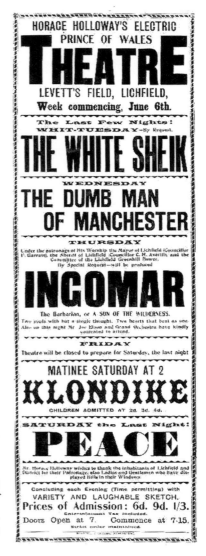

Though the text of the Holloway version is not known, Charles Peace must have been a popular subject, being presented on Saturday evening (The Night For The People). The incident singled out is 'the exciting Struggle between Charles Peace and Detective Robinson' and perhaps a notion of where the sympathy of the country folk who handed over their coppers resided is indicated: 'Come and See and the downfall of the Police.' The Audience (who are, of course, 'held Spellbound') certainly got their money's worth as the Peace play, which presumably ended in the tragic scene on the scaffold, was 'followed by the screaming farce *My Turn Next*', where singing was promised to complete the night's entertainment.

Another playbill for Horace Holloway's Electric Prince Of Wales Theatre, now playing Lichfield, also advertises 'Peace' but this time with no description.

This programme contained two of the most popular plays of the age. *The Dumb Man of Manchester* by B.F. Rayner, first produced in 1838 and (By Special Request) *Ingomar The*

Barbarian, Or A Son Of The Wilderness (Two souls with a single thought. Two hearts that beat as one.) This hardy perennial was adapted by Maria Lovell from Friedrich Halm's *Der Sohn der Wildniss* and had been a success for Henry Irving. It is known today, if at all, from D.W. Griffith's film version made in the first year of his career as a movie-maker for Biograph — filmed in September 1908 it was his twenty-seventh picture that year (the title reversed as *The Barbarian Ingomar*).

If any further proof were needed of the direct continuity between melodrama and early cinema were required, suffice it to say that the great William Haggar filmed scenes from both of these dramas in 1901 and 1902 respectively — unfortunately both are missing believed lost but these plays must have been in his repertoire as well as Holloway's. Haggar will be encountered at greater length when Charlie's further transformation into a cinematographic hero is considered. Before he became a film pioneer, Haggar's company, based in South Wales, also presented a Charlie Peace play which, presumably, formed the basis of his film masterpiece which is all we have to give us a flavour of the sets and performances of the portables. If only the text of Haggar's play were extant so a comparison could be made between stage and screen!

***

Until 1968 every play in Britain had to be scrutinised by the Lord Chamberlain's office for censorship before public performance was allowed. This draconian stricture, naturally detested by playwrights and impresarios, means that there is a wonderful repository of every play text submitted. They can be consulted in the Manuscripts Room of the British Library where they are, after a suitable wait, delivered to the researcher in huge, dusty volumes bound according to the order of their submission.

This is a both an exciting and depressing way to spend a few days in London. There's an undoubted thrill in searching for the forgotten text, wondering whether you're the first to turn these fragile, yellowing pages since the Chamberlain's man scrawled upon them with his thick blue pencil. But the sight of all these unremembered plays can't help but put you in your place. Shows that were still-born before they were conceived; shows that might have been better off dead; shows into which their progenitors poured their hearts and souls; shows which it is hoped at least some spectators paid for seats and were rewarded with a night out which meant they didn't have to shovel shillings into the gas meter; shows whose writers, however deluded, considered themselves, at least in the time of writing, quite the equals of Sophocles, Shakespeare, or Shaw. And now, who knows or cares? It is almost a duty to open the binders, to breathe in the powdery detritus as the sheets threaten to crumble beneath your white-gloved fingers.

There are six post-1900 plays in this invaluable collection dealing with Charles Peace — which does not, of course, mean there may not be others without his name in the title (which seems improbable as it is that name which is the draw). For those few who might, unlikely as it seems, wish to follow in my footsteps I give the date and Lord Chamberlain's reference number.

J. Hodson, *Charles Peace* (L.C. 1919/18)
F. D'Albert, *Charles Peace* (L.C. 1927/41)
C. Rean, *Charles Peace* (L.C.1927/49)

W. Hargreaves, *Charles Peace* (L.C.1927/51)
E. Percy, *Life and Misdoings of Charley Peace* (L.C. 1929/36)
G.H. Walton, *Charles Peace* (L.C. 1939/26)

Joe Hodson: Charles Peace, the Man that Helped the Poor

Before I wrote *Charlie Peace — His Amazing Life and Astounding Legend*, the only previous drama I had set eyes on was this work by Joe Hodson of Swallownest, not far from Charlie's home town. The text was undated but it bears all the lineaments of a portable play, performed by those travelling fairground shows carted from town to town whose strolling players were often members of large extended families.

This was a slightly incomplete copy, without the first and last pages, so I couldn't wait to read the missing passages. I was really surprised to find the submitted version was, unlike the battered type-script copy I had seen, written in longhand by Joe himself in an ordinary notebook which, when filled, the writer had simply turned the book around and completed scrawling the text on the empty verso pages. The British Library copy is dated June 24th 1919 'for production at The Comedy, Sawhill, Rawmarsh'. Perhaps Hodson had to submit it to the Lord Chamberlain for a later outing at a fixed theatre building? On the final page is written: 'Sole Property of Joe Hodson, Perm Address: 57 Millstone Hill Swallownest, Yorks', a village a few miles east of Sheffield, and Rawmarsh is now a suburb of Rotherham. It would, therefore, be playing to an audience for whom Charlie was a local lad. The subtitle gives the game away — this is never going to be a condemnation of a dangerous criminal!

At the end of the hand-written script is a note written by J.R. Hodson: 'This drama is not taken from any novel or tale of any kind in Books. I only know that Peace many many years ago was a Burglar. I have written my story Round it.' Though the spelling, punctuation and syntax are ropy throughout, this remains my favourite of all the plays because it seems so close to the species of entertainment working-class patrons would have expected and enjoyed in its chaotic alternation between violent action, knock-about slapstick, asides to the audience and digs at authority. Though the story departs so much from reality in its mythologizing of Peace, nevertheless some obligatory scenes remain. It confirms what the populace already knew about the real Charlie Peace whilst constructing a fictional protagonist whom they could cheer and take to their hearts.

Act One opens on an 'Extreme Back Road Scene with House Left' where Constable Cox (not Cock) fails to apprehend the Poacher Abrayum (not Habron). Charlie comes out of the house and makes his first aside to the audience (note: all playscripts are quoted as they were presented, with their numerous mistakes):

Peace: Good, that's an easy crib, the owners away and no-one to disturb me, it's a pity I spoiled his door, but never mind I'll send him a cheque with the compliments of Charlie Peace, written on the back in big letters for repairs of damage done on my friendly visit.

When Cox challenges him Peace pretends to be a locksmith, but when he tries to arrest him: *Charlie takes out his revolver... Fires Cox falls.* Enter Inspector (not Constable)

153

Robinson at back who sees Abrayum and arrests him for the murder. So at the end of the first short scene there has already been a violent murder and an innocent man accused.

After such an action-packed opening comes broad comedy with Constable Birdie, a gormless cop, attempting to woo Sal Thompson (!) with much business. She is described by her clothing: *Loud dress, big feathers in hat: Sal picks up squashed hat and box and hits Birdie on head with empty box pulling it well down if possible and then pushes him down*, engaging in hilarious badinage:

> You undersized good-for-nothing blue-bottle, I'll shake you out of your tunic — you — you — you Rabbit pie destroyer.

It's a while before Peace makes a reappearance in Scene 3. He drugs Sal's employer, Mrs Baker, and threatens Sal, brandishing his revolver:

Sal:	Would you murder me?
Peace:	Oh no, Peace never killed in cold blood. My wish is to injure no one, I never pull the trigger without cause, but enough of this. I have led you to believe that I am John Ward a Picture framer from Manchester, that is not true.
Sal:	*(surprised)* Not true.
Peace:	No, I'm here to help myself to your Masters belongings, and I am no other that Charlie Peace.
Sal:	Great Heavens, No — You Charlie Peace.
Peace:	Of course — why not...? You'r a good girl and I don't want to harm you, I think a lot about you, Sal, look here — give up this slavery business and come with me, I have money, I can keep you like a lady buy you fine clothes.
Sal:	Fine clothes.
Peace:	Furs, jewels, diamond rings, everything that you desire.
Sal:	*(melting)* Everything that I desire
Peace:	Will you come with me — what do you say.
Sal:	It is very tempting — fine clothes, jewels, money — to buy anything I choose.
Peace:	Yes.
Sal:	To leave this life of nothing but work and misery.
Peace:	Yes, if you love me Sal now's your time to prove it.
Sal:	*(hesitates)* Well — yes — I'll go. *(shakes hands)*
Peace:	Good, the safe and then we'll clear.
Sal:	You'll find it under the Stairs on your left.

Hardly a difficult seduction.

In Scene 1 of Act Two familiar characters are introduced in Banner Cross. In this version Dyson is the stage cuckold who has moved his young wife to a lonely spot to protect her from 'the man whom I once loved'. But then: *Peace climbs over the wall.*

(Chord). This is the first indication of the use of music, which must have been a significant element of the production, though there are no songs contained in the text.

Mrs Dyson:	Oh Charlie why do you come here, I'm a married woman now, and if my husband saw you here it would be my ruin
Peace:	Yes, and if I had depended on you my ruin would have been complete — you accepted the money I gave you — the rings and other valuables... why you are still wearing sme of them now.
Mrs Dyson:	Yes, I know I have not been fair to you, you gave me everything I desired, I loved you, I swear I did, but the life you led made me afraid. I could'nt stand the strain of it all — I thought some day you would be caught — and...
Peace:	Oh you could see me hanging on the end of a rope, eh, and you were afraid that your turn would come next — you wronged me — no woman shall ever suffer for my faults — *(pause)* you say you loved me.
Mrs Dyson:	Oh no Charlie *(rushes towards him throws her arms around his neck)* don't leave me like that — I am sorry deeply sorry. Take me back, I have made a mistake by tying myself to this old man. *(Mr. Dyson listens)*
Peace:	*(releases himself)* It is now too late Mrs Dyson you are a married woman now and this old man's happiness depends on you and you must stop here
Mr Dyson:	Yes, I'll see she does that:
Mrs Dyson:	Heavens! My husband you have heard all.

In this robust fairground production the representation of the cuckolded Arthur Dyson draws upon the tradition of Pantaloon who migrated from the *commedia dell'arte* to the English pantomime.

Mr Dyson:	Not all but enough to see how things are. *(to Peace)* Go sir before I shoot you, like the cur you are.
Mrs Dyson:	Stop husband, you don't know who you are addressing. You would be like a child in his hands, let him go while you are safe I implore you.
Peace:	Yes, I'll take my leave. *(going)*
Mr Dyson:	Stop! *(pulls out revolver)* or I'll fire. He must stay here & apologise to you and me for his cowardly conduct.
Peace:	Oh that's funny I must say, look here Mr. Dyson, I'm not in the habit of apologising to anyone — you an old man, I don't wish to argue, go inside my good man and be sensible.
Mr Dyson:	Why, you talk to me as though I was a child. I say you shall answer me here and now, or I will kill you where you stand
Peace:	Oh you threaten me do you? Look here I don't wish to harm you, Mr. Dyson, as your grey hairs protect you, I always respect old age, besides you have a wife. Good night *(going)*
Mr Dyson:	Stay I tell you, you shall not go until I have had satisfaction. In my wife's good name, I demand it so. *(during these speeches Mrs. Dyson becomes pleading)*

155

Mrs Dyson:	*(to Mr. Dyson)* Husband desist for your own sake or you may never leave this spot alive, do you know you are speaking to the renowned Charles Peace.
Mr Dyson:	Charles Peace *(surprised)* this cannot be. *(recovers himself)* So it is Charles Peace the house breaker that I am dealing with. *(pulls his wife down corner L; Charles Peace bows)* Charles Peace, thief and murderer. Charles Peace — the wife stealer.
Peace:	Stop. I have had enough of your parley. You were old and I spared you, don't goad me too far or — but there you have not long to live in this world, so I will not rob you of what time you've got *(climbs on wall)*. Good-bye.
Mr Dyson:	You sharn't go. Take that.
Peace:	Oh! You mean business. Very good. *(Comes down stage)* you shall have what you require.

They struggle. Peace trying to get possession of the revolver.

Such productions cannot stay still for long. Whoever played Charlie Peace (as well, no doubt, as half-a-dozen other parts during the week) had to be possessed with uncommon agility.

Mr Dyson:	Let go my hand, curse you, I will kill you like the hound you are.
Mrs Dyson:	Oh spare him Charlie, spare him.
Peace:	Drop the revolver, you old fool, you'll hurt someone.
Mr Dyson:	And that someone is you. *(the revolver is turned towards Dyson, he pulls the trigger. Shot. He moans "You've killed me", falls.)*
Peace:	I told you you would hurt someone and you have done so.
Mrs Dyson:	My husband, my husband.
Peace:	Yes, dead. He pulled the trigger himself. He caused the quarrel and when the verdict is read at the trial it will be "by some person unknown", then there will be a hue and cry for the murderer — the murderer — that's justice — the murderer of a man who killed himself. *(pause)*. I'm sorry, Mrs. Dyson, you saw that it was not my fault, did'nt you. *(gets on wall)*. Oh Peace, Peace what a devil you are for luck. *(exit behind wall. R.)*
Mrs Dyson:	This is all my doing. Had I not left Charles Peace this would never had happened. But I must have a doctor, perhaps there may be hope for him yet, life may not be extinct. *(shakes him)*. Speak to me, Dyson, speak to me. *(stands up)* Oh help, help.

History is rewritten: Dyson is the instigator of his own demise, killed with his own revolver; Peace is defending himself; Mrs Dyson lies to save the man she still loves.

Who in that Yorkshire crowd could have remained unmoved? But would any of them have been convinced by this incredible revision? For the duration of the drama, if for no longer, Charlie Peace has been redefined as a hero 'for the people', more sinned against than sinning. Actuality is exposed as dramatically deficient; the facts on the legal record must not be allowed to stand in the way of the expected demands of a good yarn.

The next scene is set in Charles Peace's home:

Back flats door and window at back table two chairs. L. pint pots on table, wash tub, rubbing board, clothes inside ect, R. Sal Thomson and old Mrs. Peace discovered. Mrs. Peace drinking. L. Sal washing. R .

After a doubtless hilarious cat fight between the women two other persistent tropes are introduced once Charlie has entered:

He brings violin out of case and stands at back on chair, one of the band stands behind flat and plays, Charlie keeps time on his (this is if Charlie ca'nt play violin). Short country dance arranged between Mrs Peace and Sal. Robinson knocks on door. Peace hands violin to Mrs Peace, who runs off with it, Sal gets disguise from. R. side white wig, dressing gown and large handkerchief.

This presumably side-splitting 'deaf old woman routine' with its deliberate punning mis-hearings recurs throughout the plays and becomes an essential fictional element to illustrate Peace as a master of disguise, bamboozler of the law. When was its first appearance? This disguise has passed into folklore.

Nottingham Evening Post Tuesday February 11th 1930:

KISSED BY PEACE
Mrs Adams, of Darnall, has clear recollections of Charles Peace, and a very real admiration for some of his characteristics. 'I have had many a kiss from old Charlie Peace,' she said; 'he was one of the best old men who ever lived. He gave my father, who was a watchmaker and repairer, pounds worth of work.' She remembers on occasion when Peace visited a sick-bed clad in woman's clothes. 'I thought it was Charlie's Aunt,' she said, laughingly.

This scene contains plenty of opportunities for improvised 'bus' (comic business) and, once the coppers enter, the text parenthetically spells out performance reactions and choreographs the action.

Robinson:	I say old lady, have you seen Charles Peace round here?
Peace:	Eh? Was you speaking to me? Did you say can I hear.
Robinson:	*(louder)* No, Charles Peace. *(Points to Mrs Peace)* That Lady's son.
Peace:	*(In ladies voice as near as possible)* Eh, did you say will I have a bun?
Robinson:	Oh I can see its useless wasting time.

Walks away from bed and looks round stage.

Birdie:	Leave her to me sir, I'm good at this Fog Horn Business... Look here Mother Shipton, has Charlie Peace been here?
Peace:	I don't mind if I do.
Birdie:	Don't mind if you do, What?
Peace:	Have some beer.

Sal & Mrs Peace get each side of Birdie. Peace gets out of bed behind and takes things off.

Peace:	*(pointing revolver — they stop)* Keep off all of you, the first one that advances meets his death... Let me tell you this, that the prison is not built, that will hold Charles Peace.

(NOTE — IF NO REVOLVE SET FINISH ACT HERE)

Picture at Window, Peace keeping them back with revolver. then Black out, quick change to house tops this set is made to revolve from kitchen, the two centre flats turn inwards towards front of stage. Showing house tops at the Back. Lights up as soon as set is ready. Charles Peace, climbs through window on to roof, Robinson, Birdie & Buttons, following slowly, when Peace is in Centre Robinson seizes him, and they struggle, Buttons comes to Robinson's assistance and they both struggle with Peace, Birdie comes forward to lend a hand & Peace pushes him with his foot, and he falls over the top into net below. Peace throws Buttons from him and hits him, and he falls through sky-light they roll up and down roof of House.

Haggar's 1905 film has an exact same sequence, though without dialogue of course! This raises the question: Did Haggar use the Hodson text or vice versa? The switch from the interior of the Peace household to the rooftop demands a fair bit of stagecraft and the use of a revolve which, as Hodson indicates, not every theatre would have been able to achieve. So much easier to accomplish by the new medium with a simple cut.

Whilst the obligatory characteristics are out on parade Hodson's play makes one further addition to the Peace mythos before his inevitable journey to the gallows — one incident which cannot be altered. At the beginning of Act Three, which takes place in a Wood, a character is introduced who seems to have stumbled in from an entirely different play: *Jack Hobs, waif with brush, lame limps.*

Jack:	Aint much doing to-day, I've not earned much. Road sweeping ain't any cop no time, and if it was'nt for the bit of begging I does, my mother would go short many times. Its only for her sake that I try — if we depended on Father, the workhouse would soon claim us all — he thinks of nothing but Beer, the public house is his home, and mother and me don't count in his eyes, — its perhaps not good for me to say, but mother would be better rid of him.

The poor young sweeper is brutalised by his drunken father, Bill, who *lashes him with whip*. But salvation is at hand for *Peace rushes on L. takes whip from Bill and knocks him down.* Charlie's revised role: protector of the poor and weak, distributor of wealth to the oppressed!

Jack:	Why let me look at you. *(gets up feebly)* Yes you are the gentleman that comes round the slums and helps the poor.
Peace:	*(surprised)* How do you know that?
Jack:	*(look at him up & down)* Although you've got strange clothes on — I can tell by your eyes — that you are he; the man that as saved many a poor family from Starvation, also kept a roof above their heads — my mother is always talking of you, and I myself say a little prayer for your safety.
Peace:	I do nothing but what is right, besides I like my task.
Jack:	But where does all the money come from, you must be rich?

Peace: It comes from those, my boy, that can well afford it...

Who can these characters be but reduced transpositions of two Dickensian creations, familiar enough from theatrical adaptations if not from the original versions in the novels? Charlie Peace has become a latter-day Robin Hood and earned the soubriquet of 'The Man Who Helped The Poor' by rescuing Poor Jo the Crossing Sweeper (from *Bleak House*) out of the clutches of Bill Sikes (from *Oliver Twist*).

Peached on by the faithless Sal and caught by Robinson after a desperate struggle, Peace is banged up in choky and is about to be taken to trial by train. Then who should enter but young Jack selling papers, shocked to see the man who has been such a Good Samaritan:

Peace: Its all over now my lad, the man of Peace will soon rest in Peace, you will perhaps not see me again, your friend of the Slums is no longer yours — tell them all when you go my lad, that none of them must worry over my arrest — it had to come sooner or later, so why not now? Tell them all that whatever they read about the exaggerated reports in the papers, they will sometimes think kindly of poor Charles Peace. *(Jack weeps)* Don't cry my lad, I'm not worth that, crime must be paid for, although a man may be forced to do it, I did nothing but in self defence.

Jack: Oh please let him go sir — please let him go — spare my govenor — *(falls on knee)* he's gone, he's gone. *(weeps)*. What will they do with him, I know, take him to a prison, a vile dungeon, there to be held in chains, like some dog, and then, and then — what then, perhaps the rope — no, no not that, not that poor govenor — ah if my real father had been like him, a man like him, then I should have been proud to call him govenor, but he his cruel and heartless. He that goes yonder has been more like a father to me in every way God bless him for all he's done, my govenor, my govenor.

Hodson has now given up any attempt to number scenes sequentially but has to bite the bullet in staging a further exciting incident which cannot be shirked — even though it is sure to test all the resources of the poor theatre. He cannot risk the disappointment of the paying customers so is undaunted in taking on the theatrical challenge of The Escape From The Train.

Change of scene. Back scene made to revolve on rollers so it will pass along at back. There is two painted carriages stood on stage, with wheels made to revolve. and as the scene goes up, the Back scene is passing along, the wheels going to make it look as if train is moving. Plenty of noise off side to imitate rattle of train. Peace, Robinson and Birdie discovered in one carriage, two passengers in the others.

Far simpler to write than to stage, Hodson's handwriting optimistically adds:

INSIDE OF CARRIAGE EASY TO MAKE.
Charlie Peace starts a struggle in train, at the finish he works himself through the window. They catch hold of his legs, he forces himself free, drops on stage. The two carriages are then pulled off side R. the scene at back stops moving. Peace lays on stage a moment, or two. Lights down.

At last, the long-anticipated climax with the final revelation that kept the miscreant in the public eye:

Prison scaffold at back with rope. Enter warden, governor of prison, prison chaplian with book, bell tolling throughout this scene. Peace enters from back of stage R.

Peace: The end as come. Well get you to work quick and sharp and let the outside world know that it is all over.

Chaplian: Have you anything more to say?

Peace: Yes, I have a confession to make — you arrested Abrayum for the murder of Constable Cox — I believe he is serving a term of imprisonment. It was a big miscarriage of justice. You were wrong. I did that — so now you can liberate the poor lad and compensate him for false arrest. I'm ready for my journey to the grave... Charlie is no coward and will die game. Now hangman place your noose. One word. Tell the people when I'm gone although I'm charged with murder, I only fired in self defence. The money I stole from the the big pots I spent freely with the Poor. Many a poor mother will Bless the name of Charles Peace. Now pull the lever, I am ready for the Golden Secret. Farewell.

Warder pulls lever. Peace falls into very strong nett. Drop as arranged.

ANYONE HIREING THIS SCRIPT KINDLY KEEP AS CLEAN AS POSABLE & KINDLY RETURN BY REGISTERED POST.

I wonder how often that happened?

Can this amazing text give the modern reader, nostalgic for a world never experienced, a sniff of the long lost portable fairground theatres?

Popular fiction must continually feed upon its predecessors, regurgitating barely digested morsels, half-familiar to greedy, starving diners, mistrustful of exotic dishes which demand an educated palette. What other fare was on offer?

Fred d'Albert: Charles Peace

On October 18th 1927 The Fred d'Albert Repertoire Co. (High-Class Plays and Comedies By The Best Authors. Any Length of Season arranged) apparently presented this show at the Miner's Institute Barkworth (I presume this is Backworth, a colliery village inland from Whitley Bay).

The text runs to ten scenes in thirty-nine pages and contains many familiar moments:

ACT ONE.
1 — Exterior of Arthur Dyson's House.
2 — The Police Office.
3 — Hannah Ward's Kitchen.
4 — The Police Office.
5 — The Manager's Office.

ACT TWO.
1 — Interior of Railway Carriage.
2 — The Railway Embankment.
3 — A Street.
4 — The Condemned Cell.
5 — The Scaffold.

The murder of the *pale, consumptive looking* Dyson is the subject of the first scene which begins with Mrs Dyson, *in a continued state of fear*, reading a clandestine letter:

> 'Meet me again at the old spot. Don't fail me for if you don't come to me I will come to you.' I dare not go but I am determined, if he carries out his threat I shall tell my husband all.

This is the only one of the versions, in any medium, in which Katherine is shown as a mother. Robinson, again promoted now to Detective Inspector, is present from the off as Dyson complains to him told about being pestered by 'Arthur Ward', which is, of course, the pseudonym of you-know-who. 'Charley' (in this version) makes his appearance, leaping over the wall, and gives his first soliloquy, letting us in on his *raison d'être*:

> Money, money, money, my decrepit old mother would cry to me in her wildest ravings. Charlie, my boy, get money. Scheme for it. Plot for it. Only get it. Money the all in all of our existence. With it you're worshipped. Without it you're nothing, despised... Who's talking about robbery? I go in for borrowing without asking consent.

There is no suggestion of love or desire between Peace and Mrs Dyson; his aim is to blackmail her with the letters and a photograph which will destroy her marriage.

In Scene Two Robinson defines Peace to his fellow detectives, Smart and Brown:

> He has the cunning of a devil. One day you may meet him as a beggar in the streets, the next take your hat off to him as a minister. But I'll hunt him out of all his skins and the proudest day of my life will be when I place the bracelets on the hands of Charley Peace.

For no apparent reason Sue Thompson enters the police station and Robinson learns she lodges at 9 Woodhouse Court, Darnall, where the landlady is a Mrs Ward.

Robinson: What's her Christian name? She is a Christian, isn't she?

Sue: No, she's a Wesleyan.

This is what passes for humour in the d'Albert oeuvre.

The next scene begins with a cat fight between Sue and Hannah. Then Charley enters:

Charley: Why don't you take a lesson from them texts in your bedrooms? Love one another and I'll love you. Do you know where I've been these last three weeks? I've been down to Nottingham to Robsons lace mill. Got myself up as a sweep and got a job to sweep the offices chimney and when the clerk's back were turned I got an impression of the key of the safe. I've made a key. There's about £800 in that safe every weekend to pay the hands on Saturday. I'm going down there tonight. I'll clear out that safe and be back before morning. Now what do you think to that?

Sue: Champion, Charley.

Hannah: Don't go, Charley, think of the danger.

When Robinson arrives Hannah produces the old woman masquerade:

Hannah: Here, Charley, put these things on quick and get into bed.

And the routine is reprised, with different gags at the expense of the hard-of-hearing:

Robinson: Now, my good old woman, attend to me. Do you know Charles Peace?

Charley: Oh no, she's my grand-daughter not my niece.

Robinson: We want him.

Charley: I don't mind if I do.

Robinson: Do? Do what?

Charley: Have a drop of gin.

Robinson: Have you seen him anywhere about?

Charley: No, I never drink stout.

Needless, to say a fight ensues and, once again, Charley legs it.

Alone on the stage, about to make 'my last haul' before fleeing the country, Peace lets us in on his deepest anxieties, displaying a fear and a conscience which is rare in any of the many accounts:

How I tremble, cold drops of sweat stand on my brow. I seem to hear again Dyson's dying groan, to hear her oath of vengeance — life for a life, blood for blood... I'll give up the job, but, no. Sue Thompson would jeer at me, say I'd turned weak and coward. But since I talk in my sleep for the future I'll sleep alone, my door locked, my key under my pillow, doors they say have ears. Well, let them hear as much as they like. Success, Charlie my boy, success. Now for home and my fiddle.

But Robinson appears:
Nay, lad, Pentonville and oakum.

After a lengthy tussle Charley is eventually handcuffed.
This mélange of fact and fancy continues in the first scene of the Second Act: The Escape From the Railway Carriage. This is achieved wordlessly:

Peace half faints, signs to the warders that the carriage is too hot. As soon as the window is opened he dives through. They catch him and hold him by the boot which eventually comes away in their hands. Peace disappears. Quick black out and on immediately with next scene.

Peace is on the train tracks with the lights of Kiverton Park Station in the distance. A haunted man, he shares his thoughts in another soliloquy:

I've about finished myself this time but I couldn't bear the torture of being in the train any longer. As we tore in through the night it seemed as though the carriage wheels were shrieking out: 'Murderer, you are going to your doom'. As we passed the ceme-tery I fancied I saw my mother standing on her grave, clad in her grave clothes. As the train was passing her she stretched out her hand: 'Don't let them take you to Armley Gaol. You know what it means, Charley, if they get you there: it's the rope.

162

Jump for it, lad. Jump. And before I knew what I was doing I'd dived through t'carriage window. It were a wonder I weren't cut to pieces as t'wheels ground along the metals, they seemed to be giant hands clutching at me, but they didn't catch me. Now if only I can get back to my mother's grave and die there they can do what they like with my body.

But Robinson catches up with him and, dispensing altogether with the trial, the next scene takes places in the condemned cell on his last day on earth.

> Charley: By eight o'clock I shall be dead and know the great secret. What sort of drop do you think they'll give me?
>
> Robinson: Oh, about seven feet.
>
> Charley: Ah, well whether it's a long drop there's sure to be peace at the end of it.

The play wants to have its cake and eat it too when Charley entreats his step-son, Willie Ward, not to follow in his footsteps:

> You'll be a credit to your mother. You'll be an honest man. Keep to the straight and narrow path of honesty and respectability. It's the only way to succeed in this world.

There's a moment of anger when he tells Charley:

> Willie: Outside itinerant vendors are selling details of your life and trial and some photographs of yourself.
>
> Charley: Here's folks getting money out of me and I'm getting none of it.

The actress playing Mrs Dyson has her final moment in the limelight as she is brought on to identify him and he calls out: You she-devil!

His last visitor is Hannah who never expresses any opinion about the other women in his life. I was taken aback to read that the author of this play had made a uncannily similar decision to one of my own:

> There's a chest in my framing shop at Darnall. You'll find plenty in there to reward you your troubles. Get my fiddle and all else together and advertise that you are going to sell relics of Charles Peace, the Bannercross murderer. Oh don't be afraid, you'll get plenty of bidders and you'll be surprised at the folks as'll come forward. Folks as would shrink in horror at the thought of coming near me will tumble over each other to get them bits of things as curios.

But this Peace is more penitent than mine:

> Mine has been the sin but yours will be the shame and if one so wicked as me dare lift his eyes to heaven and say God bless you I do with all my heart and say God bless you and keep you safe.

Alone and awaiting the arrival of the executioner — his name here has, for some reason been changed to Marlow — there is time for one last soliloquy, rather movingly expressed:

One minute and then death. I've often wondered, Mister Death, how you and me would come together. Whether you'd come to me suddenly or whether you'd sit on my bed for weeks waiting until the poor frail body couldn't hold the spark of life any longer. But I never thought in all my life that I'd walk out to meet you. But I don't fear you, Mister Death. I've never feared anything in my life. But, Oh dear Lord, I'm afraid of you – I am afraid of you. *(kneels)* God, it's a long time since I spoke to you and your name sounds strange coming from my lips, but will you please listen to me now? I was innocent once, when I was a baby in my mother's arms. I'm guilty now but I'm going to die soon. Will you please, God, take my soul and make it pure and white again?

The ultimate scene: The Scaffold; but not before this final declaration (in which, as in the Hodson, the policeman's name is altered — could it be his real name might provoke unwanted laughter at this most serious of moments?).

Wait a minute, don't touch that lever. I've got a confession to make. You've got a man called Haburn in prison for the murder of police constable Cox. Well, he didn't kill him but I did. See that justice is done to that lad. Don't let the innocent suffer for the guilty. Now I am ready. Can I take a drink of water?

Marlow fixes the noose. ('Here! The rope's too tight.') Marlow places the white cap. The bell strikes eight. Marlow pulls the lever. Another theatrical Peace makes the long drop.

Who is the Charlie in this show? There is none of the comedy of Hodson's yarn, nor any attempt to turn him into a champion of the poor. He is an out-and-out rogue with whom it is impossible to identify, inspiring fear and trembling rather than any kind of sympathy. One of his first lines is the oft-quoted: 'My father was a tamer of wild beasts. I'm a tamer of wild women.' But his dominant motivation seems to be solely gain. What pleasure did the Northumberland miners and their families derive from this sketchy depiction?

Alas, there is no way of knowing.

Clifford Rean: Charles Peace

This is a genuine oddity — not a play but a skit produced for Collins Music Hall, which ran from 1863 until 1958, the façade still surviving on Islington Green. The author (address 108 Crystal Palace Road, Sydenham, London SE26) presented this text, typed in purple ink, to be passed by the censor passed on 30-11-1927. It is twenty-two pages long, so the show must have lasted for something under half-an-hour. What other acts were on the bill remain unknown, unless to be unearthed by footnote delineators of the London halls. As the sole purpose was to get laughs, and comic business can at best only be insufficiently suggested in prose, it's hard to know quite how funny it might or might not have been in the playing. Apart from the escape from the railway carriage there is scant reference to any documented reality.

In this show Peace is a turn, a comedy criminal, simple if not pure. There are only four other speaking roles, all unique to this production: Bill Snape; Jerry the Diddler; Warder Hackett and Old Moll. It would be interesting to know who took these parts or whether any of the players were Collins regulars. And there are only four short scenes: ONE: A Corridor at the Sessions. TWO: A Railway Carriage. THREE: A Field. FOUR: Old Moll's House.

In the first scene Peace is already inside for burglary but murder cannot be proved against him. He is being escorted to prison when Jerry and Bill, evidently two former associates, front up to assist in springing him.

> There ain't no prison, Dartmoor or Portland or Newgate, as can hold him for even seven days if Charlie Peace says he's going to get out.

Charlie *(a very little man with pale, cadaverous face and grey prison crop in convict dress, handcuffed)* is held between two warders. One of them, Hackett, nails him as: 'The wretchedest old villain in England.' But Charlie ingratiates himself by declaring to the doubtless raucous crowd:

> Charlie: *(in a preachy voice)* Ah, my young friends, take warning from my fate. Always follow the straight and narrow path. Always go to church on Sunday and say Amen. Never pinch the coppers out of the plate, make sure you get the silver... And may my last words be ever engraved upon your hearts: Always remember to take the last trick.

Jerry palms him a handcuff key so getaway is certain. But that famous railway journey is not to unknown northern parts. No, this flying leap will happen 'near Reading' (!) But how to explain the opening of the window? Certainly the real pretext of the opening of Charlie's bowels would never have survived the blue pencil. So Rean has the Warders filling the carriage with their tobacco smoke:

> Smells to me like old rag. For the love of Heaven open the windows. Your orders are to take me to Dartmoor, not to smoke me to death like a kipper.

Then, with one mighty bound, he's out of the window and into a field where, ingenious as ever, he senses possible salvation in the immobile shape of a prop Scarecrow, which he addresses:

> I say, old feller, have you got a pair of unmentionables as you could lend a poor old fellow who ain't struck on the pattern of his own... I never could abide broad arrows. A bit drafty about the sit me down but as I ain't expecting to go into company they'll do. Now ... I'm afloat. Hope you won't catch pneumonia. Not bad. Plenty of holes in it and lots of mud. Hope there ain't much company as well. Now I'll trouble you for your cadey, old boy *(examines hat)* not exactly Lincoln and Bennett.

These celebrated milliners remain to this day makers and purveyors of fine silk headgear.

With Warder Hackett on his track and with a cracked ankle Charlie must have recourse to his well-known powers of camouflage:

> Only one thing, Scarecrow old boy, I'll have to be your understudy. As Shakespeare says: One man in his time plays many parts.
> *He sticks some straw down the back of his neck and takes some in each hand which he withdraws up sleeves ... and assumes pose as Scarecrow.*

Another eerie moment. Imagining I'd made this up, I had Charlie fooling the cops by hiding in a waxwork show and unable to remain completely immobile. Here the Warder splutters, in almost the same words I would use eighty odd years later:

165

Hello, I'll swear I saw the damned thing move.

Now, with *the hue and cry all over the country* he has to hole up in Old Moll's Crib in his former stomping ground of South London, where Jerry and Bill treat the Islingtonians to a ditty:

Work, boys, work and be contented
Rouse your little tootsies with a will
For you may rely you'll be happy by and by
If you only keep a climbing on the mill.

This would have been recognised as a take-off of an acquiescent air, here sung by erst-while prisoners who must have been subjected to that fortunately long-since discontinued instrument of state punishment on which they were forced to spend many a toilsome hour: the treadmill (a.k.a. Colonel Chesterton's Everlasting Staircase). Harry Clifton's original chorus, designed to keep the workers in their place, ran:

Work, boys, work and be contented
As long as you've enough to buy a meal
The man you may rely will be wealthy by and by
If he'll only put his shoulder to the wheel.

Unsurprisingly, this had, already been irreverently mocked by music hall supremo Harry Champion:

Work, boys, work and be contented
Making ammunition for the war
Help to make the shot and shell
Blow the Germans all to hell
Though you've never done a stroke of work before.

Back in Old Moll's crib where, for some unknown reason and especially troublesome and unnecessary to stage, the old girl has a pet song bird in her wardrobe with *no water and devilish little seed.* And then: *Enter Charles Peace, fiercely.*

Throw up the window and show the glad tidings for all the town to hear.

The Man On The Run evokes a distant memory of otherwise long-abandoned actuality:

Charlie: I must get back to the old crib at Peckham and become the respectable old gent with one arm again. The cops have never penetrated that disguise... Where's the old fiddle?

Moll: I dusts it every morning with my flannel petticoat.

And here, I'm afraid, it comes again, the still point in an ever-turning world. Hearing the Warder outside, Charlie hides — yawn — in bed, donning nightshirt and cap. Yes, it's time for that omnipresent deaf business — though, as might be expected for metropolitan spectators, this bit is a trifle more elaborate than in versions hith-erto.

Hackett:	You're an old fool.
Charlie:	What? Sit on a stool? I can't. I've been bed-ridden for forty years, ever since I had my last pair of twins, two beautiful boys and one went bandy through having rickets and the other went for a soldier and got shot in the Indies.
Hackett:	What's your name?
Charlie:	What's my game? I'm too old to play games now. But I used to be very good at shove ha'penny... I'm a respectable married widow woman I'll have you know.
Hackett:	How long have you been a widow?
Charlie:	Why ever since my husband died.

As he pulls his clothes around him he uncovers his boots which are sticking out the bottom of the bed.

Hackett:	Got you at last, Charlie Peace.
Charlie:	Have you? Not yet. Quick, Bill, douse the glim.

BLACK OUT.

Everyone was surely either in stitches or at the bar as Jerry gives a running commentary on what seems to be happening off-stage as Police apparently chase the wanted man:

> He's stolen a dog cart. He's whipped up the horse. He's round the corner. Hurrah! Good old Charlie!

But then, dah-dah... Who else but Charlie steps out of the wardrobe to take a bow in an iconographic guise, wearing: *the well-known makeup of wide-brimmed hat, old frock coat and hook instead of one hand.* He coolly finishes the card game, and the sketch, by trumping Jerry with the Ace of Spades.

> I always like to take the last trick.

What a card. Such a chirpy chappy. One of us, eh? Is he what we would desire to be? Wouldn't it have been wonderful to have chortled along and to have marvelled at the acts which surrounded this show? Maybe not. Perhaps it went off like a damp squib; maybe this was a dud, long past its sell-by date, having them clamouring for their money back. Who's Charlie Peace, mam? Some old waxwork in the Chamber of Horrors.

***

A tantalisingly curt cutting on an otherwise unknown drama from Tatton Press Cuttings, Sheffield Local Studies Library (Volume 2, Page 187):

> Last week on January 30th (1927) the play of *Charles Peace* was performed [theatre unspecified]. Sir William Clegg was present. He was the solicitor for Peace at his trial and saw himself as one of the characters in the play. Peace frequented the Meadow Inn, Darnall. A clock disappeared from Darnall School but reappeared on Peace being threatened.

W. Hargreaves: the Adventures of Charles Peace

Should there be an apology for unearthing this cack-handed effort? The author, or his representative, surely possessed an impressive address: Player Productions, Suite 57, 26 Charing Cross Road. However, William Hargreaves's play, dated 1-11-27 for performance at the Grand Theatre at Gravesend, might well be worthy of disinterment from the mustiest depths of the Lord Chamberlain's archives, because this is a drama for which there is fascinating extra-textual confirmation and, indeed, controversy. This show was reported, one hundred and fifty miles north of the performance, in the news pages of the *Derby Daily Telegraph* of Tuesday December 13th:

> **HANGMAN ACTOR — JOHN ELLIS TELLS OF HIS WORK — EXECUTED 200 PEOPLE**
> Grim tales of the gallows were told today by Mr. John Ellis, who during the 23 years he was public executioner, hanged 203 people. Mr. Ellis last night made his debut at the Grand Theatre at Gravesend. He took the part of a hangman in a sensational execution which brings to a close the melodrama called *The Adventures of Charles Peace*. A real gallows was used on the stage.
> Mr. Ellis is rather below average height. He has a brown moustache, merry eyes, and a soft voice, with a Lancashire accent. Notorious people he has hanged include Crippen, Seddon Smith of 'brides in the bath fame', Roger Casement, Armstrong the poisoner, and Mrs. Thompson. [note: Edith Thompson and her lover Frederick Bywater were executed for the murder of her husband; the case provides the basis for F. Tennyson's Jesse's novel *A Pin To See The Peep Show*.]
> 'I started in 1901, and altogether I executed, I think, 203 people in England, Ireland, Scotland and Wales,' he said. 'In 1924 I retired. It is often rumoured that I did so through the Mrs. Thompson case; really it had nothing whatever to do with it, although it was certainly a terrible task. The reason for my giving up was altogether different... People do not realise the jeers and insults which hangmen have to put up with. In company some people get up and won't sit in the same room with you. I was proposed as a Mason, but owing to my position as an executioner they could not accept me — I had to withdraw...'
> Mr. Ellis, who is 53 years of age, was born and bred in Rochdale, where he has a hairdresser's business.

This is the first of the dramas to depict Peace's shooting of Cock and the unjust imprisonment of William Habron, including a long scene of the young Irishman's trial — though his ethnicity is never referred to. This is largely copied out from the transcript and Charlie expresses no pity or remorse for this miscarriage and wants the boy to be hanged (There'll be no rest for me till they do.)

Peace's own process is not shown, though obligatory scenes of the shooting of Dyson and the escape from the railway carriage are, of course, included. His noted propensity for disguise is indulged as he appears variously as a blind beggar and a one-armed man. And there is even some slight attempt to elicit audience sympathy by providing the old lag with a degree of motivation for his crimes.

In the first scene he appears up north after a stretch in the stone quarries at Portland and confides to an invented criminal confederate, Slimy Harris:

> Back once more in my native Yorkshire, where happy days were once my share. Happy days untainted by prison solitude and gloomy walls... I was only a lad when I first got jugged, a kid not twenty one in 1853.

I broke into a crib at Mount View, Sheffield, got nabbed and sentenced to a month. In 54 I did my first penal servitude, four years. Four years of muttered curses, bitter anger, blinding rage... On my release I resolved to go straight. I was willing to toil fair and square. But every man's hand was against me, every job that I sought was refused. They laughed as they stood by and mocked me, crying Gaolbird and Ticket-of-Leave till my soul cried aloud full of anguish and my poverty urging me to steal. I took to the road for new cities where none would know me, as I thought but the old mocking cry was awaiting: Gaolbird and Ticket-of-Leave. Like a whining cur that's whipped and thrashed by a drunken bully, I crawled away sad and heartbroken, back to the gutters, back to the land of dark despair... It's too late now, too late... The thieving desire creeps through my blood like some strange disease that you can't explain.

Before he kills Dyson he ponders aloud in a quasi-poetic vein:

Tis strange how men's professions vary and strange that each should have his hour. For one hour differs from another according to each man's affair. Honest men love light and sunshine, hours 'twixt dawn and sable dusk; cunning rogues love darksome shadows, midnight grim and stilly house. The crude philosophy outspoken holds a tinge of sad remorse for I, yes I, a rogue and scoundrel, common thief and crafty knave have shed not tears of bitter sadness like a frail and tender maid. The world would laugh, laugh loud and merry. Grin like some half-witted fool were I to speak of tender passion, sentiment and woman's love. Woman's love — how SHE enthrals me. Catherine Dyson thrills my soul; thrills me with a youthful frenzy, lustful greed and mad desire. God! I've never known such passion, yet this woman scorns my love, tries to openly avoid me and treats me with a cold disdain. 'Tis not my nature to be thwarted or lose a thing that I desire. By God, I'll have you Catherine Dyson if all the world stood by your side.

There's no shortage of comic coppers to leaven the solemnity. Seeing a London Postman Constable Robinson punningly confides:

I wish I was knocking off as soon as he is. His job is easy compared to mine. All he's got to do is handle the mails. I've got to handle the males and the females as well!

Sergeant Brown enters to enumerate the expected qualities of a policeman in relation to historical leviathans who, though famous enough, were hardly topical in the late 1920s:

Brown: These days robberies night after night are causing a general alarm. Every time I pick up a newspaper there's some paragraph blaming the police for stupidity... A policeman should have the heart of a giant. The brain of a genius. The tact of Lord Beaconsfield. The talent of Shakespeare. The craft of Napoleon. And the wisdom of Solomon.

Robinson: Yes, and he'll get twenty seven shillings a week.

There's another irrelevant comic scene before the journey north with the Just Married couple Sally Shuttle and Sam Sowerberry (yet another Dickensian surname!) waiting on the platform for a train to take them to their marital hotel. The Railway Porter tells them:

Porter: I went to Margate for my honeymoon.

Sam: With a face like yours you should have gone to Saint Helena.

Another up-to-the minute gag about Old Boney! The hilarious twist is that they're on the wrong platform and have missed the train for Blackpool. Why, why, why must we submit to such torture? This is a schizoid text with no comedy at all in the delineation of Charlie's character, but with a strange desire to draw out the drama by inventing neither-here-nor-there scenes and characters.

The play text ends with Marwood entering to escort the condemned man to face the long drop. The scaffold scene itself does not at all appear in the submitted version. But that newspaper report told a different story:

> After dealing with the various dramatic episodes in the life of Charles Peace, the play shows him in broad arrow clothes, standing in the condemned cell. There was some applause last night as Ellis, playing the part of Marwood the executioner, walked on and pinioned 'Peace's' arms and led him out. The last scene was brief and startling. 'Peace', with feet and hands tied, stood on the scaffold, and Marwood, who wore a black morning coat and trousers, drew the noose around his neck. Suddenly Marwood smashed down the lever, the trap flew open, and Peace vanished with a crash amid the shrieks of women and children in the audience.
> A chaplain in cassock and and surplice and warders stood near the condemned man. It was a realistic scene. 'It is a real gallows and there is no make belief about it,' said Ellis. 'You could really hang a man on it... I said to Mr. Tom Morris, who plays the part of Peace, "You are the first man who has ever spoken to me after I hanged him."'

Two days later the same paper followed up with this account:

> **THEATRICAL MANAGER SEES LORD CHAMBERLAIN**
> The appearance of John Ellis, the former public executioner, in the play dealing with the life of Charles Peace, now being produced at the Grand Theatre Gravesend had a sequel today when Mr. Stanley May, the manager of the company, called on the Lord Chamberlain. Several protests were made against the hanging scene in which Mr Ellis appears, but the nature of Mr. May's discussion with the Lord Chamberlain, which lasted about half-an-hour, was not disclosed. Mr. May said he could not state the result of the interview, and no statement was issued from the Lord Chamberlain's office.

It looks as if the company manager had been trying to pull a fast one on the Lord Chamberlain. Is there no ignominy to which the theatrical profession will not resort to make a quid or two?

The actual appearance of Executioner Ellis becomes even more disconcerting given, despite his own denials, his apparent disturbed state of mind at the time. This account (from which the sensitive might wish to avert their gaze) is by an anonymous biographer and culled from Ellis's Wikipedia entry:

> The ordeal of executing Edith Thompson in 1923 had a profound effect on Ellis. Thompson had collapsed in terror at the prospect of her hanging and, unconscious, had to be supported on the gallows by four prison warders. Various accounts report 'that guards had to tie her to a small wooden chair before drawing the noose around her neck', and that 'she was hanged in a bosun's chair'. When the gallows trapdoor opened and Thompson fell, the sudden impact of the noose caused her to suffer a massive vaginal haemorrhage. The large amount of blood spilled, combined with the

fact that Thompson had gained weight during her imprisonment even while resisting food, led to conjecture that she might have been pregnant, although no post-mortem examination was made.

All women hanged in Britain after Thompson were required to wear special knickers made of canvas to prevent a recurrence of the massive bleeding suffered by Thompson. Traumatised by the Thompson execution, Ellis took to drinking heavily, and attempted suicide the following year by shooting himself in the jaw. Suicide was at that time a criminal offence, and Ellis was charged and bound over for twelve months at Rochdale Magistrates Court. Eight years later, in September 1932, after another bout of heavy drinking, Ellis succeeded in his suicide attempt, cutting his throat with a razor.

Edward Percy: the Life and Misdoings of Charley Peace — a Robustious Melodrama in the Old Vein, in Four Acts

This is the longest, fullest, and most accurate and legitimate drama, by a noted playwright, submitted to the Lord Chamberlain's office on 12-9-29 for performance at the Ambassador's Theatre, though a poster shows that it must have later transferred outside the West End.

It is the only play for which there is a full cast list, including some notable character actors; though perhaps only Roger Livesey, in the small part of William Habron's older brother, is fondly remembered today for his splendid performances in Powell and Pressburger's films.

Edward Percy had a long career but this play is never included in the catalogue of his oeuvre. On November 13th 1947 he gave a lecture on *The Art of the Playwright* at the London Polytechnic which was later published by the English Theatre Guild with illustrative extracts from his plays — though none from *Charley Peace*. Perhaps he was embarrassed by this early, baggy effort. *Trials of Charles Frederick Peace*, by W. Teignmouth Shore, had been published in 1926 and it seems likely that this was Percy's primary source text. At the start of the text in the Lord Chamberlain's collection he appends a note:

At least ninety percent of the play adheres meticulously to fact; for the odd ten percent I must invoke the dramatist's licence.

The scope of the piece is shown by the locations of the fifteen scenes:

ACT I
Scene 1 — A Framer's and Gilder's shop at Darnall, Sheffield 1st August 1876.
Scene 2 — The crossroads at Whalley Range, Manchester 1st August 1876.
Scene 3 — An outhouse at Deakin's Nurseries, Whalley Range 1st August 1876.
Scene 4 — Framers etc. 3rd August 1876.

ACT II
Scene 1 — The Manchester Assizes Court 27th and 28th November 1876.
Scene 2 — The yard of the house at Banner Cross 29th November 1876.
Scene 3 — The little eating house at Hull 30th November 1876.

ACT III
Scene 1 — A tavern in South London October 1878.
Scene 2 — No. 5 East Terrace Peckham 9th October 1878.
Scene 3 — the Garden of No 2 St. John's Park Blackheath 10th October 1878.
Scene 4 — No 5 East Terrace Peckham November 1878.
Scene 5 — The 5.15 a.m. express from King's Cross to Sheffield 22nd January 1879.

ACT IV [hand-written in the LC text]
Scene 1 — A corridor in the Sheffield Police Station 24th January 1879.
Scene 2 — The Leeds Assizes 4th February 1879.
Scene 3 — The Condemned Cell at Armley Gaol 17th February 1879.

At this point any aspiring impresario would have been cranking the handle of the adding machine in increasing despair. But not to worry, Percy pens a reassuring note:

From Author to Producer:

Lest any producer should turn aghast from this play at the thought of its fifty or so speaking parts and its twelve separate sets let me hasten to explain two facts:

(i) There are only five characters which either go through the play or else must be kept strictly individual, namely: Charlie Peace; Hannah Ward; Willie Ward; Kate Dyson and Sue Thompson. The rest can not only be doubled, trebled, quadrupled, quintupled and even sextupled — like characters in a revue. Actually seventeen speaking players are needed. A certain numbers of 'supers' is however inevitable.

(ii) Although (if we assume that Act II scene 1 and Act IV scene 2 are the same set re-arranged) there are twelve sets required, yet the following six: Act 1 sc2; Act 2 sc2; Act 2 sc3; Act 3 sc3; Act 4 sc1; Act 4 sc 3 are little more than front cloths; while Act 1 sc3; Act 3 sc2 are of the simplest description. Even the stage mechanism of Act 3 sc5 presents no insuperable difficulty. The important built-up sets, occupying most of the stage, are three in number, namely: Act 1 sc1; Act 2 sc1 (also Act 4 sc2) Act 3 sc1. Or, in other words, one in each act. These arrangements have been devised in order to facilitate speedy changes.

The career of Peace was kaleidoscopic; its presentation must be kaleidoscopic also. At the same time redundancy has been avoided. The main incidents of Peace's history are so marked and individual and embrace so many different places that the episodic method is the only means of treating them effectively. But there must be no wait; the audience must be hurried breathlessly along. EP

He even appends a useful diagram to save potential directors from tearing out their hair with a detailed inventory of characters in each Act outlining practical suggestions for doubling. Seventeen players are needed to fill the sixty speaking parts.

Any Peace piece demands music, so this is Percy's rather vague and unimaginative suggestion:

> In view of the fact that with the best stage staff in the world, there must be some inevitable 'waits' between several of the scenes in this play, music will occupy an important part in the production. As the play is essentially one of 'period' I would suggest the employment of tunes and pieces which were current musical coin in the eighteen seventies; also the music of *The Beggar's Opera* with which we must assume Peace to have been familiar and which, seeing that he was in a sense the last of the highwaymen, seems peculiarly appropriate as an adjunct to his 'life'. Lastly, all English songs catches, glees and country dances are applicable to one who, in his odd moments, went round the countryside fiddling at fairs and in taverns... EP.

Indeed, the very first tune is from John Gay's show as Charlie is introduced playing and singing *Let us take the road*. But who is the Charlie in this show? What are the spectators to make of him? His philosophy is expressed in the first scene:

> Why there's no enjoying anything where there's no risk. Tommy Atkins likes his job. For why? 'Cos he may get pinked in India or Egypt or somewhere tomorrow — or else pink t'other beggar! Your merchant likes to speculate. For why? Cos he may lose his money, ay or scrounge a bit without working for it. And me, well, I may be nabbed or I may bring home a belly full o' swag. It's the risk, my girl, that whets your appetite. I like my profession. By God, I'm proud of it! Hark ye, I put my brains — one man's brains — against every man as owns goods and pays other men to make locks and bars for him and other men agen to walk up and down outside, day and night, a-guarding of him — and yet I can break through under their very noses and pick the kernel out of the nut! It gives a flavour to life, Hannah. By thunder it does!

He's motivated by the prospect of thrill, danger makes life worth living, telling his step-son: There's only two things as count in life, Willie, brains and boldness. And in the next scene he puts his ideas into action when, disguised in evening dress, he is nabbed by P.C. Cock and has no compunction in shooting the young bobby.

Back in Darnall he faints when he hears Cock is dead but soon rallies and plays a hornpipe:

> *Mrs. Peace and her son dance helplessly to his relentless scraping which goes quicker and quicker. He shouts down their remonstrances, capering around like a goblin as he fiddles. The great macaw stretches her wings and screams shrilly. And on this mad picture the curtain falls.*

Armed with his copy of W. Teignmouth Shore, Percy provides a lengthy account of the trial of William Habron at Manchester Assizes. The 'dramatist's license' is exercised in the creation of two comic northerners in the public gallery acting as a Chorus before Charlie enters as *a little clean-shaven old gentleman with twinkling gold spectacles who might be a bookseller or tutor.*

> It's a weakness of mine to attend trials. I'm, er, highly sensible of the majesty of the law. Then again, I'm fond — for a whim ye know — of fancying myself in the position of the accused. I'll try to enter his feelings. Sometimes I'll go so far as to devise his defence. A harmless pastime.

173

After the Banner Cross shooting (which is not staged) Charlie moves his operations to London where he has already taken up with Sue. He wears a hook instead of left hand (I lost that old pal to a crocodile in the wilds of California when I was gold prospecting) and has a 'mahogany' complexion:

> In Inja I was in charge of the hemerald mines of the Maharajah of Cooch Behar. Life's nothing out there, you know. I was too soft-'earted. I couldn't stick it.

Another persistent legend, adapted from Shore's trial book, is now dramatised:

> I shall now deliver a short hexerpt from 'Amlet, which I see Mr Irving is going to put on at the Lyceum Theatre this winter. There's an actor for you... See him while you're in London. Yet, by Heaven, there's a thing or two I could teach Irving.

He makes good on this boast by performing the whole of the graveyard scene, playing both the Gravedigger and the Prince!

The second scene of Act Two came as something of a surprise. At an Evelina Road soirée Sue plays the harmonium and neighbour Mrs Brion sings... *The Young May Moon*. This favourite, one of Thomas Moore's Irish Melodies, was, by an amazing coincidence, the very air I chose for Sue to perform in the Nottingham Music Hall!

> *Charley Peace accompanies on his fiddle. He is in a brown coat with a velvet collar buttoning close in to his neck around which a coloured handkerchief is knotted. His feet are thrust into beaded slippers.*

> Peace: That song always makes a special appeal to me. I often 'um it to myself when I'm up late working.

More of his belief system is articulated in this version of an oft-quoted remark, something the real life model was reported to have said:

> I believe in God but I ain't afeard of him. I believe in the Devil but I ain't afeard of him. No, by thunder, the only person I'm afeard of is — myself!

How does Sue discover the real identity of her 'Jack Thompson'? And why does she turn on her lover? After the party, at which drink has been taken, Sue expresses her suspicion that 'Your money isn't honestly come by' and he threatens her with his horse whip. Later she hears him talking in his sleep:

> Now, Kate, be kind to me. I'm going to have you, Kate. Nothing'll stop me.

After he goes out to work Sue conveniently finds the reward notice.

Then there's the inevitable arrest at Blackheath and the police's discovery of what prize they've bagged (By God, we've got Charley Peace!) When Peckham denizens are told of life in London SE, neighbour Brion is naturally shocked:

> Always a petticoat in the case. Conjugal infidelity, that's the snake at the root o' life... What was this place: The Abode of Love?

(The reference is to the Agapemonites, a Somerset Vicar's Sex Cult, providing persistent prurient fascination for readers of salacious Sunday rags.)

On the train to Sheffield, how does he persuade the Warders to open the window, given the indelicacy of the real pretext? There's dirt on the glass of the railway carriage and he begs the Warders to pull the window down so he can see the old church spire at Darnall where he was baptised and married. When they refuse he protests:

> God forgive you. You refuse a man the sight of his birthplace, the last chance he's got of seeing it. Why, I'd not refuse my dog the half of such a prayer. O God, who am I fallen among? Turks and Injans? O God, have pity on me! Within a few miles of my old home and not allowed to see it. What are you afraid of? That I'll jump out? From an express train? Handcuffed? With door locked? In broad arrows? God forgive you! I forgive you.   I bear no malice. It's just ignorance.

When, after argument, they finally agree to his demands:

> *Suddenly like lightning he dives through the window. There is something demonic in his intensity. He falls in the snow.*

For the trial scenes Shore comes again to the dramatist's assistance (as, I confess, he did to my own), before he's in the condemned cell, manifesting gallows humour:

> Got the carpenters about, 'ave you? That's a noise that would make some men fall to the floor. They're working on my scaffold. I've not worked so long with wood without knowing the sound of deals.

Another confession: I also used a version of this sentiment, so there must have been a common source — but I can't now remember exactly what it was. It appealed to me as a perfect demonstration of what Sigmund Freud acutely defined as 'the operation of the kind super-ego' in his short paper on 'Der Humor' (a short addendum, written in 1927 to his monumental 1905 study *Jokes And Their Relation To The Unconscious*):

> When, one Monday morning, a criminal being led out to the gallows remarked: 'This week's beginning well,' he is producing humour for himself and evidently affording himself some satisfaction.
> As a listener I am affected, at long-range as it were, by this humorous production of the criminal; I share, perhaps, in his yield of humorous pleasure.

The only use of the blue pencil from the Lord Chamberlain's office is a large question mark by Charlie's confession where he pleads for God's forgiveness and redemption. Was this considered blasphemy? It was evidently allowed.

> I forgive my judges and jailers, my executioners and slanderers. I hope to meet them all in the Kingdom of Heaven before long. Thanking you, O Lord, for the grace which has come to me in these prison walls and has made me see myself as I was and detest myself and has helped me to become a new Adam and put on the armour of Righteousness and look forward to better times in a 'appier spot. From your most wretched creature and sinner Charles Peace *(fervently)* Amen.

175

Percy, perhaps under the influence of the Gravesend controversy, eschews an execution scene. Instead the play ends with a visit from Hannah. It is to his long-suffering wife that Charley expresses a confounding conundrum:

> I've learnt two things in my life, Hannah. The first is that crime is no career for a man with brains. The second is that there's more brains wanted in crime than in any other profession.

The curtain comes down and hides them — together again.

Charles Peace on the Stage — Murderer 'Hero' of a New Play

Thanks to the *Play Pictorial* article there is, for once, some indication of how this drawn-out drama, running for over three hours, was received by metropolitan critics, if not by audiences. From *The Times*:

> Here is a report in sixteen [actually fifteen] instalments of the life of Peace between August 1, 1876, when he was working as a framer and gilder in the neighbourhood of Sheffield, and February 17, 1879, which saw him in the condemned cell at Armley Gaol. It is a report that has every appearance of accuracy. You might, indeed, be reading a contemporary newspaper. Whether it is worth while to devote three and a half hours to the misdoings of Peace is a question everyone must answer for himself. Certainly this reporter knows his business; there is not one of the instalments that is not full of various incidents.

The *Daily News:*

> [O]n the whole, the play held my interest, in spite of the heat and the scrappiness which never quite brought off the thrill the author intended. Some attempt has been made to depict the character of the arch criminal — his vanity, his love of music, his sudden fits of ferocity, his wry sense of humour, his indomitable will and his unshakeable courage.

The *Morning Post*:

> Although some of the fifteen scenes could be spared as redundant and unnecessary, Mr. Edward Percy's *Life and Misdoings of Charley Peace* presented with complete and almost welcome success at the Ambassadors last night, is a far, far better thing than one had expected. It is more than a chronicle-play. It is full at once of fascinating memories of the seventies and at the same time of genuine psychological suggestion...

Finally, the *Daily Telegraph*:

> The episodic method has its difficulties, but it should be said at once that, in spite of the small size of this stage, they were triumphantly surmounted — though one could have endured the excision of a few at least of the episodes contained in a programme lasting for some three hours and twenty minutes. The performance of the principal actor, Mr. Oswald Dale Roberts, was also not only a success, but a remarkable one — particularly when it is remembered that he was a last-minute

choice after the breakdown of a predecessor of wider reputation. His own, however, should after this achievement, be very definitely established. Physically he is well suited to the part, and he played it both with confidence and with convincing effect. Here and there, perhaps, there were somewhat noticeably melodramatic touches — but then, after all, was not this essentially an affair of melodrama?

A tragic postscript to this production was reported in the *Singapore Press and Mercantile Advertiser* for June 16th 1930:

THE ACTOR WHO LIVED HIS PART 'CHARLEY PEACE' — WINDOW LEAP TO ESCAPE PHANTOM POLICE
This is the story of... a brilliant actor and a brave man — and of how Fate intervened to add a tragic, real-life chapter to his career of make-believe.

Oswald Dale Roberts... was lying in St. Mary's Hospital, Paddington, yesterday seriously injured as a result of a fall of 50ft. from the third-floor window of his home in Hampstead.

His wife told a *Daily Express* representative that Mr. Roberts climbed out of the window, believing in his nervous condition that he was Charles Peace and was being pursued by the police. He clung to the window sill for a few moments before he fell, while Mrs. Roberts, who was in the back room, made desperate efforts to drag him back.

HIS LEAP IN THE PLAY
Mr. Roberts recently acted the name part in *Charley Peace* at the Ambassadors Theatre and in the play Peace leaped through a railway carriage window to escape the police. He did so at only three days notice, learning a long part and acting it with such skill that the following morning Mr. Hannen Swaffer said of him:

'Oswald Dale Roberts, a little-known actor, who had stepped into the leading part at a few days notice, gave a performance which in the circumstances was a brilliant one — full of character and psychologically accurate. His task was difficult, even as a feat of memory. We see Charles Peace, in his picture-framer's shop in Sheffield, committing his two murders, watching another man sentenced to death for one of his own crimes, being charged with murder in prison, and then awaiting his end in the condemned cell. The last scene in which he moralises in the condemned cell in the presence of the wife he has treated so badly was a fine piece of writing — humorous, tragic, full of drama.'

Mr. Roberts suffered seriously from nerve strain brought on by war service... His condition is stated to be improving.

Another casualty of the war to end all wars.

Gladys Hastings-Walter: Charles Peace the Master Criminal

Although her address is given as 14a, Thorngate Road, London W9, this — the final play in the Lord Chamberlain's collection — has something of a northern bias. Its production was at the Hippodrome, Salford on April 4th 1939. She trumps Percy, for this play has seventeen scenes. Whatever prompted this show, a commission or a punt? The question dangles, as it does to all of us who have paddled in these waters: Does it add anything to the mythic corpus?

Music is to the fore as in Scene One Peace turns up in The Pig and Whistle, as The Great Ethiopian Musician or The Modern Paganini, to play on his one-stringed fiddle.

I would suggest a green focus or blue from flies as if coming from skylight so as to get a gruesome effect. It is optional as to whether to make him slightly humpbacked in this disguise but he should certainly limp just a little.

(One tune mentioned is the lovely *Gypsy's Warning*:

Do not trust him, gentle lady, though his voice be low and sweet
Heed not him who kneels before you, gently pleading at thy feet
Now thy life is in its morning, cloud not this thy happy lot
Listen to the gypsy's warning, gentle lady, heed him not.)

Peace attends Habron's trial in the guise of *a very old man, dressed in a long frock coat, top hat, looking something like an old 'Gospel' preacher... He has a packet of sand-wiches in his hand and pretends deafness.*

Though this was written by a woman, Gladys Hastings-Walter provides no great insight of female psychology in Charlie's dealings with his *amour fou*:

NOTE: Her name is Mabel Katherine Dyson which is why she is sometimes called Kate Dyson. She was an Irish-American by birth — wed in the States in her youth — and is said to have spoken with a slight American accent.

Charlie appeals to her with an enticing prospect:

Charlie: This is no life for you — you come away with me — to Manchester — to Leeds — anywhere. I'll set you up like a fine lady — fine silks and satins to wear, jewels as many as you like... There shan't be another lady in England as fine as you.

Kate: Why, you ugly little monkey you. I loathe you — I detest you.

For once his sojourn in Nottingham is mentioned if not depicted, mixing fact and fancy:

In Nottingham I lodged next door to the police station. I saw a house with Room To Let in the window so I took it. I knew that was the very place for me — the police never think of looking under their noses for a wanted man. Very comfortable place it was too — kept by a widow woman, a Mrs Thompson, with a daughter, a luscious piece. We got very friendly. I was quite sorry to leave.

In a rather fine speech, dealing with the troubling Jekyll and Hyde clash of psychologies in one body, there is an explanation for what every member of the audience wants know: Why?

Give up night work? Not while I have life. Hark 'ee, Hannah, I'll tell you something.
    I only live at nights. In the day time it ain't me — there's a jumble of queer person-alities all mixed up in this body o' mine and sometimes one comes to the surface and sometimes another — that's why I'm good at disguises. I just call on one or another of my personalities and out it comes popping — all ready to oblige. But at night the real me leaves. Charles Peace goes slipping through the streets like a shadow, none

seeing me pass — creeping into houses — welcoming me like a dog welcomes its master — up the broad stairs through the friendly darkness. Sometimes the stairs give me give me warning. 'Take care' they say 'we creak here, dodge this step, Charles, that's it.' Turn honest?

That's what I got for honesty, a maimed hand and a twisted leg, got in the machine when I was young. No compensation. Honesty? *(spits)* That for it. Give me my houses and the friendly shadows that hide my ugly face and mis-shapen body and hail me as King.

The second half opens in Peckham after two years have elapsed:

He has dyed his hair and coloured his face with walnut juice. He wore spectacles and looked a thin wiry benevolent old buffer who had spent some time in the East.

Charlie, now a Church Warden, treats the women in his *ménage* to a reading from the Bard whilst his lover Sal (this writer's name for Susan) *is lolling on a sofa looking bored to the teeth.* His wife wants to know:

Hannah: Couldn't you read the *News of the World* — a nice juicy murder or one of them spicy divorce cases?

Charlie: Not on a Sunday. That's not the literature for a Christian house.

Willie Ward is reading an article about fingerprinting, recently invented in France by M. Bertillon, and out in the stable Tommy the pony needs extra oats and a nice warm mash.

Difficult narrative problems are dealt with without undue anxiety: Sue gets the key to the drinks cabinet and finds the Reward notice. (How strange we dramatists all come up with similar solutions). After he is caught at Blackheath Mrs Dyson simply turns up!

Policeman: I thought you were in America.

Kate: I came over on a visit.

And Sal (Sue) enters, not quite sober, to identify the man in custody and to claim the reward:

Police: Impossible... This man's a half-caste. Well, he went in dark brown and he's come out about ten shades lighter. If we keep it up he'll be a nice pink before long.

The obligatory scene of the Escape From The Railway Carriage, so challenging to stage, causes no great difficulty with these stage directions:

Fill in as arranged. This and the next scene at the Embankment can easily be omitted.
All that remains is a well-worn canter through familiar locations of the Condemned Cell (I wish they'd build that scaffold a bit quieter. Government labour I suppose.) *And the Scaffold* (I say, this rope's too tight. You're hurting my neck!)

A THUD... THEN SILENCE.

Michael Eaton: Charlie Peace — his Amazing Life and Astounding Legend

Modernism set itself up to clean out the Augean stables of trite sentimentality... which so often led to a snobbish rejection of entertainment apparently beneath the dignity of the over-educated. Perhaps if the high priests of Culture had looked a little closer, or experienced a little deeper, they might have found such 'low cultural forms' which made the populace laugh, cry (and, of course, pay) to be more psychologically complex. Could it be that these despised genres also make us think? As William Blake aphoristically maintained: 'A tear is an intellectual thing.' Who would be so confident to subscribe to the conventional wisdom that popular art has proved to be less significant, less plausible than the avant-garde?

So my own contribution to keeping the memory green was inspired by the repertoire of the late nineteenth-century portable theatres — shows which I could never have seen and can only possibly imagine. But this play in no way looks down upon or camps up this little-known form, which in its heyday truly proclaimed itself as 'A Theatre For The People'. On the contrary, my contemporary homage attempts to embrace this neglected 'drama of attractions' which could only have thrived for so long because of an awareness of the desires of its audience whose participation it encouraged. But if the style evokes a theatrical past then the thematic sub-text is, I trust, as valid today: Why are we so frightened of crime yet so fascinated by stories of crime?

This was a co-production between Nottingham Playhouse and the Belgrade Theatre Coventry, directed by Giles Croft, Artistic Director of the former, and premiered there in October 2013.

As previous playwrights instinctively realised, any attempt to stage the life of Charlie can never adopt the lineaments of the 'well-made' three-act drama — it is, as Percy put it, inherently 'kaleidoscopic'. Our production had a company of eight taking on thirty characters in fifty-one scenes. Only two performers played one part only: Peter Duncan as the lithe and agile Charlie, and Norman Pace as the disgruntled Showman struggling to maintain some degree of control over the trickster hero. The female performers each took on two roles: Bridie Higson as Katherine Dyson/Susan Bailey and Mia Soteriou as Hannah Peace/ Ma Adamson (the first time this character had even been, to the best of my knowledge, represented). The company of four male actors (Charlie De Bromhead; Nicholas Goode; Alex Mugnaioni and Philip Rham) personated the remaining twenty-four parts. Music and song would undoubtedly have been a characteristic of the fairground theatre experience, so the company were all

multi-instrumentalists. Ballads, songs and hymns were featured throughout under the musical directorship of Jonathan Girling.

The look of the piece was contributed by the great graphic novelist Eddie Campbell. Long before I came to know him I had always admired his images, especially for *From Hell*, Alan Moore's vast revisiting of the forensic actuality and the legendary speculations of the Whitechapel murders. Though Eddie had never before worked for the theatre, and was based ten thousand miles away in Brisbane, his knowledge of late nineteenth-century illustration was conveyed electronically to be animated by

William Simpson for front and back projection onto designer Barney George's set which represents a Showman's booth at Nottingham Goose Fair shortly after Peace's execution.

Scenes could be changed instantly at the press of a computerised button, leading to startling transformations without the need for cumbersome props and furnishings, thus giving a drawn impression not unreminiscent of the sets of William Haggar's film.

For instance, the difficult but obligatory moment of the escape from the train was effected by a reverse angle 'cut' from inside the railway carriage to chase along the track without the necessity of a revolve.

The concept is that amongst all the fun of the fair a flamboyant Showman is pitching *THE EXECUTION OF THE MURDERER CHARLES PEACE — Tableau Vivant In Living Exactitude. With the Very Rope Used At Armley Gaol!!!*

It's no surprise that it was important to feature Peace's sojourn in my own neighbourhood and the local lass who was the recipient of his silver tongue. Whilst trying to steal a turquoise gown for the Nottingham Nightingale Charlie has to fool the blue lobsters by hiding in a waxworks show as Spring Heeled Jack, The Terror of London. And how does he gain Sue Bailey's affection? Years ago, when trying to track down the current whereabouts of lost Peaceiana, I entered into a correspondence with someone who had once worked in Tussaud's storehouse where he had personally handled 'one of Charlie Peace's ventriloquist dummies'. One of? The first and only mention of yet another performative accomplishment which could not be denied:

Charlie hears steps coming up the stair. Instinctively he takes his pistol from under his pillow. Then there's a quiet tap on the door.

Susan: *(from without)* Mester Thompson? Jack?

Could it be? It is her! Charlie secretes the revolver back under his pillow and takes a case from under the bed. A voice, not his usual tones, calls out mournfully:

Charlie: Come in!

Sue enters — wearing the costume he has stolen from the shop window — to be confronted with Jack Thompson holding... a Ventriloquist's Dummy! It is this grotesquely carved little creation which does all the talking in a strange, strangulated voice:

Charlie :   *(as the Doll)* They call me Sunny Jim. But my disposition is far from sunny because my best pal is so sad. Can Sweet Sue make Jack jolly again?

(singing)
Susan, Susan, lovely dear,
My vows shall ever true remain
Let me kiss off that falling tear
We only part to meet again
Change as ye list, my mind shall be
The faithful compass
That still points to thee.

Does Sweet Sue like the pretty garment Jolly Jack sent her?

Susan :   It's lovely... I don't deserve it.

Charlie : Say you'll never go away again. Tell him you'll never leave him!

Susan :   You'll settle for second-hand goods?

Charlie : *(as himself)* I don't care where you've been or what you've done. Stay with me, my darling. I'll make you a fine lady!

She comes closer to him — they kiss.

In this version Charlie gives rebellious voice to his anti-authoritarian *modus vivendi:*

The morning sun streams through the lace curtains. Charlie and Susan are in bed together making passionate love. Well, certainly passionate for him, though Sue, as ever, seems not so much passive or even indifferent but as if she's forever going through the motions of life, content to go along with it, letting him do whatever he wants, satisfied when it's over and done with. And when it is over she gets out of bed and dons a beautiful silk dressing gown.

Susan: Best be off. Must get to work.

Charlie: Susan... Susan! Don't you understand? You're mine now. You never have to do a day's work ever again.

Susan: They fine us a ha'penny if we're not in chapel for prayers five minutes before morning shift.

Charlie: So this is 'honest toil'?

Susan: Only what we all have to do.

Charlie: Let me give you a lesson in the fruits of honest toil, my darling. Summat I've never told any living soul afore: When I was a lad I was apprenticed at Millsands Rolling Works — Dante's In-adjective-ferno! The Overseer took again me from the second I entered that hell-hole. On the very day of me fourteenth birthday that sanctimonious chapel-going Pharisee accidentally on purpose bumped into us and shoved us hard by the smelter at the exact moment as a strip of white-hot steel shot off the line... Went straight through the back of my knee — that accounts for the horrible scar on my leg. I reached down to tug it out – that accounts for why I've only got two fingers on this hand. No words can describe the pain. Fourteen! Happy bastard birthday! I were lucky not to have my leg cut off. Ecod, I were lucky to be alive!

And as I lay on that filthy cot in that vermin-infested infirmary — watching my poor deluded father down on his knees by my bedside muttering pious prayers to the Good Lord to spare me — without considering that perhaps his deity might have thought twice before causing me all this suffering in the first place — I swore that from that day forth no man would be my master... Nor no god either!

Took me the best part of two year to be able to walk again — not crippled, not lame but lithe and more supple than ever! 'Work'! Work's the word the Gaffers use to cover up their murder. They might kill us in a blinding flash through a pit-fall or a steam engine explosion. But, most like, they kill us by slow degrees one day at a time.

Why should a lovely lily of the field like yourself toil and spin to make the Lace Merchant fatter? Why should the Owners possess, as if by right, such fine things what the likes of us can only dream of? I don't believe in dreaming, love. I go in for getting.

183

Later it is Susan who will reveal Jack Thompson's true identity which she had discovered whilst attempting to ransack a cabinet in search of the mother's ruin when she comes across the 'In Memoriam' card for his dead son.

In the condemned cell he meets Hannah for the last time, prompting her in the sale of memorabilia which will both provide for her and ensure his immortality: ('You always was a good provider, I'll say that for you — despite what other short-comings').

The play ends where it began, on the scaffold at Armley. But this is where the form allows for the greatest departure from documentary-drama reality. Never persuaded by the piety of Peace's last words, a different, unconscious manifesto could not be resisted. History is rewritten as Charlie addresses the Reporters (and the Audience) who have come to see him dance the Armley jig:

> You came here today to see me swing, didn't you? You think you can be shot of Old Charlie, don't you? But you can't cast me off so easy. I'll wager there's hundreds outside these walls this bitter morning turned up to give me a good send off. Every window over-looking Armley Gaol is full of faces. I can even hear the kiddies singing songs about me as they skip in the cobbled street. What more could a body ask for? The common folk'd be frit to death if they caught me lurking up their entries, but they devour every word written about me. True or false — what do I care?
>
> What's to admire, you might wonder, in someone like me? Why should such a bred to the bone villain become a poor man's hero? I'll tell you!
>
> When judges and magistrats cover up their own guilty secrets by preaching that prosperity comes as a consequence of a virtuous life, I say: No!
>
> When up-standing members of the police force safeguard the sanctity of private property whilst pocketing back-handers, I say: No!
>
> And when self-righteous parsons in their pulpits who've never known the sweet taste of forbidden fruit sermonise about the sacred ties of holy matrimony I say: No! No! And No again!
>
> My life gave the lie to all that sanctimonious sabbath gas. If I wanted summat — be it silver plate or another man's wife — did I ever ask permission? I lived out the desires of the down-trodden, those secret longings harbouring in the deepest, dark depths of your souls.
>
> I was what you want to be — even though you're all too scared to admit it. I let my genie out of the bottle. Now try and stuff back the stopper.
>
> To me walls were never obstacles but opportunities. Locks were only there to be picked. A safe? Anything but. I was the shadow on the bedroom curtains, the uninvited guest lurking under the mattress, the breath on the face of the sleeping bride. Mine were the footsteps in the dew on your lawn, the muddy hand-prints on your fresh-painted portico.
>
> Plush possessions some wealthy Banker — who'd never done a day's 'honest toil' in his fat life — imagined were his own when he went to bed... in the morning mine, all mine!
>
> I wouldn't swap places with any of you —
>
> I really wouldn't. I feel sorry for you —
>
> I really do. What have you ever had out of life? When have you felt the joyous delight that comes from snatching summat never rightfully yours, summat you've done darn all to deserve.
>
> To grasp with clawing hands material goods mounted up by some miserly merchant and to make them your own, to have and to hold. To destroy forever the deluded sense of security of some factory-owning tyrant with the gall to think his wealth puts him above the rest of us. To whip his Turkey carpet right from under his feet. What greater pleasure could there be? Hang the consequences.
>
> When I'm gone there'll be others, I'll be bound. Some of them are probably taking this opportunity to enter your houses while you're out at this very moment —

rummaging through your cabinets of curiosities, fingering the contents of your under-clothing drawers, rattling the skeletons in your moth-infested cupboards. Does that give you something to fret about? I do hope so. But they'll be pale imitations — entirely lacking in finesse.

None of them will ever be as loved, as feared as Old Charlie. Who among you can deny life's been richer since I came into the picture?

Fare thee well, brothers and sisters. See you in your dreams... your nightmares.

(he cocks one last snook then turns to Marwood)

Executioner, pull that lever! I'm ready to learn the Golden Secret! Turn this Life into Legend. Turn this Man into Myth.

Will this be the last time Charlie takes to the stage?

Charlie Peace — Cinematograph Star

The Life of Charles Peace — William Haggar, 1905

No-one deserves a place in the pantheon of British 'early cinema' more than William Haggar. Most of his films are missing believed lost, though there is always hope that further instances of his work remain to be rediscovered in archives throughout the world. Fortunately, the career of this portable theatre showman turned cinema maker and exhibitor has been fully recounted by his great-grandson Peter Yorke in *William Haggar — Fairground Film Maker: Biography of a pioneer of the cinema* (Accent Press 2007).

Though he was born in Essex, the travelling theatre troupe of William Haggar, his wife Sarah and their eight surviving children worked the fairgrounds of south and west Wales 'following the coal.' In 1898, only three years after films were first exhibited by the Lumière brothers at the Regent Street Polytechnic, William embraced this new medium of narrative sensation by investing in a cinematograph to exhibit films in his booth. Within a couple of years he was making his own experiments.

At first these were 'topicals' in the Lumière mould and scenes from plays in his repertoire. But then he became more ambitious, filming well-structured fictional narratives using real locations. Made in 1903, *Desperate Poaching Affray* (which still survives) is a fast-moving chase culminating in a realistic fight in a river between police and poachers. The pace and originality of these films led to a distribution deal with the French company Gaumont. And in 1905 Haggar made his undoubted masterpiece, *The Life Of Charles Peace*.

Charlie was ubiquitous in the fairground, and not only as a subject for the stage. The *Ilkeston Pioneer* of November 13th 1908 reports:

On one occasion Charlie Peace, set up as an effigy to be shied at, came in for a good deal of attention at three balls a penny, and the figure, almost as tricky as the original, was not always to be 'nobbled', but when a boy was fortunate enough to knock him over with a 'basher' he was generally rewarded with a 'real Havana cigar'.

187

No mere abbreviated record of a stage play (though that in itself would have been something special), *The Life Of Charles Peace* is an impressively innovative moving picture, for the time a real blockbuster epic, running for over eleven minutes. William's son Walter plays Charlie as a white-faced villain whose outrageous exploits the working-class audiences in the mining communities of the valleys must have taken to their bosoms. He's always on the move, a shape-shifter incarnate. The relish with which he metes out violence towards a variety of comic policemen is especially prominent. The final scene of Peace's execution was considered particularly shocking.

It wasn't just the son who had a starring role for, unsurprisingly, this was very much a family production. The full cast is as follows: Walter Haggar as Charles Peace; Lily Haggar as Peace's accomplice; James Haggar as Dyson; Violet Haggar as Mrs. Dyson; Sarah Haggar as Peace's mother; Henry Haggar as First Policeman; Fred Haggar as Second Policeman and Joe Giddings (a family friend) as Third Policeman.

Peter Yorke quotes his great-aunt Lily:

> Pembrokeshire was Father's favourite site for making films and there he made *The Life of Charles Peace*, the notorious burglar and murderer. This film was a classic of its time. All the parts were played by members of the family. My brother Walter took the part of Charles Peace and my twelve year old self played a minor role. I have never been able to understand why — I had a brother two years older — he didn't take the part I took. But I think it was that the brother who took the part of Charles Peace was short, although he must have been twenty-two, and I was shorter than him and the brother next to me was a big fellow, and I think they wanted someone shorter than Charlie Peace as his henchman. I wore my brother's suit and I had long hair, all under my brother's cap. I didn't do much. All I did was stand outside... This woman loaned us her house and they used a window for Charlie Peace to open and climb in and do his burglary act, and I needed to be on the outside and hold his tools and give them to him. Another scene was him making merry, making love to a married woman, she was his mistress. He was playing the violin and everyone was dancing. My mother was in it — all the family was in it, except my father.

Gaumont advertised the *Life* in *The Era* (September 23rd 1905) as: 'Specially suitable for Fair Ground business.' Presumably the violence of the fights with authority figures, the frequent shootings and the shock of the scene on the gallows caused them to add: 'Not recommended for Sunday School exhibitions'! It is even rumoured that London magistrates attempted to remove the picture from distribution — another instance of Charlie's supposed baleful influence upon the suggestible young and ignorant.

Of the many studies of early cinema, two works deserve special consideration for their in-depth analyses of *The Life Of Charles Peace*. Michael Chanon, in *The Dream That Kicks*, published in 1980 (Routledge and Kegan Paul) and subtitled *The Prehistory and Early Years of Cinema in Britain*, pays particular attention to Haggar's graphically bold title cards: 'among the first [film] to make sustained use of such inter-titles as a narrative device.' These scene-identifying titles obviate the need for a Lecturer or Dramatic Describer, the character who would have stood at the side of the screen interpreting the action and directing the spectators' attention — for film was never silent, only non-synchronised. Nevertheless, Chanon argues that there must have been some degree of 'foreknowledge, without which the film would hardly have been conceivable in the form Haggar gave it.' But members of the audience would already have been aware of the basic lineaments of the Peace story — if only from seeing a fairground play by Haggar or one of his competitors.

In Noel Burch's *Life to those Shadows* (University of California Press 1990, translated by Ben Brewster) he writes that the Haggar film is:

> [C]ertainly one of the true masterpieces of primitive cinema anywhere... it makes the notorious criminal a kind of superman, both villainous and sympathetic, fascinating and brutal, obstinate and epic... The Peace character... is a kind of acrobat-clown straight from popular music-hall... and the way he ridicules the police, in particular, makes him a character manifestly close to the popular audience — who are also assumed to be quite familiar with the historical Peace's deeds.

Burch also remarks on the contrast between the interior scenes, played against stylised painted backdrops, and the exteriors 'arranged to make admirable use of depth of field'. I assume that these interiors must have made use of sets from the portable theatre play. Burch goes on to speculate:

> I am tempted to see in this coexistence of two types of representation of space a pendant to the coexistence of two forms of popular art and the unbridgeable gulf between two 'social temperaments', Peace being a kind of force of nature astray in an insipid lower-middle milieu. No doubt I am reading too much into this film.

Not at all. For me, this is the very basis of Charlie Peace's troublesome being. This is why popular entertainment continually returned to this character in so many media, struggling to transform Life into Legend, Man into Myth.

Though the film consists of sixteen shots it is more accurate to describe it as consisting of eleven distinct sequences:

1. <u>PEACE'S FIRST BURGLARY</u> — INTERIOR. A woman is in a room; Charlie parts the curtain, revealing a painted crescent moon on the backdrop; he enters through the window followed by an accomplice; they jemmy a chest; the woman goes to get three men; a fight ensues; Charlie escapes out of the window; the woman shoots his accomplice with a rifle.

    An 'invented' scene with no historical basis but getting the picture off to a an action-packed opening

2. <u>PEACE AT DYSON'S HOUSE</u> — INTERIOR. Charlie plays violin to Mr and Mrs Dyson (and their dog); the curtains are open and the moon is still out; he mimes drink and Dyson goes off; Mrs Dyson at first resists then kisses Charlie; Dyson returns enraged; they fight and Dyson knocks him down; Charlie shakes his fist and exits.

    The first scene to draw on a factual incident with which the audience would doubtless have been familiar — everyone knew he was a fiddler.

3. THE MURDER OF MR DYSON — EXTERIOR. Charlie leaves a letter in a bush and hides; Mrs Dyson retrieves it and holds her hand against her cheek; Dyson enters and finds the letter; Charlie can be glimpsed in the background and Dyson finally sees Charlie and knocks him to the ground; Charlie has no compunction in taking out his revolver to shoot him; Dyson falls; Charlie is triumphant; Mrs Dyson swoons.

The scene is shot in a rustic setting with no attempt to reconstruct the back yard of the house at Banner Cross where the actual murder took place.

4. CHAS PEACE AT HOME — INTERIOR. In a set with a painted background on which an industrial scene is sketched as if outside the window Peace plays his violin to his wife and two daughters; a lad enters and points outside; Charlie dresses as an old woman in a bonnet and shawl and hides in bed; four Coppers enter and search; Charlie stupidly reveals himself; the family fight them as Charlie climbs a ladder. CUT TO:

5. [NO TITLE] ON THE ROOF — SET OF AN EXTERIOR. Charlie shoves one PC down the roof then another through the (paper) skylight; he hides behind the smoking chimney stack; shoots the third policeman; the second re-emerges; a long tussle follows at the end of which Peace shoots the copper off the roof; the fourth PC enters; one chimney pot (accidentally?) falls off;

they grapple; Charlie throws the other pot at him, before shooting him when he falls down the skylight; Charlie looks chastened as he exits.

This is one scene split into two shots with a continuity of time between the action in the house and the following action on the rooftop, so it should be considered as a single sequence. The first shot replicates the incident in so many of the plays of Charlie's 'deaf old woman' routine, though here, of course, without any punning misunderstandings. The scene on the roof is packed with so much action, suggesting that either it was very well rehearsed before the film was exposed in camera or, perhaps, that it was an oft-played scene from the drama. However, on stage it would not have been possible to make such a smooth 'cut' from an interior to an apparent exterior. This is the language of film, not of the theatre.

6. BURGLARY AT BLACKHEATH — EXTERIOR. A terrace house; Charlie enters with the young lad as his accomplice; he jemmies a sash window and enters; a PC arrives before two others who drag off the lad; Charlie chucks out his swag which the waiting copper throws to one of his mates; another copper comes back; Charlie hits them with a club and escapes; the PC whistles. CUT TO:

7. (NO TITLE) ALLEY — EXTERIOR. Charlie leaps over wall; two PCs are waiting and another arrives; a vicious, long fight before he escapes by running down the alley away from the camera. CUT TO:

8. (NO TITLE) ALLEY — EXTERIOR. Another angle on the alley as the three police chase Charlie who runs over a pile of rubble.

These three shots are edited together to form a sequence which is very precisely choreographed so, although the camera never moves, there is considerable movement within the frame and between the shots producing the effect of the protagonist's body continually changing size. The house he burglarises in no way resembles the villa at Blackheath. Charlie's exploits took place at night so presumably this sequence would have been tinted blue.

9. PEACE THE PARSON AND THE POLICE — EXTERIOR. Charlie rushes into a country lane from the back left of the frame; he disguises himself as a parson throwing away his broad-brimmed hat and donning a top hat and spectacles; one of the cops runs in and mimes: has he seen anyone? Charlie points off screen but stops him to hand out a tract; another policeman comes from another direction and the business with the tract is repeated; then a third, same again who knocks the tracts into the air before running off; Charlie walks right towards the camera and cocks a snook with his thumb on his nose; then he turns around and legs it sharpish.

This scene lasts less than a minute but packs a punch, playing on the audience's knowledge of another of Charlie's well-known traits: his mastery of disguise. This is the only time the film resorts to trick photography, stopping the film before continuing cranking to produce the illusion of quick-change. A close-up is produced not by moving the camera but by having the actor approach it.

10. PEACE CAPTURED BY P.C. ROBINSON — EXTERIOR. In a field with houses in the background Charlie is picking up a bag of swag; a PC enters and takes out his truncheon; Charlie hits him and he stays on the ground; Charlie shoots Robinson in the arm; a third PC is shot at and runs away flailing towards the camera; a long struggle with Robinson before Charlie is eventually collared and led off.

This is the longest shot in the film and there is no holding back from the violence. It also contains the 'biggest close-up' as the third policeman runs away.

11.   PEACE BEING TAKEN TO SHEFFIELD FOR TRIAL — EXTERIOR. On a railway platform Charlie, in arrowed prison garb, is escorted between two police; he tries to run away as he is shoved into a compartment; a railway worker shuts the door.

Peter Yorke notes: 'The railway station in the film was the Birdcage Halt, Pembroke Dock — it no longer exists... Walter later related that at Pembroke Dock, during the filming of their Charlie Peace story, a railway guard had loaned them his train as well as helping to catch the elusive Charlie.'

12.   STRUGGLE IN THE RAILWAY CARRIAGE — EXTERIOR. Shot from outside Charlie can be seen grappling with his warders and they hold him by the legs as he tries to escape out of the window. CUT TO:

13.   (NO TITLE) TRAIN — EXTERIOR. Shot from side on, the train is moving; Charlie's upper body emerges out of the window; he is pulled back inside; he emerges again; then his body leaps out of the train window; one of the PCs is holding one of his shoes and they gesticulate for the train to be stopped. CUT TO:

14.   (NO TITLE) TRAIN LINE — EXTERIOR. Charlie hops along the line, trying to escape; he is chased by the two cops who easily catch up with him and he is dragged off towards the camera.

This sequence, of the most famous incident in the life of Charles Peace and not one which could ever be ignored, is truly marvellous, ensuring the film's reputation as a masterpiece. Always an issue as to how this effect could be produced on stage, this was the first time it was attempted on screen and must have taken much thought and careful preparation. The result is nothing less than a fully realised early instance of continuity editing. The action is broken down into three separate shots which have to be edited together to make sense as a representation of the seamless passage of time and space. The first is shot from outside with the camera presumably on a tripod on the station platform as the reflection of buildings in the window shows the train is not moving. And then... a match cut! A side-on angle of the following action; now the train is moving (so the camera must have been held out of one of train's windows?); the figure that emerges is evidently a dummy but the pace is so fast that this effect is by no means laughable. Finally the action continues and concludes on the track through movement within the frame — the only problem is that the train cannot be seen behind them. All in all these few seconds represent nothing less than the mind of a film-maker who, though steeped in the conventions of the theatre, is figuring out how to tell a tale in a completely different, a completely new way. Triumphant.

15. <u>CHAS PEACE IN PRISON</u> — EXTERIOR. In a prison yard a Warder walks in with Mrs Dyson; another Warder leads in five Lags; she shakes her head at each in turn; the sixth is Charlie; when he is identified, uncowed, he makes to attack her.

16. <u>THE EXECUTION</u> — INTERIOR. On the scaffold: the Chaplain; the Warder and Charlie with his hands tied; the bearded Executioner restrains his feet and fits the noose; the Condemned Man recoils; the white mask is placed over his head; the priest intones; the lever is pulled; the long drop. THE END.

A final family anecdote as Peter Yorke adds: 'Walter Haggar, playing Peace, said later that he had a very narrow escape from being choked to death.'

On November 11th 1905 another advertisement for the *Life of Charles Peace* appeared in *The Era*, stating:

This is the ORIGINAL and FIRST picture taken dealing with the life of the "Modern Ishmael" and must not be confused with another film of the same title issued by another firm some weeks after us.

For Haggar had a competitor.

Life of Charles Peace — Frank Mottershaw, 1905

Most of the films produced in the silent era are no longer extant, so their existence lives on only in catalogues and trade journals. In November 1905 *The Optical Lantern and Cinematograph Journal* reported:

> The Sheffield Photo Co. are coming out with a new subject called *The Life of Charles Peace*, and whilst it is a matter of regret that it should so closely follow a film with a similar title issued by another firm, these gentlemen inform us that they have been working on the subject for a considerable time, and that the scenes are original and totally distinct from the one already referred to. Officials who had charge of the case have been interviewed with the object of getting the details as correct as possible. The Banner Cross murder and Peace's sensational leap from the train were taken on the actual spots. By a strange coincidence the same engine driver was driving the train who conveyed Peace from London to Sheffield, when he made this sensational leap to escape.

It was evidently this notice of a forthcoming 'drama-documentary' which must have stimulated Gaumont's advert on Haggar's behalf. It is quoted in *The History Of The British Film 1896-1906* by Rachael Low and Roger Manvell, based upon research of the History Committee of the British Film Institute. This post-war publication (George Allen & Unwin 1948) remains an invaluable inventory of both the companies making films and a description of the kind of films they were producing.

Frank Mottershaw, founder of The Sheffield Photo Company, was not forged in fairgrounds but owned a respectable photographic business before he and his son ventured into film-making with a camera of his own devising. It is particularly sad that this early 'bio-pic' is now lost given that the real house on Eccleshall Road and the real stretch of the line at Shireoaks were used as locations. In the Sheffield Local Studies Library there is a cutting in which Harry Mottershaw, a later chairman of the family firm says: 'The parts were played by local amateur actors. The whole production cost less than one hundred pounds.'

Fortunately, however, a full shot-by-shot description does survive in the trade press, so a fair comparison between the two productions might be made. However, there is no way of knowing what attitude the film takes towards its local protagonist and the police, or whether the overall effect of the Sheffield film would have been as subversive in effect as the South Wales production. The Mottershaw advertisement was possibly produced in such detail as a necessary aid to the Describer.

THE LIFE OF CHARLES PEACE, THE NOTORIOUS BURGLAR — FRANK MOTTERSHAW, SHEFFIELD FILM COMPANY. 870 feet. ALL THE SCENES ARE TITLED. THE SCENES OF THESE INCIDENTS WHICH OCCURRED AT NIGHT ARE ARTISTICALLY PRINTED BLUE.

> A film of intense interest and excitement. Every attempt has been made to make this film as exact in detail as possible. The Banner Cross Murder, *taken on the actual spot;* the Sensational Leap from the Train, *taken on the actual spot.*
>
> Scene
>
> 1. The opening scene shows the Prince of Burglars at work as a Picture Framer.
>
> 2. Whilst Peace was living in Darnall, a suburb of Sheffield, he became on friendly terms with a neighbour, Mr. Dyson, and his wife, and was in the habit of calling

and entertaining them with his violin, playing on which he was very clever. Unfortunately he became too fond of Mrs. Dyson, and on one occasion Mr. Dyson caught him embracing his wife. Enraged at this, he turned Peace out of his house. These incidents are depicted in this scene.

3.   Shows Dyson throwing a note into Peace's garden, which forbids his unwelcome intrusions into his family. Peace is enraged, and from this moment he evidently formed an intense hatred of Mr. Dyson.

4.   *The Murder At Banner Cross.* Peace conceals himself in Dyson's garden at night. Mr. Dyson hearing a noise comes out of his house, and Peace runs away towards the street, Dyson following. Peace turns round and fires at Dyson, and at the second shot he falls mortally wounded. Peace makes off over the fields.

5.   Peace commits a burglary at Manchester and is captured by the police.

6.   Peace approaches a house at night, carrying his Violin Case, in which he usually carried a Rope Ladder to enable him to scale high walls, etc. He throws the ladder on to the wall and climbs over.

7.   The Interior of the House. After fastening up the door, he ransacks the Safe of its silver and jewellery.

8.   Whilst hiding his spoil in a field he is watched and captured after a desperate struggle.

9.   *How Peace Deceived The Police.* After the last incident Peace was convicted and sentenced to a long term of imprisonment. This scene illustrates the cleverness of the man in disguising himself. The police being on his tracks he finds a quiet spot, and taking from his Violin Case a change of clothes and make-up, he completely disguises himself as to be able to put the police off the scent when they meet him.

10. A desperate encounter with the Police.

11. Peace commits a Burglary at Blackheath; the Attempted Murder of P.C. Robinson; and Final Capture. Peace is here shown breaking into a house at Blackheath. Two Policemen on their night beat notice a light in an upper window, and being suspicious, keep watch. P.C. Robinson sees Peace leaving the house. Peace sees him, and fires several shots, the last hitting the constable in the arm. The plucky constable however sticks to his opponent, and is successful in holding him until the arrival of his comrade, when he is hand-cuffed and taken to the lock-up.

12. *The Sensational Leap From The Train.* When Peace was brought from London to Sheffield for trial he conceived the idea of escaping by jumping through the window. In this scene, just as the train is passing between Kiveton Park and Shireoaks, Peace is seen to suddenly make a leap through the carriage window, but Peace manages to kick off his shoe and falls on the line. Unfortunately for himself he is injured by the force of the fall, and is unable to crawl into the wood (which was his intention) before the train had been stopped, and he is in the hands of the warders, who carry him away and place him in the guard's van.
     This was the last incident in Peace's criminal career before his Trial and Execution at Armley Gaol, near Leeds. It has been decided NOT to reproduce the Execution Scene as we believe it is too ghastly and repulsive.

The final sentence explicitly distances this more tasteful enterprise from the previous production. But there is no reason to expect that this would not have been a lively picture with a strong narrative drive if it was anything like the Mottershaw-produced *Daring Daylight Burglary* from 1903. This, too, had been made entirely on outside locations in western Sheffield — the very places their Peace film would be shot.

Adventures of Charles Peace, or Charles Peace, King of Criminals — Ernest G. Batley, 1914

All that is known about this lost picture, which at 2000 feet would have run for about twenty minutes, comes from an advertisement and synopsis in *Pictures and Pleasures* of September 7th 1914.

Jeff A. Barlow, an actor who, like Charlie Peace, was a master of facial manipulation, was cast because of this uncanny aptitude. In his quotidian case he appears bald, smiling with round Crippen-esque specs. There are three stills 'Controlled by J.D. Walker's World Films Ltd.': Charlie confronting a copper in a street scene; Charlie with two Warders in the train; a platform exterior with Charlie being dragged into the train. The synopsis bears merely a parallel relation to reality:

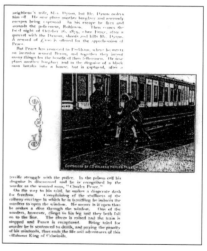

THE STORY

Consequent upon a term of ten years' imprisonment at Sheffield, Charles Peace embarks upon a determined career of crime. Making the acquaintance of Fanny Binkhorn, the maid servant, he gets invited to the servants' hall and on New Year's Eve, the family being away, he entertains the servants. He supplies drugged wine for the party, and when the wine has taken the effect, he ransacks the house. He then returns to the hall and, pretending to fall asleep, awaits the awakening of the servants, with the stolen jewels and silver in the violin bag at his feet. The butler raises the alarm and goes off to inform the police.

He now terrifies Hannah Ward, a destitute woman, and commits another burglary, securing valuables to an enormous amount. Later on Peace falls in love with his neighbour's wife, Mrs. Dyson, but Mr. Dyson orders him off. He now plans another burglary and narrowly escapes being captured. In his escape he fires and wounds the policeman, Robinson. Then comes the fatal night of October 26, 1875, when Peace, after a quarrel with the Dysons, shoots and kills Mr. Dyson. A reward of £100 is offered for the apprehension of Peace.

But Peace has removed to Peckham, where he meets an inventor named Breon (*sic*), and together they invent many things for the benefit of their fellowmen. He now plans another burglary, and in the disguise of a black man breaks into a house, but is captured, after a terrific struggle with the police. In the prison cell his disguise is discovered and he is recognised by the Warder as the wanted man 'Charles Peace'.

On the way to his trial, he makes a desperate dash for freedom. Complaining of the

196

stuffiness of the railway carriage in which he is travelling he induces the warders to open the window. No sooner is it open than he makes a dive through the window. One of the warders, however, clings to his leg and they both fall on to the line. The alarm is raised and the train is stopped and Peace is recaptured. Being tried for murder he is sentenced to death, and paying the penalty of his misdeeds, thus ends the life and adventures of this villainous King of Criminals.

From *Pictures And The Picturegoer*, March 20th 1915:

THE MAN WITH A HUNDRED FACES — FACILE FEATURES ON THE FILM

If you have seen Charles Peace, the notorious king of criminals on the screen you have seen an actor whose features are so remarkably loose that he can easily and comfortably make at least a hundred different faces in not much more than as many seconds.

His name is Jeff Barlow, a well-known actor who after thirty years' stage experience is now adding to his laurels by playing for the pictures.

It was Mr. Barlow who conceived the idea about a year ago of picturising some of the exploits of Peace, the man who as burglar and murderer was the talk of the country in the seventies and as a result the B. & C. Company produced the fine film (with himself in the title role) which is now drawing crowded houses throughout the country. Mr. Barlow... has recently made arrangements, he tells me, to appear at an early date in a second Charles Peace picture.

The
Adventures of Charles Peace

This Film shows a faithful representation of the character of the King of Criminals,

His thrilling experiences,

Facial Contortions and Quick-change Artistry,

His abilities as a Musician, Burglar, and Inventor.

Nothing gruesome or objectionable.

It shows the triumph of justice over evil, even when perpetrated by an exceptionally clever man.

NO FANCY PRICES

Controlled throughout Lancashire, Yorkshire, Cheshire, and Ireland, by

The Clarion Film Agency Ltd.

Kinema House, 12, Cannon Street, Manchester

[I]t goes without saying that Mr. Barlow is a character-actor of no mean order, and during his stage career his amazing faculty for making different faces has doubtless been of the greatest service to him as it must obviously be in film work also.

'How did you first discover it?' I asked.

'By practising in front of a mirror' he answered 'and as a boy I got more kicks than ha'pence for doing so. Many a time in my touring days,' he continued 'I have amused myself and a friend or two by using my face to keep the public out of our railway carriage. On some occasions big crowds have collected on the platform and taken me for a madman or a looney, according to the face I had elected to make. It was my brilliant India rubber features,' said Mr. Barlow 'that caused me to think of Charles Peace as a popular subject for a film drama. He had just such another face, and had many times escaped the clutches of the law by changing it. But Peace was really, you know, a born genius, a clever musician and one of the kindest-hearted men who ever lived. Had he turned his talent in the right direction he might have made himself a pillar of society instead of the dastardly criminal he actually was.'

'Is it really Charlie Peace in the picture?' asked an old lady the other day after gazing at the poster outside a cinema. 'Certainly not, madam,' answered the manager 'pictures were undreamt of when Peace was alive.' But the dear old lady seemed far from satisfied. 'I thought they might have made a moving picture of him before hanging him,' was her final retort.

Yet another anecdote to keep the legend living.

Pimple in the Whip — Fred & Joe Evans, 1917

What, we might ask, is Charlie Peace doing in a parody of play about the fixing of a horse race?

The Whip, a four-act drama by Henry Hamilton and Cecil Raleigh premiered at Drury Lane in 1909 and was an immediate success with not one but two sensation scenes. The first was a spectacular train crash and the climax was the Newmarket Gold Cup with twelve mounted horses racing on a treadmill worked by hydraulic ramps. The plot involves an attempt by the villains to nobble the eponymous favourite by arranging for his horse box to be crushed by a speeding express train. A clue to

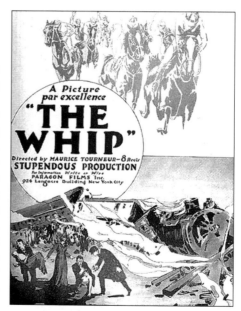

Charlie's later comic appearance might be gleaned as a crucial scene takes place in a waxworks where The Whip's trainer overhears the details of the dastardly plan before finding himself locked in overnight.

In 1917 the play was thrillingly adapted for the screen under the direction of Maurice Tourneur, relocated to the USA with Saratoga standing in for Newmarket and the Eden Musée replacing Madame Tussaud's for the excellent Chamber of Horrors scene. It is the film which received parodic treatment from another forgotten hero.

Fred Evans and his brother Joe made over two hundred quickly churned out slapstick shorts in the silent era, many of them featuring Fred as Pimple, a clown whose white face derived from his circus background. In England his comic popularity is said to have been eclipsed only by Chaplin. The comedy of the Evans Brothers can best be described, in technical terms, as bonkers. The scripts were characterised by outrageous punning intertitles, so this is verbal as well as visual humour. No sacred cow is safe from their send-up.

Rather than risking insanity by attempting to make sense of this mayhem, I shall defer to this deft synopsis by Bryony Dixon, Curator of Silent Film at the British Film Institute:

> Lord Elpus (Pimple) is penniless and puts all of his money on The Whip, a race horse. The villain, Lord For-givus (Joe Evans) follows him to a secret trial of The Whip (represented by a pantomime horse). Later, the villain goes to The Whip's stable and tries to poison him by sawing his leg off, and then his tail, but Elpus intervenes. At Madame Tussaud's, Lord Elpus and the heroine see wax figures of Von Tirpitz, the Kaiser (a pig), Von O'Clock and Charles Peace. The villain locks Elpus inside, but he escapes with the help of a genie from Aladdin's lamp. Elpus cycles after a train containing The Whip. As he is releasing the horse, the train behind crashes into the carriage too soon, and the scene has to be repeated twice before Elpus rescues The Whip, only for the train to crash into them both. At Newmarket, Lord Elpus himself rides The Whip in the race (the other competitors also being pantomime horses) and seems certain of victory when the horse throws him just before the winning post and refuses to move any further.

Lord Elpus and his fiasco, Lady Jones, visits Madame Tussaud's.

So Peace's presence is explained: any comic scene in the Chamber of Horrors must include the favourite waxwork villain.

Pimple as Lord Elpus enters Madame Tussaud's Chamber of Horrors with his 'fiasco' and dragging a toy dog on a lead — a not uncommon money-saving device. A lady walks in unseen by them.

> **Isn't it wonderful how natural they get these figures up.**

Thinking she is another wax figure Pimple whacks the lady with his stick and she turns and bashes him before leaving. In turn they examine the figures with grotesque papier maché heads. First is Von Tirpitz (head of the German navy at this time of war). *This is the man who invented Turpentine.* Next is Von O Cluck: *The man who invented dinner time.* Then the hated Kaiser Bill, who has the head of a pig:

> **Fancy putting the Kaiser in here. What an insult to Charlie Peace.**

They go over to examine the figure of Peace, who bears more than a passing resemblance to the original as he was depicted at his trial.

> **This is Charlie Peace. the man who invented Peace Pudden.**

When Pimple turns his head Charlie seems to dislocate his jaw to thrust his face forward.

Pimple is shocked and points: *Did you see his face move?*

But when he turns again the face has returned to its previous disposition. Pimple grasps hold and manipulates the jaw back and forth to great hilarity. There is, sorry to say, no credit for the competent gurner who played Peace.

Ever the patriot, Pimple did not shirk from doing his bit.

The Case of Charles Peace — Norman Lee, 1949

From the *Spectator*, February 12th 1937:

MONEY FOR FILM STORIES BY NORMAN LEE

On the occasions when the kings of Hollywood and Wardour Street emerge from their fortresses to make a public pronouncement, as often as not it is to speak of the crowds of writers who, lured by reports of the vast sums to be gained by the fortunate, form permanent queues outside their premises in the hope of securing employment — in most cases to no avail, for most of the poor creatures are ignorant of the rudiments of the trade to which they are trying to gain admittance. Mr. Norman Lee, who has had experience as a film-director has now come to the aid of these unfortunates with this admirably clear and practical book (Pitman, 7s. 6d.), which describes precisely what is wanted, from the story in its first draft to the finished scenario, and in what way it should be presented. A wider knowledge of the cinema than can be gained by casual visits is of course necessary for anyone who is going in systematically for writing for the films, and Mr. Lee cannot supply the reader with the knowledge or intelligence to learn technique as he watches the film. But for those who are prepared to take some trouble, this is the perfect guide.

Anyone reading the several volumes of memoir written by Norman Lee might be fooled into thinking that this writer/director occupies a hallowed place in British cinema alongside such renowned contemporaries the like of Alfred Hitchcock, Michael Powell & Emeric Pressburger or Frank Launder & Sidney Gilliat. He is every bit their equal... if only by his own account.

Nevertheless, he did have a long, if not entirely distinguished career with over a score of films, silent and sound, to his credit, mostly quota-quickies. His *Log of a Film Director* (1949) displays photos of such Hollywood luminaries as Robert Montgomery, Frank Sinatra, Greer Garson and Spencer Tracy. Only when the small print is examined is it revealed that these are stock shots from M-G-M and 20th Century Fox — Lee had directed none of them. The book does, however, contain one picture of him working on a film whose title then was known as *The Trials of Charley Peace* though the text never mentions the production of this picture.

On July 14th 1948 the *Nottingham Journal* reported:

THE TERRIBLE CHARLES
When Mr. John Argyle, a British film producer who has several times visited Nottingham, begins a series of films based upon famous British trials it is announced that the first trial on the list will be *The Trial of Charles Peace* and that action sequences in the story will be filmed as much as possible in the actual places where the events occurred. In this event Nottingham could expect to be pleased for Peace, arriving in Nottingham in January 1878, took up his residence in the Sussex-street area, lodging with a Mrs. Anderson, a notorious receiver of stolen property. He committed many burglaries in the city, and on one occasion, when caught stealing

blankets, he escaped by flourishing a revolver. Later in his career, when wanted for the murders of P.C. Cock and Mr. Dyson and with a reward on his head, he lay hiding in one of the caves behind the Trip to Jerusalem. Another of his Nottingham lodgings, a house in Red Lion-street (now Cliff-road) was pulled down in August, 1931.

If the people of Nottingham were expecting to host stars of the screen they would be disappointed, for the film was made entirely at Merton Park Studios in Wimbledon. This production (available on DVD) remains the only cinematic representation of Charles Peace since the introduction of sound and, though definitely low-budget, as a 'drama-documentary' it manages to pack a lot of factual material into 88 minutes.

The titles, superimposed over the statue of Justice at the Old Bailey, state that the film is 'Based on the Records of British Justice' and that the trial scenes are 'supervised by Christmas Humphreys K.C.' a Buddhist convert and barrister, later judge, who is known for his works on Zen. The mellifluous tones of Valentine Dyall, credited as 'Storyteller', provide the voice-over narration, leading from the Central Criminal Courts to the Hendon Police Training College where a monocled, stiff-as-a-board Sir Clement Barnes (another K.C.) lectures the recruits on 'The Trials of Charles Peace.'

> He was a very remarkable character, a veritable Jekyll and Hyde. A respected trader and a man of evil living, as it were, side by side. In all the history of crime there has been no-one quite like him, before or since.

There follows a dissolve from an illustration of the trial before Justice Lopes to the courtroom set, establishing the structure: the story will continually flashback from the courtroom drama to incidents from Peace's life in 'the days of horse-hair sofas, hansom cabs and penny-farthing bicycles'. The film also has the ambition to represent not only the story of Peace but also the parallel tale of William Habron and the quest of his family and their priest to secure justice for this wrongly-convicted lad and to overturn the miscarriage of justice.

Interestingly, the two main parts are both taken by sons of celebrated actor-manager theatrical knights. Peace is played by Michael Martin Harvey, son of Sir John who was most famous for his role as Sydney Carton in *The Only Way*, an adaptation of *A Tale Of Two Cities* in which Harvey toured, initially with his wife as co-star, for over thirty years until he was well into his seventies. It was in the 1925 version directed by Herbert Wilcox (the last silent Dickens picture) that Michael, or 'the boy Jack' as his parents called him, movingly made his film debut as a foppish aristo bravely facing the guillotine. Michael Martin Harvey (aged 52 at the time of production) capably embodies all Peace's well-known traits, scraping the one-stringed fiddle, playing with pets, switching from benign codger to vicious brute, from stern paterfamilias to jovial pub entertainer, working on his monument and expressing the expected penitence.

Habron is played by Peter Forbes-Robertson, son of Sir Johnston of that ilk, a famous Hamlet who twice took the role of the Dane in silent cinema, in 1913 and 1915. For once Habron is depicted as (slightly) Irish but he is anything but a Fenian hot-head, rather a sad apologetic victim, expressing due deference to authority when he is finally pardoned, displaying no spite or resentment at the unfairness of his treatment which brought him to the brink of judicial murder.

The glamorous Chili Bouchier, who also began her career in silents in Anthony Asquith's delightful *Shooting Stars* (1928), plays an alluring Mrs Dyson, capturing Katherine's initial fascination which in time turns to terror.

The film hits all the high spots: Charlie with his one-stringed fiddle; entertaining his mistress in a Sheffield pub; the murder of Dyson; his disguise as an old woman; the Peckham soirée where Sue (played by Roberta Huby) entertains the neighbours; Sue's descent into drunkenness; the daring escape from the railway carriage; and Peace in the dock.

But a question remains: What did the post-war welfare state world want from this miscreant? Is Charlie Peace a conscious warning or a subconscious aspiration?

The 'factual-drama' genre removes the need to represent the central character as a 'hero'. Charlie can remain an enigma, ultimately incapable of explanation. There's always a problem with a Trickster as protagonist. Such a character can *change* — that's the shape-shifting nature of the beast — but can he *develop*? Does he go on a life-changing journey or is his only rite of passage the voyage from freedom to captivity, from life to death? And, if so, what can he learn *en route*? What is his quest? For money? For women? For fame? For an end to boredom? Is he ultimately sociopathic, relishing causing confusion and chaos, not playing by or caring for the same rules as normal humanity? Is he inherently subversive without being in any way politically rebellious?

And Charlie's character is not the only psychological conundrum. Why does Hannah stick with him? Why is Katherine attracted to him? Why does Susan stay with him?

If there is a critical edge to *The Case Of Charles Peace* it is doubtless unconscious. After Charlie walks from the condemned cell towards the off-screen gallows there is a cut back to first image: Blind Justice with her sword and scales. Though the workings of this allegorical figure seem to have prevailed in the case of Peace do we wonder whether we can have ultimate faith in the forces of legalised retribution she represents?

This was Charlie's last cinematic outing. Is it not time for a twenty-first century production which does full justice to this amazing life, these amazing times? Before anyone asks: Yes, this is a pitch.

Postscript: What connects the King of the Lags with the Fab Four? Well... in *A Hard Day's Night*, knowingly written by Alun Owen and exuberantly directed by Richard Lester in 1964, Ringo tries to escape the excesses of Beatlemania, resorting to disguise in order to elude the mobs of screaming fans. Egged on by Paul's tricksterish grandfather, played by Wilfrid Bramble, Ringo's loner exploits result in arrest for loitering with intent. At the cop shop the world-weary Desk Sergeant tells the drummer: 'Go and sit down over there, Charlie Peace'!

Another ballad, this one in the first-person:

THE TRIAL AND EXECUTION OF CHARLES PEACE

Alas! my trial is over now, not many pity me
The jury has found me guilty, I shall die upon the tree.
Charles Peace it is my name, farewell to all so dear
I sentenced was for murder, now is stopped my wild career.

For robbery they tried me first, they sentenced me for life
For that crime I done at Blackheath God help my injured wife.
The crime against me was thought clear, for murder I must die
In my dreams my executioner appears before my eye.

My poor old mother little thought when she gave me birth
As I grew up I'd turn so bad while upon this earth.
From the railway carriage window to escape I did try
Now for the murder at Banner Cross Charles Peace soon must die.

My guilty conscience knew no rest, I plundered night and day
I knew Missis Thompson well, many hours we passed away.
Missis Dyson swore I was the man that took her husband's life so dear
The brand of Cain is on my brow, my sad end it draws near.

I little thought my trial so soon, alas, it would be o'er
In my prison cell my weeping friends seldom I'll see them more.
My wife perhaps she will break her heart when she thinks of my bad end
So young me all be warned in time, it's ne'er too late to mend.

The evil one was near me, he tempted me each day
I'd sooner die upon the tree than linger life away.
And when I'm gone all good friends remember my career
Charley Peace the Blackheath Burglar before his Maker must appear.

So sons and daughters dear as on through this life you go
Take warning by Charles Peace, his former life you know.
Charles Peace the Blackheath Burglar for murder I must die
My trial was rather quickly o'er, to all I bid goodbye.

'A black flag was hoisted outside the gaol to denote that the execution had taken place.'

The Comic Hero

The legend never dies. Charlie underwent yet another massive transformation when he burst into prominence once again as an anti-hero in a comic strip which ran for an amazing ten years, from 1964 to 1974, with reprints continuing into the 80s. When folk of my age heard I'd written a drama about Charlie Peace many had no idea he was an actual historical character — they knew him only from the pages of *Buster*, which kept the myth alive for kids of my generation.

On June 20th 1964 (when Cilla Black was at the top of the charts with *You're My World*, which could have been Susan Bailey's theme song, chased by Roy Orbison with a far more gloomily appropriate ballad *It's Over*) *The Astounding Adventures of Charlie Peace* made a debut in *Valiant:*

Why was a late nineteenth-century burglar and murderer considered fit for purpose as the continuing character of a children's comic strip? The first few tales, beautifully drawn by Eric Bradbury, were dark, gothic and not a little subversive. Once again it was now-forgotten, always-neglected writers and artists who gave us a weekly dose of Peaceiana. I thank and applaud them from the core and depth of my being.

In these early strips ('a complete story in every issue') elements of the iconography of the 'arch-rogue' are disinterred and resuscitated. In that first *Valiant* offering the double nature of Peace is instantly framed: brilliant violinist/most notorious thief the world has ever known.

At ten years old I was gripped — this was the very fellow my grandma used to tell me about! It was only a shame the tales took place in London rather than Nottingham.

How to make a comic hero from such a miscreant? How to avoid perennial accusations that the glorification of crime would lead easily influenced youth onto the path of crime? The protagonist must have antagonists. So the representatives of the forces of law and order must forever be on Charlie's trail, in the shape of a bluff, handle-bar moustachioed constable, subtly nominated P.C. Thick, and his superior, the square-jawed, bowler-hatted Inspector Tim Bannion. A gauntlet is thrown down:

Go on then, Charlie Peace... Back to your rat- hole! But it's war between us now! One of these nights I'll make you pay for your crimes — if it's the last thing I ever do!

And, of course, Charlie cannot survive in this environment if he is to be, as in life, 'base and bad'. To ensure longevity as any kind of long-running hero his image must be cleansed, as it was in the plays which succeeded his execution. He must mutate into a latter-day Robin Hood, robbing from the greedy, miserly, undeserving rich to share, anonymously, his booty with the deserving poor. Thus it is that at the end of this very first strip Charlie tosses the fruits of his booty through the window of a poor mother, Mrs Foster, whose poverty means that she and her sleeping son, Alfie, are on the threshold of the workhouse. *A sovereign! Enough to keep the little 'uns in grub and clothes for the next six months! Where did it come from?*

Needless to say there is no depiction of the Peckham *ménage à trois*!

The spine-chilling adventures of Charlie Peace will appear every week in BUSTER starting next Monday! Thrill to the dramatic meeting between the notorious burglar and Fang Chu, the ruthless pirate of Hangman's Wharf! THIS SENSATIONAL STORY APPEARS IN NEXT MONDAY'S BUSTER... Price 6d.

In the first *Buster* tale (AN EXCITING NEW SERIES THAT CANNOT FAIL TO THRILL!) another criminal archetype is evoked in the shape of Fang Chu, a barely disguised version of Sax Rohmer's Fu Manchu, with 'a face that was even uglier than his own!' Charlie uses his amazing powers of disguise to impersonate 'the ruthless pirate of Hangman's Wharf' who vows vengeance: *You got the better of me that time, Charlie Peace! But some day we shall meet again — and then I swear you shall die the Death of a Thousand Cuts!*

Over the following weeks we were treated to a tale involving a juvenile gang led by the Fagin-esque figure of Mister Jake and another set in a fairground where Charlie's adversaries are the denizens of a freak show (the pay-off comes when a top-hatted dandy on a penny-farthing mistakes Charlie for 'the Wild Man of Borneo' — shades of Pongo). Aspects of his true nature are evoked: not just his love of music and his ability to alter his appearance but also his love of animals (his pet goat Hannibal proving to be a useful side-kick) and his association with the waxworks (where he disguises himself as Sir Francis Drake). All in all a most worthy and respectful addition to the mythos.

But the chiaroscuro mood of Victorian *noir* could not be sustained. By the start of the new year the stories have been shortened to two pages, another artist has taken over, the art-work is broader, more 'cartoonish' and the tales have become not so much comic as downright daft. But a tone of subversion remains: Charlie undergoes the complete transformation into a loveable rogue whose antagonists are not the 'Crushers' (police) but Scrooge-like exploitative capitalists and criminals far more hard-hearted than himself.

And then, on one adventure... Charlie pulls a stunt on a Quality Street thoroughfare then breaks into in the laboratory of a mad scientist, Professor Desmond Date, where he finds an odd-looking safe. He opens it to discover it is empty just as Bannion and his men show up to imprison him in this chest.

Little do they know, however, that: *I have been trying to tell you, gentlemen... the minute Peace set foot in my incredible 'time-transporter' he began travelling towards the future! He should be in the year 1968 by now!*

And sure enough, like TV's Adam Adamant before him, the Victorian hero finds himself in Modern London where fings ain't wot they used to be. This is a world of skyscrapers and the Post Office tower; of concrete mixers and Routemaster buses; of Bingo Halls, Discos and Ten Pin Bowling Alleys; of TV crews and long-haired pop stars; of mini cars and mini-skirts — a world which, needless to say, he will find far more confusing than his own times past. *The world's gorn flippin' crazy! Where the 'eck am I?*

213

His first exploit in January 1968 involves his lack of knowledge of the etiquette of supermarket shopping, unaware that the contents of his trolley have to be paid for. He hi-jacks perhaps the one remaining horse and cart (belonging to TIPTOE & SON RAG 'N BONE MERCHANTS) and finds his way back to his old dockland haunt.

Over the next few years he would zig-zag between the two eras.

What a sustained act of the collective imagination of the Fleetway/IPC employees to keep the old lag alive for ten years, week in week out plus annuals and holiday specials.

But this was not to be Charlie's final appearance as a comic book hero.

Albion was a six-part series running between August 2005 and November 2006, the result of a unique deal between IPC and DC comics to revive many of the eccentric figures from the British strips of our youth. It was written by Alan Moore with his daughter and son-in-law, Leah Moore and John Reppion, and illustrated by Shane Oakley (the main instigator of the project, according to Leah Moore) and George Freeman, with cover art by Dave Gibbons, Moore's collaborator on *Watchmen.*

The premise is that leading characters from British 60s and 70s strips have been moth-balled in a secure government facility on a remote Scottish island... naturally they are destined to awaken, rebel, escape and run rampant. Who knows what American readers made of creations such as Robot Archie, Cap'n Hurricane, Janus Stark and the Steel Claw — none of which exactly fit the stateside superhero template.

(For those unfamiliar with the density of reference *Albion* has been exhaustively annotated by Damian Gordon, Pádraig Ó Méalóid and *the Bash Street Contributors*, accessible via the *Albion* page on Wikipedia.)

The story begins with Danny, a young collector, finding a treasure trove of rare comics in an antiques shop run by an ugly old curmudgeon Charles Love — those of a certain vintage immediately suspect this must be a *nom-de-guerre.* In issue 3 the heroine, Penny Dreadful, immediately recognises him. But *Albion*'s Charlie Peace is far from the amiable scamp of his *Buster* days. He appears on the cover of issue 4 (with the inevitable title 'Peace In Our Time') posed between two tower blocks, a vintage revolver in each hand.

The historical Peace is evoked in a back-story of how he evaded the hangman's noose... but there is no mention of a time machine to explain his existence in contemporary Liverpool.

Albion brought Charlie alive again from Olde England to Blairite Britain in yet another incarnation.

But not the last. For the most recent appearance of His Nibs as a Comic Book 'Hero' has been yet another collaboration between Eddie Campbell and myself. *Inside the Mind of a Master Criminal* is a contribution to *Dawn of the Unread*, a laudable initiative devised and edited by James Walker to promote literacy through the literary legacy of our native city of Nottingham. This project began as an ever-expanding and still-searchable website before all the pieces were collated to be published as a graphic novel.

Our conceit is that an ageing and over-weight archivist (surely not based visually on this writer?) purchases a fly-blown waxwork of Charles Peace from a defunct show under Skegness Pier which will be the centrepiece of his exhibition at the Museum of Crime and Punishment. Naturally, the figure will come alive to infect the mind of the impressionable curator and will provide a self-serving justification of his nefarious criminal celebrity. As an ironic nod to Charlie's rebirth in our childhood in the pages of *Buster*, this is another instance of how Peace won't leave us in peace. Perhaps this may not be his final illustrative manifestation.

"BACK IN THE GOOD OLD DAYS I WAS THE BEST THERE WAS. THEY USED TO TALK ABOUT THINGS BEING 'PEACE PROOF.' HAH! THERE WAS NO SUCH THING, LET ME TELL YOU.

"GOT INTO SOME VERY TRICKY PLACES, I DID. PLACES THEY SAID WAS IMPOSSIBLE. NICKED STUFF YOU COULDN'T EVEN IMAGINE THE WORTH OF.

"I THOUGHT I WAS UNSTOP-PABLE, BUT I GOT SLOPPY. I LET MY GUARD DOWN AND THAT BASTARD *ROBINSON*... HE GOT ME GOOD AND PROPER.

"THEY DIDN'T %£¢* ABOUT IN THEM DAYS, NOT LIKE NOW. THEY WERE GOING TO STRING ME UP. I BELIEVED IT, TOO. COULDN'T SEE ANY WAY OUT.

"EVEN *I* THOUGHT I WAS A GONER, FOR A MINUTE THERE.

"'COURSE I GOT AWAY. I ALWAYS GOT AWAY. A NEW NAME, A NEW TOWN, A NEW TIME, IT'S ALL THE SAME TO ME. WHEN I FALL I LAND ON MY $%¢*IN' FEET.

217

CHARLIE PEACE
INSIDE THE MIND OF A MASTER CRIMINAL

written by
Michael
Eaton

drawn by
Eddie
Campbell

MUSEUM OF CRIME
AND PUNISHMENT.

Why Charlie Peace?

Charlie Peace is dangerous. He worms his way into your brain. He takes over your life. He won't let go. He makes you do things against your better nature.

Nottingham Evening Post, Thursday May 28th 1891:

EXCITING SCENE AT A STATION

At Barnsley, yesterday, a boot finisher belonging to Armley, named Arthur Mayo, was charged with being drunk in a carriage on the Midland Railway at Cudworth. Detective-Inspector Evans, of Leeds, who prosecuted, said defendant was a passenger by the 8.40 p.m. train from Bristol to Leeds.

At Cudworth the porters heard some of the passengers calling for assistance, and going to the off-side they saw a man hanging head downwards out of the carriage window, the occupants of the carriage holding him by the legs to prevent him falling. The defendant shouted out that there were three devils and Charlie Peace after him. Police Constable Wood said the defendant was mad drunk. He was suffering from *delirium tremens.* The three occupants of the carriage were commercial travellers on their way to Leeds. The Chairman said that great credit was due to the three gentlemen who had undoubtedly saved the defendant's life. He strongly advised him to give up drinking and sign the pledge, which defendant agreed to do. Fined ten shillings and costs.

A final ballad struggles to have the last word on how posterity will judge Charlie — it could almost be sung to the tune of *What A Friend We Have in Jesus* :

LINES ON THE SAD FATE OF CHARLES PEACE

The scaffold now has done its duty
And sent a murderer from this world
Charles Peace has been executed
And to eternity is hurled.

On the twenty fifth of February
Upon the drop Charles Peace did stand
To be sent before his heavenly maker
For breaking of the Lord's command.

For the murder of Mr. Dyson
Charles Peace met an awful doom
And his career at length has ended
He sleeps forever in a felon's tomb.

He made a full and free confession
When he found his guilt was known
That his crime so sad and cruel
Upon his trial was clearly shown.

He had no mercy for his victim
And none to him the judge could give

He had disgraced the name of man
And was no longer fit to live.

Day and night he has been guarded
By the warders in his cell
As each lonely day departed
With fear of death his courage fell.

He's been a burglar and a murderer
But his career it is now run
At Armley he was executed
And suffered for the deeds he's done.

From his cell out to the scaffold
Thro' the chilly morning air
The Bannercross murderer was conducted
And looked a picture of sad despair.

His sad career was quickly ended
As the fatal bolt was drawn
Beneath his feet the drop descended
And Charles Peace died a death of scorn.

But death was anything but the end. And scorn was not the final verdict.

Why has this common criminal been the focus of such multitudinous metamorphic makeovers? Could it be that Peace's life and crimes offer a resounding 'No' to his society's sanctimonious illusion that honest toil leads to material prosperity? Charlie cocked a shameless snook at notions of the sanctity of private property and domestic, matrimonial bliss. Accepting no authority but his own, he lived out the unspoken desires of the down-trodden — the Rampant Id, the Troubling Trickster, the Dionysiac Bringer of Chaos, ambiguous focus of disconcerting fascination.

He refuses to lie down. When will he rise again?

Appendices:
The Women in Charlie's Life

Appendix A: Who was Hannah Peace?

What can be known of the life of Hannah Ward, before she met the man whose name she subsequently took as her own? Who was her first husband, the father of her son Willie? Did she ever legally tie the knot that binds with Charles Peace or was their supposed marriage 'over the broomstick'? Why did she remain ever faithful? Loyalty? Or fear? To what extent was she implicated in the procurement and disposal of his felonious articles? How did she react on learning that her man had shot and killed the husband of his mistress — a woman she seemingly abhorred?

Did she, as some accounts attest, retreat to her native town of Hull to open an eating house for the working man? And if so, did England's Public Enemy Number One track her down there while he was on the run and convince her to harbour him? What ruses then did 'Mister Thompson', transformed into an apparently respectable dealer in musical instruments, employ to cajole her to join him in the metropolis? How did she feel about sharing their suburban London residence with his new paramour? What effort of will must it have taken for Hannah to maintain the subterfuge in the neighbourhood that the younger woman of the household was her husband's loving 'wife' whilst she passed herself off as his doting 'mother'?

These must remain matters of speculation.

What follows is a verbatim account purportedly from Susan, 'Mrs Thompson' — but to whom she gave this testimony about her rival is not revealed. If true, she could only have gleaned this information from Charlie himself. Peace is said to have married Hannah Ward in July, 1858, although this seems doubtful as he may well have remained in incarceration until October of that year.

> He went long distances sometimes. It was on one of these excursions that he first met Hannah Peace — not Hannah Peace, if you please, but Mrs. William Ward. I will tell you what he told me about their first meeting.
>
> It was at the side of a canal on the road to Hanley, in Staffordshire, he met Hannah, who had a baby in her arms, then six months old. She stated, after they had got into conversation, that she was going along that way to find out her brother-in-law, who was the only friend she had in the world. She was then a widow of William Ward, a pensioner, and she told Peace so. He asked her what she was going to do if she did not find her brother-in-law, and she answered: 'I think of committing suicide.' Peace said, 'You are surely not going to do that — a nice-looking woman like you.'
>
> She was much older than he was, and I have no doubt was a good-looking woman. Peace said that they stayed all night at an inn. He promised her that if she would live with him he would prove a good father to Willie. They went to Worksop for a while, and when there he perpetrated several burglaries in the neighbourhood. I can't tell you how many... That child is now Willie Ward, who is twenty-one years of age, and

221

Peace is not his father. He never showed strong affection for Peace, but when he came to live at our house in London he would do anything for me. I think Peace took Mrs. Ward and her child to Sheffield and introduced her to his mother as his wife there.

The anonymous reporter offers his own gloss:

> The testimony of Mrs. Thompson, however, it must be admitted, must be looked upon with distrust, if not with suspicion and whether this is the true story of the meeting it is not so easy to determine. It is, however, quite certain that after his marriage or connection with the woman whom he always acknowledged as his wife, that he resumed his old courses.
>
> He professed at this time to be earning a living by hawking spectacles and cutlery, but his ingrained fondness for entering the houses of others and for appropriating goods that did not belong to him had not been eradicated by the prison discipline to which he had been subjected. His unhappy wife soon found out the character of the man with whom she had formed an alliance...
>
> It was not many weeks after her marriage that Mrs. Peace's eyes were enlightened as to the extra professional avocation of her husband, by a visit of the police to her house. His alliance with this ill-fated woman did not appear to have any influence over him, in the shape of turning him from his evil courses.

Little else is known to explain the fidelity of this forgotten wife.

All that remains on the record is the transcript of her trial at the Central Criminal Court — the Old Bailey — on January 14th 1879, whilst Peace was still in custody in London, less than three weeks before he faced the murder charge at Leeds Assizes.

Hannah Peace *Alias* Ward (58) was charged with 'feloniously receiving seven pocket-handkerchiefs and other articles... well knowing the same to be stolen.' These goods, identified by South London witnesses whose homes had been burgled, variously consisted of: a clock; twenty-three pounds worth of wearing apparel; two caskets, one tortoiseshell and one cornelian, value about thirty or forty pounds; two dessert knives; a pair of bracelets; an Indian table-cover; a silk dress and (what else?) a pickle fork.

She had been arrested back at Darnall, at the house of their daughter, Jane-Ann, who was attempting to pursue a righteous, law-abiding existence. (I have been informed by more than one of her living descendants that she remained until her death a stern and pious proprietess of a sweet-shop). Her husband, William Bolsover, a miner, was unwillingly dragged into these hearings to testify that his mother-in law:

> ...came to my house and said she had left a large box at Sheffield station. She said she had seen something in the paper relating to a man who was apprehended, and she supposed it was her husband. I took her in and... went to Sheffield and brought her box, which was heavy. There were eventually two brought to my premises. I saw them searched. All the things that have been identified as found on my premises had been brought there by the prisoner. I had nothing to do with them.

In court Hannah insisted that she had been lawfully wed at St. George's Church, Sheffield but that — rather conveniently — 'the old man burnt her marriage certificate some time ago... and that the two witnesses to the marriage, John Clark and Clara Clark, were dead.' The mitigating judgement she made, presumably somewhat wearily, was: 'He has been a great deal of trouble to me and seems to harass my life wherever I go.' This is her only publicly quoted statement about Charles Frederick Peace.

Mr. Forrest Fulton K.C. (for the Defence) submitted that there was no case to answer, inasmuch as the presumed marriage between the prisoner and Charles Peace had not been disproved by the Prosecution and, assuming the marriage to exist, the accused had acted under the coercion of her husband. Mr. Justice Hawkins concurred in the opinion that the charge could not be supported, as there was reasonable evidence to show that the prisoner was Peace's wife and, as such, acted under his authority.

The Jury followed the Judge's direction to return a verdict of Not Guilty. And with that she walked free into obscurity. It is to be hoped that the rest of her life was long and uneventful.

Appendix B: The Tale of Katherine Dyson

Before she left England after the trial the erstwhile Mrs. Dyson seemed adept at using the press as her mouthpiece to ensure her saintly reputation as a grieving widow would remain unsullied. One such hack introduced her apologia thus:

> Mrs. Dyson was desirous, before leaving this country, of contradicting in the most emphatic terms the imputations which had been freely cast upon her character and her morality. She accordingly left the following narrative behind her with an earnest request that, by its publication, she would be set right in the estimation of her husband's townsmen.

So at last eager readers were provided with an amazing autobiographical sketch and self-vindication — copied out in full in Chapter CLIV of the Penny Dreadful. Katherine's exciting young life in the New World and her tragic relocation to Sheffield reads as if it had been taken down in shorthand; this sounds how people really talk, though doubtless well-rehearsed:

> I was born in Ireland, at Maynooth. There I remained until I was fifteen years old. There, having just left school, I started off by myself to see my sister, who had previously gone off to America. She was living at Cleveland, Ohio, and is the wife of Mr. Mooney, captain on one of the Lake Erie steamers. Though I only went originally to see my sister, I stayed at Cleveland, for I liked the place, the people, and the life. It was there that I first met my husband. He was then a civil engineer, in the service of Sir Morton Peto, and was at that time one of the engineers on the Atlantic and Great Western Railway.
>
> We married, and spent our honeymoon on a visit to the Falls at Niagara. Coming back from our honeymoon, we went into housekeeping at Cleveland, but we did not remain there long. We stayed only until the section of the line of which Mr. Dyson had charge was finished. Then he received another appointment — that of engineer to the St. Louis Railway, known as the Iron Mountain Road, and went to reside there. He subsequently became the engineer of other lines in course of construction, and his last engagement in America was as superintendent engineer of the magnificent bridge which spans the Mississippi, and here his health broke down.
>
> He had been often compelled to lead a very rough kind of life, and it began to tell. His duties made that necessary, for the railways on which he was engaged opened up quite new country. The life, however, had many charms for me. I am a good hand at driving, and am fond of horses.
>
> I always used to drive Mr. Dyson. He used often to say that I could drive better than he, and he would sit back in his buggy — they call them buggies there — whilst I held the reins and sent the horses along. I liked the excitement of driving him to and from his work, and especially when we were in new country, and he was out surveying. I have driven him through forests where there were bears, and over creeks — they call rivers creeks in America — that were swollen by the floods. The horses have often had to swim. I remember on one occasion sending the horses and the buggy across a river, and then coming over myself on a piece of timber. Of course such a life has some drawbacks, but I was young and strong, and it possessed for me considerable fascination.
>
> My husband loved me and I loved him, and in his company and in driving him about in this wild kind of fashion, I derived much pleasure.
>
> Afraid? Not I. I did not then know what fear was. Besides, I have a good deal of courage. I think I have gone through sufficient *(here Mrs. Dyson's tone was tinged with some sadness)* of late to show that — and I always felt safe. To be in positions

attendant with danger caused me not fear, but a kind of excitement which, if not always pleasurable, certainly possessed some kind of fascination.

But, as I have said, Mr. Dyson's health broke down, and he was compelled to return to England. This was about four years ago. We first lived at Tinsley, with Mr. Dyson's mother; then at Highfield, nearly opposite the police station; and afterwards we took a house in the Alexandra-road, Heeley. Then we went to Darnall, and it was there that my troubles began. But for our going there, Mr. Dyson would probably have been still alive, and I should have been spared all that has happened since.

Not for the first time has an espousal resulting in a sojourn the English provinces led to the unravelling of a wild colonial woman. There is still no attempt to explain what Charlie could possibly offer her? Drink? Adventure? The exhilarating recklessness of sexual misadventure? The interviewer presses her: 'It is impossible for you, Mrs. Dyson, to be unaware of the rumours afloat as to the terms on which you and Peace were at Darnall. Would you like to say anything about that matter?'

That is just what I want to speak about. *(Here Mrs. Dyson spoke under some emotion and her face became quite flushed with excitement.)* I want you to do me the justice of writing down just what I state. The public of Sheffield — the vulgar public I mean — have been prejudiced against me. I have been tried in every shape and form since I came over here to give evidence, and my character and credibility have been made light of. But I want the people of Sheffield to see that I am a different kind of person from that which they have taken me for. They have classed me with Peace and Mrs. Thompson, and others of his gang, but I wish to show them that I am far superior to any of them...

The journalist persists: 'The statement is not true that your husband was jealous of you and Peace?'

Why should he be jealous? There was no cause, for all this time that we were at Darnall I was doing my best to withstand Peace. I know what has been thought and what has been said. *(Here Mrs. Dyson spoke excitedly and in a tone of much bitterness.)* I think no woman has ever been tried as I have. Why, ever since I came from America to give evidence, they have been trying me, not Peace. I want the public to understand that I have been tested to the utmost, and yet what has been proved against me?

Why, absolutely nothing.

All that has been said about myself and Peace is a lie, and I wish it to be put down as a lie. If you could draw three strokes under the word, so as to make it plainer I should like it done. I wanted this opportunity of saying what I have on this matter. I had no one to speak up for me, I had to speak for myself. I deny what has been said and imputed with regard to Peace and myself, and I dare and defy any one to say with truth that my conduct with regard to him was anything but what was right.

This first-person account must have been elicited by the same reporter at the very same time as her lengthy description about her life in Darnall, reproduced in the earlier Chapter LXXXIX. This, of course, may well be the product of self-serving hindsight, but, if true, it is a terrifying account of stalking.

When we went to Darnall our troubles began... You will naturally ask how I became acquainted with Peace. It was impossible to avoid becoming acquainted with him. Besides, at that time I did not know the sort of man he really was. He lived the next

225

door but one to us at Darnall, and he used generally to speak to Mr. Dyson on going in and out. Mr. Dyson was a gentleman, and, of course, when Peace spoke to him he used to reply. But Peace wasn't content with a merely speaking acquaintance. He wanted to force himself upon us. He did all he could until he succeeded in accomplishing this. One of his favourite means was to place his parrots and his other birds upon a wall. He would then call our attention to them, and to what they could do, and thus get us into conversation with him...

There was no introduction. He introduced himself, and would have you to talk with him whether you would or no. At first Mr. Dyson did not object, and Peace became a constant visitor to the house. He was plausibility itself. To hear him talk you would have thought him the most harmless of men. I am certain that much which he has succeeded in doing, both before and after the murder, is the result of the power which he has been able to exercise by his tongue and manner.

Of course, when we went to Darnall we did not know what he was. To us he appeared to be simply a picture-framer in anything but good circumstances, for he had but little business to do... We considered they were poor. I am, of course, now speaking of the time when we first went to live at Darnall. Mr. Dyson soon begun to tire of him. My husband had travelled much, and could converse well on many subjects.

Peace was plausible enough, but his language was not good; in fact, he very soon began to show that he was anything but a gentleman.

Mr. Dyson could not stand that; and, besides, he had seen something which disgusted him.... it was some obscene pictures, and my husband said he didn't like a man of that kind, and wouldn't have anything more to do with him. Besides, another thing greatly repelled Mr. Dyson. It was this. Peace wanted to take him to Sheffield to show him what he called 'the sights of the town.' Mr. Dyson knew what that meant, and being, as I have said, a gentleman, he became much disgusted at Peace and annoyed that he should force his company upon us.

My husband had been accustomed to different society. But we couldn't get rid of him. We were bound to show him common politeness. Though he must have seen that we didn't want his company, he forced himself upon us. He would, for instance, drop in just when we were sitting down to tea, and we were compelled almost to ask him to have a cup. His constant visits to the house at last became intolerable to us, and then it was that my husband placed his card in the garden, desiring Peace not to annoy him or his family.

When he found that he could no longer gain access to the house, Peace became awfully impudent. He would, for instance, stand on the doorstep and listen through the keyhole to what we were talking about, or look through the window at us. His persecutions at this time became almost unbearable. He did everything he could to annoy us. I was not afraid of him, and should have taken the law into my own hands, but my husband would not hear of such a thing. He always advised me to keep quiet.

I could not stand his impudence and the way in which he went on. I had not been used to such society as his proved to be, and I rebelled against it. I can hardly describe all that he did to annoy us after he was informed that he was not wanted at our house. He would come and stand outside the window at night and look in, leering all the while; and he would come across you at all turns and leer in your face in a manner that was truly frightful.

His object was to obtain power over me, and having done that, to make me an accomplice of his. I have told you that when I knew him first I thought him to be a picture-framer, and nothing more. Since then, however, I have learnt a good deal, and much that was difficult to understand has been made plain. He wanted me to leave my husband! Positively to leave my husband.

'What should I do that for?' I said. 'If you will only go to Manchester,' he answered, 'I will take a store (American for shop) for you, and will spend £50 in fitting it up. You shall have a cigar store, or a picture store. You are a fine-looking woman. You

look well in fine things, and I will send you fine clothes and jewellery, and if you
wanted to pawn them it would be easy. The pawnbroker would think everything all
right. Suppose, for instance, you had a grand pair of bracelets on, all you would have
to do would be to go into the pawnbroker's, take them off your wrist, and say, "I want
to pawn these things." If you will only do what I want, there shall not be such another
lady in England as you may be.'

At the time I couldn't understand what was his object. Of course, I see it plain
enough now. I did not suspect be was a burglar.

Only the stoniest of hearts could remain unmoved by her temptation into the web in
which she became ensnared. 'Will you come into my parlour?' said the Spider to the
Fly.

He was living at Darnall, making picture frames whenever he could get any to make, and his wife was apparently assisting to keep the house together by washing bottles at a wine and spirit merchant's. How could I know that he was anything other than he represented himself to be?

I was suspicious. I remember on one occasion he offered me a sealskin jacket and several yards of silk. Of course, he couldn't have come by them honestly. I now know they must have been part of the proceeds of a burglary. And well I should have looked if I had accepted them! I should then have been quite in his power. But I knew better than that. I declined his present, and told him that if he had a sealskin jacket and some silk to spare, he had better make a present of them to his wife and daughter.

I also told him that they wanted them much more than I did, and that if I desired to have a sealskin jacket, I would wait for it until my husband bought it, and that if he couldn't I was content to go without. Some time afterwards he offered me a gold watch; but I wouldn't have it. That, of course, was stolen. I consider that he offered me these presents as one means of getting me into his power. I would have nothing to do with him, and so he tempted me with sealskin jackets, and silks, and watches.

I remember when he was speaking to me about Manchester, he said:

'If you will only go, I'll fix you up there nice. You will have a splendid business, and will live like a lady.' 'Thank you,' I said, 'I always have lived like one, and shall continue to do so quite independently of you.'

I was getting downright mad with him, because of his constantly bothering me. What he wanted me to go to Manchester for was to pass off his stolen goods — at least that is my opinion. He never said so in so many words, but he could have had no other object. To do this, he needed first to get me in his power, and not only did he try, but other members of his family did their best. When he found that he could not succeed by fair means, then he tried what threats and persecutions would do.

He once came into my house, and said as I would not do what he wanted, he would annoy and torment me to the end of the world. 'Don't you ever come into my house again,' I said, 'or ever darken its doors.' But it was no use my saying that. He still came whenever he could get in, and when he couldn't, he watched for me and followed me wherever I went, I have known him to go to the railway station and say to the booking clerk after I had taken my ticket, 'Give me a ticket for where she's going.' That's how it was he followed me to Mansfield, and then came into the same house there where I and my companion were staying. That was, too, how it was that he was seen with me in the streets.

So it was as regards his being with me in the fair ground, about which so much has been made. I went to the fair with a neighbour and her children, and when we got into the photographic saloon my intention was to have the children photographed. I had no intention whatever of having myself taken with Peace, but he stood behind my chair at the time my likeness was taken. That was quite unknown to me, though, at the time. You can have no idea, unless you know the man, how he persecuted me and attempted to get me within his power. I remember doing something in the kitchen, and my back was turned to the door. Hearing a slight noise, I turned round, and then I saw Peace standing just inside the door. The expression on his face was something dreadful. It was almost fiendish — devilish. He had a revolver in his right hand, and he held it up towards me and said, in an excited and threatening manner: 'Now, will you go to Manchester? Now, will you go to Manchester?'

I did not shriek, but I cried out 'No, never! what do you take me for?' Finding that I was firm, he dropped his hand, and went out; but I can assure you I was frightened at the time. He had a way of creeping and crawling about, and of coming upon you suddenly unawares; and I cannot describe to you how he seemed to wriggle himself inside the door, or the terrible expression on his face. He seemed more like an evil spirit than a man. I have told you that when we knew him first we thought him a rather nice old man; but I soon found out, after he had taken against me, that we were sadly mistaken in our impression of him.

He turned against me solely because he could not make me do as he wanted. I would not have done as he wished for anything in this world.

He wanted me to be an accomplice in his doings. That has been his endeavour all through, and because he could not succeed he turned round on me and was determined to have his revenge. He thought he could handle me as he liked, that I was a weak sort of a woman, and could be got over like others who have been associated with him; but he found he was mistaken. I was terribly tried by him, though, and at last I was frightened — I don't deny it. There have been times when I haven't feared him, and when I should have thrashed him if Mr. Dyson would have allowed me.

I once did give him a good hiding, because he had insulted and annoyed me, but perhaps I had better not say much about that now. I used to be especially afraid of him at nights, because he had a habit of continually prowling about the house, and of turning up suddenly. He would, too, assume all sorts of disguises. He would boast how effectually he could disguise himself; and I was afraid of his coming in some guise or other at night, and carrying out his threats.

He was very determined. I never saw anything like it in my life. I have been about a good deal, but I never saw such determination and persistency as he has. It seems to me there was scarcely anything which he couldn't accomplish if only he was determined to succeed. He once said, 'I never am beaten when I have made up my mind. If I make up my mind to a thing, I'm bound to have it, even if it cost me my life.' You could not shake him off, do what you might. The only way to get rid of him was to knock him down as I once did.

Determined as he was one way, I was equally determined the other, and that was why he never succeeded with me. He once made use of this expression to me: 'I don't care how independent you are, I'll get hold of you some way or other.' But I said as firmly as I could, 'Never!' and so I have always said.

We went to Bannercross because we were afraid of Peace. Before going there, my husband took out a warrant against him. That was in July, 1876, and as soon as Peace knew of the warrant he left the town. It was soon after this that Mr. Dyson decided to go to Bannercross.

What became of Peace I never knew, except that I heard he had gone to Manchester. He suddenly disappeared, and I did not see him again until on the very day that our furniture was being removed to Bannercross.

I and my husband saw him coming out of our new house there.

So annoyed and irritated was I at this that I really should have caught hold of him, and held him until a policeman could have been fetched. But my husband would not hear of such a thing. Just fancy Peace coming out of the house we were going into! I really felt quite mad at it. This was on the 25th October, and I did not see him again till the night of the murder.

I didn't really know that Peace was a burglar until after the murder. If I had he would never have entered our doors. But what I know now explains a good deal. For instance, when we were out walking together, if I happened to look into a shop window, he would say to me, 'Is there anything there you would like? If there is I will get it for you before morning.' He would say that if I looked into a jeweller's or a draper's shop. I did not know what he meant then, but I do now. My suspicions were aroused, for I used to see him leave his house at Darnall in the evenings with a little satchel under his arm, and he would come back early in the morning carrying a large bundle. The satchel, I suppose, contained his housebreaking implements. He often used to go to Manchester with this satchel. He came to my door one morning just as he was going to Manchester. He then had his satchel with him. Looking into the room where I was, he said: 'I'll have you alive or dead. I'll have you, or else I'll torment you to the end of your life.' On another occasion, when I had defied him, he said: 'I'll make you so that neither man nor woman shall look at you, and then I'll have you to myself.' I answered, 'Never. What can you do? What are you capable of?' 'No matter,' he replied, 'I'll do it.'

He was always wanting to get my photograph, and as I wouldn't give him it, he or some member of his family stole one out of a locket which I had. It was afterwards copied by a photographer in Sheffield, and I have fancied since that he wanted to get my features transferred in some way or other to one of his obscene pictures and so disgrace me. I cannot understand in any other way what he meant by saying that he would make me so that neither man nor woman should look at me.

This is the only suggestion of doctored pornographic photographs — an imputation which was never mentioned subsequently. But if such tampered pictures did indeed exist they would have been worth a small fortune in the Peaceiana market.

I am told that since he has been sentenced to death he has become a changed character. That I don't believe. The place to which the wicked go is not bad enough for him. I think its occupants, bad as they might be, are too good to be where he is... Not even a Shakespeare could adequately paint such a man as he has been. My life-long regret will be that I ever knew him.

But yet... but yet... There remains the vexed issue of those alleged notes, supposedly dropped in a field behind the Dyson house and denounced by Katherine as forgeries designed to implicate her. They were reproduced in full in Chapter CLXX: *Extraordinary Communications*.

> The theory of the prosecution was that the whole of the notes and letters were written by Peace for his own purpose. What those purposes were, of course can only be imagined. It may have been to get Mrs. Dyson into his power. The notes were of an extraordinary character. Most of them were written in pencil on scraps of paper. As doubtless this correspondence will be read with considerable interest, we give it in its entirety, following the spelling and other eccentricities of the writer.

The asterisks do not seem to indicate 'expletive deleted' but rather passages which must be illegible. And it would appear that the subsequently reputable shop-keeper and Sunday School teacher, Jane-Ann Bolsover, née Peace, may well have been complicit in these dangerous liaisons.

Things are very bad for people told him everything * * * Do keep quiet, and don't let anyone see you. Money send me some.

Send me a drink. I am nearly dead.

be quick * * you * * he is out now.

he is out now so be quick let us have a look at you.

Will you send me a shilling or two and a drop and keep very quiet, be quick.

Give it to me up in the garret but don't talk for fear he is not going only his sister is coming, love to all.

I will write you a note when I can perhaps tomorrow. You can give me something as a present if you like but I don't want to be covetous and take them from your wife and daughter.

Mrs. Norton is raising hell about what I * * * * Could you settle it and send me a print that is I have and * * * her to let me have a pint.

he is gone out come now for I must have a drink.

After he is going out I won't go if I can help it so see for Janey.

I have just run out of writing paper excuse the envelope. Many thanks for my book, don't mind framing the picture, let them have it without, as I have nothing to say in the matter. I will thank your wife as soon as I get a chance to see her for her kind present, tell her so, with my love. I was very sorry to hear your quarling, hope it is all settled now and * * * * having to hear the readings you should be quiet. You have a good wife, be kind to her. This was written yesterday, but could not see you.

He won't say when he is going. Not to-day anyhow he is not very well. I will write you when I have a chance and put you in the work * * * *

He only went for tobacco and he has not been out. I shall tell you when he does. You must not say I am Dr. when I am not for I don't thank you for that opinion. I shall go to Ireland if you don't be — I am washing to-day, so he won't be out perhaps. Get me paper. Love.

If you have a note for me send now while he is out, but you must not venture for he is watching, and you can't be too careful, hope your foot is better, he went to Sheffi yesterday but I could not see you anywhere were you out love to Ja.

*Have you got your handkerchief I lost mine * * pocket hank and gloves*

* * * * thanks for this money * * * must be careful and not show anything or I will let you starve.

I think I will go by 9 o'clock now, you must not go by train, go by tram because he will go down with me don't let him see anything. Meet me in the Wicker hope nothing will turn up to prevent it. Love to Janey.

If you are not at home Janey will give you this do be careful you will get yourself into trouble about the empty house don't come until I tell you there is a man over the wall says he will give you hell now I tell you this as a friend so as you may be on the look out for your familys.

How well you never told that man. I looked at you out of the window.

You left me to find out for myself, and would not put me on my guard, as

I do to you. Hope you won't omit again. Don't talk to Willie much, or give him any half pegs. * * * * Don't be a fool. It looks as if you want people to know the way you and if you are not more careful we will have to say quits. I have told you not to say anything until * * *

Saturday Afternoon. I write you these few lines to thank you for all your kindness which I shall never forget from you and your wife she is a very good one does she know you are to give me the things or not how can you keep them concealed one thing I would wish you to do is to frame his mothers photo and send it in with my music book if you please do it when he is in. Many thanks for your kind advice I hope I shall benefit by it.

I shall try to do right by every one if I can and shall always look on you as a friend, good bye I have not much time, burn this when you read it.

Dear sir, Are you at home or not, for I can't see you. I looked for you yesterday, when I went to Sheffield, but could not see you, and don't like to send if you are not in, because I know Janey have not seen you all day; but he has not been out. You are getting very with old Ned; don't blab anything to him, for it will be all over. Never speak of me. I will not set this till I know you are at home. Hope you are well, and don't fret; but I will give you the wink when the coast is clear; but you must not take notice till I tell you or you will make a mess of it, because is always on the look out. Don't know when he will go out again, but will sure tell you. Love to G — b - burn this.

Who could have made this up? Could such communications, replete with Americanisms, really have been 'forged'?

Kate's final assessment:

> My opinion is that Peace is a perfect demon — not a man.

And with these words she boards the White Star liner and sails into posterity.

Appendix C: Sue's Story

Another intrepid pressman, also anonymous, deserves great praise for securing this scoop. His personal interview with Sweet Sue, the Nottingham Nightingale who became the Peckham Prisoner, was reproduced in full in Chapter CL of *The Adventures of A Notorious Burglar*. Where else could be found in such telling detail a convincing insight into the life and psychology of an ordinary Nottingham lace worker propelled into extraordinary circumstances because of a passing attraction to the most infamous villain of her age before being cast back into oblivion and the bottle? Susan Gray/Bailey/Thompson could have been lock-stitching, ruffling or finishing off on a bench in the Lace Market next to one of my great-grandmothers. She must surely be lamented as a temporary celebrity victim. Might she be equally lauded as a heroine?

The news hound who tracked her down from seclusion back in Nottingham insists this is' a faithful chronicle'.

> The following is a tolerably accurate description of her personal appearance. In person she is tall, and considerably above the middle height. Her figure is not robust. Her complexion is fair, and was no doubt at one time good. Her hair is dark and plentiful, and her eyes of a deep blue, what is known as a violet hue. Mrs. Thompson, at the time I saw her, was dressed in a brown robe, trimmed with velvet to match; and wore a cloth jacket and round hat, becoming and neat. Both of these articles she removed in the course of conversation. Her manner was at first frank and agreeable, but as our interview lasted it changed to a fitful moroseness, which was difficult to deal with. Both in person and in manner Mrs. Thompson may be said to be decidedly prepossessing — what may be called a taking woman. She is manifestly a fairly well-educated woman, and writes a pretty, ladylike Italian hand... The woman seems to have money, but she appears to be oppressed by a dread that 'Charley' Peace will escape and cut her throat.

Small wonder!

This instance of reportage from the era leaps off the page like a treatment for a movie yet to be filmed. Though Susan's story bears all the structural hallmarks of the classic three-act play, her own words belie any attempt to reduce her to a stock character from fairground theatrical melodrama.

> My maiden name is Susan Gray, and I was born in the year 1842, at Nottingham. My parents are very respectable people, and carry on a small business in that town. I am heartily sorry to have brought this disgrace upon them.
>
> In my childhood I went to various schools in Nottingham — to the Trinity School when I was a youngster, when I was also picked out as a singer in the choir. I continued to attend the Trinity Schools until I was eight or nine years of age, when my parents removed me to the College School. There I remained until I was fourteen, when I went out to work. I should not like to state where I was employed, as it might give pain to persons living, but there are those alive who know that this statement is true.
>
> After I left my first situation I stayed at home and assisted my father in his business as his bookkeeper.
>
> When I was about twenty-eight or twenty-nine years old, a Mr. Bailey one day came for purposes of business to my father's house. He had occasion to see my handwriting, and asked me if I would make out some bills for him. I obliged him, and from that day I kept his books, and did all the writing he required. One day he asked me if I would marry him, and, in a spirit of vexation, I having had some little

disturbance with a brother of mine, I said 'Yes.'

We were married on the 10th of October, 1872, but three months after that I left him, on finding out what was his true character, and that it would be impossible for me to live happily with him. I went next to live with my married sister at Nottingham. I then worked for my living, employing my time in the manufacture of caps such as ladies and servants wear.

One Sunday evening, perhaps six months afterwards, as I was going to chapel, I met Bailey again. He stopped and spoke to me, and finally induced me to return to live with him. I stayed with him for nearly a year, when I again left him, and since that time I have not spoken to him, except to obtain from him a weekly allowance, which I continued to enjoy until I met the man Peace, but on my becoming connected with him that allowance was forfeited.

That's her Act One normality. Now comes the switch in her humble existence, the inciting incident:

I met Peace in January, 1877, I think it was. He came to the house where I was living at Nottingham about that time. One evening, just as I was returning from work, when I entered the house, I saw him there. I shall never forget the impression he made upon me. I thought him of very singular appearance, and, from what I saw at first sight, I had reason to believe that he was a one-armed man but that appearance was only the result of one of his tricks and deceptions. When I went in he said to the landlady, 'Is this your daughter?'

I was not living with my sister then. I had left home, and had not spoken to any of my family for a long time. In answer to Peace's question, my landlady, after some hesitation, gave an affirmative reply. Some conversation in subdued tones then took place between Peace and my landlady. I ought to have said that this occurred in a house in a district known as 'The Marsh' at Nottingham — a very low neighbourhood indeed. Peace had brought my landlady some boxes of cigars for sale. She said to him, in reference to myself, 'You can speak before her. She won't say anything.' Peace then asked her if she would go and see if she could sell the cigars.

This woman, who is since dead, was an accomplice of his, and used to assist him in the disposal of stolen property. Her name was Adamson. She thereupon went out and sold them, and when she returned gave him eighteen shillings, of which sum he returned her six shillings by way of commission.

After that he became a constant visitor, and we always spoke of him as the one-armed old man. He not unfrequently had there his breakfast, dinner, tea, and supper, and at last it became known to me what his real character was. At first he gave out that he was a hawker, and dealt in various little articles such as pedlars invariably travel with — spectacles, cheap finery, and jewellery, and miscellaneous goods of that description. At last he openly showed himself in his true character — I mean as a most daring burglar. He brought things into the house which it must be evident to anybody were stolen property.

There were articles of silver plate, timepieces, watches, and even quantities of tea, sugar, and other perishable articles. I do not know at all where he got these from; but I am perfectly satisfied that they were the proceeds of robberies or burglaries. This knowledge was kept from me at first. I was led to suppose he was what he seemed to be — viz. a hawker, and a quiet, respectable man.

On one occasion he went out of town, saying he had to go and see his mother at Hull. By his mother he meant Hannah Peace. Peace on that occasion took five pounds to Mrs. Ward at Hull, and stayed there three weeks. During that time he committed several robberies either at Hull or in the neighbourhood. I know that to be the case, because when I have been in Hull he has shown me the houses at which the burglaries were committed, and he also told me that on one occasion he had to run for it, when he 'fired wide' at a policeman by whom he was in imminent danger of being captured.

The property was disposed of in Hull.

He returned after a while to Nottingham. I was out at the time of his return, having business in the evening, for I was still at work and getting my own living in an honest way. I was not earning very much, for work was short, but still it was honest. On this particular night, on my return home, Mrs. Adamson said to me, 'Oh, Mrs. Bailey, who do you think has come back?' I replied I did not know, to which she made answer, 'Why, the one-armed old man, and he has asked for you. He swears he will shoot you unless you go to him.'

He was in the house of our next-door neighbour, and previously to that the lady of the house came in, and said, 'Oh, Mrs. Bailey, do come in, the old man's gone mad; he wants to see you so bad. He won't be satisfied with anyone until you go.'

When I went in I found him drunk on Irish whiskey. He said, 'Is that you, pet?' (for by that name he used to call me), 'I am so glad you have come, where have you been?' I told him I had just come in from business.

He said, 'Oh, I am so glad you have come. I thought you were never coming back. Are you not pleased to see me?' I said, 'Oh, particularly, very; I like you so much.'

People must not think by that that I loved him, or because he said in his last letter to me that I did. I got him home, and made him a cup of tea, after which he seemed better. He went back to the place where he was then residing, for he did not, as I have already said, live in the house with me.

The following day he came to me very early. That day I was rather short of work. He said he was sorry he had been in such a bad way and had behaved so rudely. He next asked me to stay at home for the day. I said 'No, that would not do. I should lose my work.' 'Never mind that,' said he. He reckoned up how much I was earning, and said, 'Look here, darling! If you will promise me not to go to work again, I will pay for your board and lodging. And if Mrs. Adamson likes, I will give her fourteen and three a week for my board, and come and stay, but not sleep here.'

There was no accommodation for him in the house. Eventually my better feelings were overruled, and I submitted myself to him. He was invariably very kind to me, and I did not live with him unhappily.

I knew that he made a living on the proceeds of burglaries which he committed, but I never had any of the goods so stolen; and my dresses were bought for me by him. He said one day he would have given me a splendid ostrich feather, but he had not got them, because the woman of the house at which he used to lodge would not give them up. I said,

'It is very strange if you have things where you used to lodge and didn't get them if you don't owe them anything.' He replied 'Never mind; I will buy you one.'

One Monday night he brought home a black silk dress, polonaise, and a long jacket, which he said he thought would fit me. I told him I did not wear such things. He offered to buy me some like them, but this offer I also declined. If I remember rightly, these things were the proceeds of a burglary at Hull, and I believe they have been given up to the police. I have since worn dresses that were stolen, but they have all been given up now to the police.

Mrs. Adamson went with him one day to look at a pawnbroker's shop, into which she wanted him one night to force an entry, but the project never came to a head. I believe he thought the premises whereon was so much valuable property were pretty sure to be watched. Mrs. Adamson would have found means of getting rid of the spoil, but he never did enter the place. I would rather not mention the name of the street in which the shop was situated.

After that he committed a great clothes robbery at one of the factories, and in the course of a week he went again and stole a great number of coats. He brought several rolls of cloth and the coats to Mrs. Adamson, who disposed of a great portion of the property to persons whom one would have thought to be of unblemished respectability.

In June, 1877, Mrs. Adamson wanted some blankets, and Peace said he could get her any amount. He went to get some, or, at any rate, to try, but was detected in the act of entering the house. He made his escape through a stable and through a wood yard. Resistance was offered by a man on the premises, but Peace pulled out his revolver and threatened to shoot him and the man, intimidated, let him get clear away,

After that he was constantly concerned in robberies until the occasion of the great silk robbery, for the perpetrator of which £50 reward was offered. That was just before we came to London. The silk was disposed of by Mrs. Adamson, and the detectives came to her house two or three days after Ward, as I then called him, and I were sitting together. We were living together you know, sir, then — the fact is we were in bed together.

I was asleep, but the noise the officers made on entering awoke me.

I said, 'Oh, Mr. G.,' that is the name of the officer who first entered the room. He stood astonished when he saw me. 'Oh, Mr. G.,' I said, 'let me get out of this.' He said, 'I am surprised to see you, Mrs. Bailey.'

The men turned to the convict Peace and said to him, 'What is your name?'

'John Ward,' was the rather sullen reply.

'What do you do for a living?' the officer next asked.

'I hawk spectacles.'

'Where is your licence?'

'I will show it to you when I come down.'

'Get up and dress,' said one of the officers.

'I shan't before you,' was the reply, in the same sullen tone and manner, 'but I will be down directly.'

They went downstairs, leaving Ward in the room. I said to Peace, 'Let me go out,' whereupon he permitted me to leave the room, and went to my next-door neighbour's, where I was very much hurt indeed at the thought of what had happened. They asked me what was the matter, and I said, 'I do not know.' No sooner had I left the room, than Peace slipped on his clothes, and made his escape through the window, squeezing himself between two iron bars which I am sure were not more than six or eight inches apart.

He ran across the road into the house of a neighbour, whom he got to fetch his boots for him, the detectives being at the time in the house waiting for him to come downstairs. At last one of them shouted out, 'Come, young man, you are a long time coming.' No answer being returned, a move was made upstairs; the door was thrust open, and the discovery made that the bird had flown.

Away from the neighbour's house he went to the Trent side, where he walked for a considerable distance. When he considered himself safe from recognition, he entered a public-house, where he gave a man 1 shilling and a note for me. The note was one asking me to go to him at the place where he was staying, but I declined, and the daughter of the house where I was living went to see him in my stead.

I sent him some money by her, and the answer he made me was that he did not care for all the detectives in England; that be would not lose sight of me; that he would not go away from the place without me. I belonged, he said, to him, and he would not leave the neighbourhood without me. He sent yet again, and then I met him by appointment in the evening time, and from that time we have always been together.

Now she is separated from her former life: she has crossed the line, no turning back. The Second Act of Susan's drama, full initiation into criminal complicity, also involves a change of location. She moves from the secure tedium of a provincial town to the seething throng of the Great Wen — though the boundaries of her being become even more constrained:

We came to London together, and took apartments in the Lambeth district, where he began again that career of crime which has made him so notorious. But here again his character to the outside world was the same as it had ever been.

Though he was always regarded as a passionate man, he was at the same time looked upon as quiet, peaceable, and inoffensive, and in the highest degree, respectable. As a performer upon the violin he was anything but a mean proficient. He mixed very little with his neighbours, to my knowledge, in this locality, and but little was known of that wonderful fund of ingenuity which be undoubtedly possessed.

Often and often have I said to him what a pity it was that he had not turned his abilities to a better account than for the purpose of committing depredations upon the property of his fellow-creatures; but though his manner to me was kind, he would always jeer and scoff at my rebukes.

It would be utterly impossible for me to enumerate all the robberies he has committed. He has told me at times of his having been into as many as four and even six houses in a single night, sometimes with success, and sometimes, of course, without.

During the day it was his custom to remain in bed, preparing himself for his work in the following evening, when he would regularly go out upon his housebreaking exploits. Sometimes he came in with a great deal of valuable plunder, consisting chiefly of silver and gold watches, rings, and various other articles.

And then... a turning point, a moment when a chink of reality illuminates her circumscribed situation as the suburban chatelaine:

One Sunday evening a knock came at the door at the house where we lived at Lambeth. I answered the door and saw before me a little elderly woman.

'Does Mrs. Thompson live here?' she asked.

I replied, 'Yes.'

She then said that she was Hannah.

I called to Peace and said, 'Jack, you're wanted.'

'Who is it?' he asked.

'Come and see,' I replied.

He did, and he found to his surprise I believe, that it was Hannah.

'What brought you here?' he asked.

I interrupted jocosely with the remark, 'I suppose the train.'

Hannah, however, said, 'Didn't you get my letter? I have been waiting two hours on the look out for you.'

I said, 'We received no letter. There is no delivery here on a Sunday morning.'

Jack said, 'Come in,' and she came in. Having looked round our apartment, she said, 'You have a nice place here.'

Jack asked her if she would have some supper. She replied in the affirmative, and this I had to get ready. She then began to talk about his friends and of the people whom they both knew, and I learned in the course of conversation that the shop at Hull had been given up, and that she had realised the proceeds.

Peace asked my permission to have Mrs. Ward and the boy Willie in London. I could not do otherwise than consent, and eventually they came. Shortly after their arrival we moved to a house at Greenwich, but as we did not live comfortable in the same house, we moved into separate habitations adjoining each other, Mrs. Ward and her son living in one, and I and Peace in the other. Whilst we were living in this manner Peace made a journey into the provinces — a thing which he now very seldom did. Whilst upon this excursion he committed a great burglary in Southampton.

The police say that the affair took place at Portsea, but I know better; it was at Southampton. By this robbery Peace cleared something like £200; £60 of the money being in gold and silver, and the remainder in Bank of England notes. These he found no difficulty in getting rid of. There is a place, I am told, where all Bank of England notes can be disposed of without inquiries being made, but I do not feel justified in stating where it is. That is reserved for the Bank of England authorities.

It was upon the proceeds of that excursion that he started his pony and trap, the expenses of maintaining which he found to be great. In the first place we had no stable accommodation connected with the house we occupied. This had to be paid for, and the cost of the food for the pony was again a very considerable item.

One day I said to him: 'I don't like this neighbourhood; let us remove from here and get where there is a stable connected with the house.' He told me he had seen a place in the Evalina-road, Peckham, and if I would put my things on we would go and see it, which we did.

We inquired next door as to who was the agent or the landlord of the house, and the lady whom we saw kindly referred us to Mr. Smith.

We looked over the house, which we both liked very much. Smith and Peace came to an agreement as to the building of a stable.

When Smith asked for references, Peace said to him: 'Oh, come down and see my house.' Smith did so, dined with us, and went away perfectly satisfied, for a few days afterwards we received a note to say that the house was at our disposal. Shortly afterwards we removed to the house No. 5, East Terrace, Evalina-road, Peckham, where my troubles commenced.

Susan echoes Katherine's bitter judgment when she moved to Darnall. But surely the seeds of her troubles had been sowed long since?

Mrs. Ward and the boy Willie came to live in the same house with myself and Peace, and her presence occasioned much trouble between us. When we were settled, Peace began his system of robberies again.

Oh! many a time have I, by my tears and by my entreaties, tried to keep that man at home.

I was not allowed to move from the house without either one or the other being with me; but though they were so afraid of me, I should never have breathed a syllable against them. I have been threatened, and he latterly at times ill-used me. I have had a pistol pointed at my head and more than once he has threatened to kill me. Peace used occasionally to ill-use Hannah cruelly, and in a way I shudder to think about. On one occasion he threatened me because I had pawned a silk dress, and he was afraid that it might be traced.

Backed by jealousy, a prey to remorse, and the object of constant suspicion, is it to be wondered that I at last took to drinking? In this respect Peace was again indulgent, for though he jealously guarded me when I went out, at home I could have what I liked, and with drink I deadened my senses, and idled from my shame and despair.

Peace, as a rule, went out nightly, unless he got a good haul, when he would stop at home for a night or two. What I call a 'good haul' was when he was able to show me plenty of jewellery and silver-plate. I have known him bring home sixty-six ounces at a time.

His method of procedure being this: he used to be driven of an evening to within a certain distance of the house where he intended to 'work.' If the nights were light, Peace used to be concealed all night and return home, say, between six and eleven o'clock in the morning, when someone would go out and meet him. He was very good to his horse, for I should like people to give him his due; and it was only occasionally that he worked it hard. He often went to his destination by train or by tram, and someone would go with the trap to meet him at the hour and place appointed. When he has come home haggard and black, as I have often seen him, he has said to me, 'Well, pet, have ye not got a smile for me?'

According as he had been successful, or the reverse, he would say, 'Well, I have not done much, my girl' or, 'I have done pretty well,' and then he would proceed to sort out the property, preparatory to its disposal. I have seen him shake his head sometimes over the proceeds of the night's takings, and say, 'I don't think they will fetch much.' Then he would tell me of his struggles and his escapes, and the number of houses he had been into.

Could the following reminiscence have provided the original derivation of that abiding image of 'Beauty and the Beast' which Purkess distributed gratis? Or was she drawing upon an already sanctioned icon of Peace's mythologisation?

Once he told me that, in order to get a gold watch and chain from under a lady's pillow, he had to shift her position slightly. The lady, he told me, muttered something fond, and turned over to her husband, whom she believed to have been the cause of the very slight disturbance occasioned. Peace abstracted the watch and chain, and came away.

I verily believe that, when such adventures occurred to him, he used to come back sick at heart, for, notwithstanding the profession which he followed, and the fact that he had always firearms which he would not have hesitated to use had he been disturbed, he was generally very kind to me, and I am sure he felt such things.

Now, as to the disposal of the property. If it was valuable, he used to send for those persons who bought of him, and obtain for them such a sum of money as he required. I am not at liberty to say who those persons were, but Peace used to swear that if ever he was taken he would do for them, and confess as to his accomplices, but I hope I shall not be mixed up in that affair.

I always told him he would go to Blackheath once too often. I cannot say more than the persons to whom he disposed of the property were Jews. Two I know of, certainly, and they will 'Jew' me, I expect, if they get hold of me. One day I went with him while he disposed of some property.

He used to take the property wrapped up like drapers' parcels — innocent and unsuspicious-looking enough.

He used to treat me with great kindness when Mrs. Ward was nowhere about. He seemed to be never so happy as when he could get me alone. We occupied the drawing-room floor, using the front room as a sitting room and the back as a bedroom, the breakfast-room below being my private sitting-room or boudoir...

It is as if she's compelled to confirm the local colour, to put herself in the picture:

The care of Peace's animals, of which, by the way, he was extremely fond, devolved upon myself. It would be as well, I think, to say what they were, as the collection was heterogenous. There were ten Guinea pigs, every one of which I gave away when he was taken; a goat, two cats, two Maltese terriers, and a cockatoo; and in addition to these, Mrs. Ward kept a Maltese dog, a parrot, a dog, and four pigeons.

When Peace went out at night to work he always took with him a revolver, a 'jemmy,' a sharp knife, and various sized screws wherewith to fasten the doors of rooms in which he was 'working,' so as to ensure his being able to thoroughly ransack them without being disturbed; but he never took skeleton keys, for he was so skilful that he would take out the panel of a door almost noiselessly and with great rapidity.

Peace never went out without leaving me with a revolver which, I dare say, I should have the courage to use had occasion presented. He had four revolvers altogether, and the three he left at home I destroyed, when I found he had been taken. Yes... I sank them.

This revelatory testimony breaks off for a while as Susan produces some remnant cast-offs from their time together. Is she expecting her interrogator to make her an offer for her scanty memorabilia? The reporter writes:

Here, Mrs. Thompson, as I shall continue to call her (that being the name by which she is best known), produced to me an old pair of Peace's trousers. In addition to the usual side pockets, they were fitted with pockets behind on a level with the hip, and in these receptacles he used, she told me, to stow away his revolver, and whatever instruments he had to take with him. The inside of the trousers on the left-hand side was filled with a piece of oilskin or glazed cloth, to prevent the iron from chafing the burglar's skin. Mrs. Thompson also showed me how, by turning in his left foot and by bending up his make-believe arm towards his shoulder, the little man used to assume deformity. I also obtained from her a description of a burglar's stick, as she called it, which Peace found useful in climbing, and an instrument still more remarkable which, she said he possessed, as a kind of portable step ladder of seventeen steps, which he was able to fold into so small a compass that he could go out with it underneath his coat without attracting attention. It was provided with hooks, for the purpose of fastening to walls and window ledges, but she said he never used it, owing, I suppose, to the fact that it was a clumsy apparatus to affix noiselessly.

Susan's narrative must perforce continue into Climax before Third Act re-incorporation. Her Rite of Passage from Innocence to Experience is almost complete. But of the active role this erstwhile passive victim most likely played after the capture of 'John Ward' she remains, quite prudently, tight-lipped.

> When we saw in the papers that he had been taken Mrs. Ward cried out, 'Oh, my poor Charlie, my poor Charlie! I must go. I dare not stay here; Willie, you must go too.' I then asked her, 'And what is to become of me then?' 'Oh,' she said, 'You are young; you can fight your own battle.'
>
> She was for selling everything, but I objected to my furniture being sold, as I thought I might be able to get a living by letting apartments. My rooms were well furnished, though I had no carpets, and Jack bought every stick that was in them. We divided all the money that was in the house, about £5, and sold the trap, harness, cushions, and rug for £8, though he had given £14 for the trap alone. It does not matter to whom they were sold, because the man who bought them did not know at that time that we were other than very respectable people, and I should not like to expose him as having had dealings with us.
>
> Hannah took all the moveables. We divided the ready money, and parted. I was very firm about the furniture, which Jack said he had bought to be my own. If I liked, he said, he would buy me more. I was to have had a piano on the 14th December last, as a birthday present.

Susan says nothing whatsoever to shed any light on how the true identity of the man arrested after the shooting of Constable Robinson was discovered; nor does she mention her claim on the reward. In fact the police specifically came to deny this — possibly to protect her or, more likely, to prevent her from receiving the one hundred pounds, which would have set her up in a new life back in Nottingham.

The reporter concludes:

> [O]ur interview lasted for something over five hours, she must have been tired and her memory confused. I was not such a barbarian as not to have offered her some refreshment during that period. She took it in the form of steak and onions, rinsed down with brandy and water. When we parted we were the best friends in the world. She shook me warmly by the hand.

Like Hannah and Katherine, Susan also offers a final sound-bite:

> When the police caught him they caught the cleverest thief and the cleverest beast that I should think there ever was in human form.

I cannot help feeling that I have made a great mistake. It has blotted my life. But there, I am not going to be sentimental any more. I am not a sentimental sort. I have my own character to redeem and if I have my health and strength I hope to do it. Heigh ho!

Heigh ho! And are we any the wiser? To use her own words, 'As I was, so I am.'

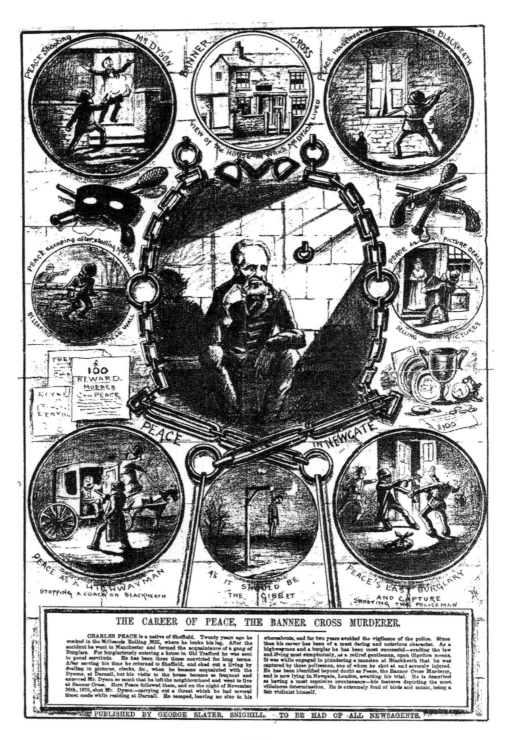

THE CAREER OF PEACE, THE BANNER CROSS MURDERER.

CHARLES PEACE is a native of Sheffield. Twenty years ago he worked in the Millsands Rolling Mill, where he broke his leg. After the accident he went to Manchester and formed the acquaintance of a gang of Burglars. For burglariously entering a house in Old Trafford he was sent to penal servitude. He has been three times convicted for long terms. After serving his time he returned to Sheffield, and eked out a living by dealing in pictures, clocks, &c., when he became acquainted with the Dysons, at Darnall, but his visits to the house became so frequent and annoyed Mr. Dyson so much that he left the neighbourhood and went to live at Banner Cross. Here Peace followed them, and on the night of November 26th, 1876, shot Mr. Dyson—carrying out a threat which he had several times made while residing at Darnall. He escaped, leaving no clue to his whereabouts, and for two years avoided the vigilance of the police. Since then his career has been of a most daring and notorious character. As a highwayman and a burglar he has been most successful—evading the law and living most sumptuously, as a retired gentleman, upon illgotten means. It was while engaged in plundering a mansion at Blackheath that he was captured by three policemen, one of whom he shot at and severely injured. He has been identified beyond doubt as Peace, the Banner Cross Murderer, and is now lying in Newgate, London, awaiting his trial. He is described as having a most repulsive countenance—his features depicting the most villainous determination. He is extremely fond of birds and music, being a fair violinist himself.

PUBLISHED BY GEORGE SLATER, SNIGHILL. TO BE HAD OF ALL NEWSAGENTS.

Acknowledgments

Paul Marygold, projectionist and cinephile, and Ann Featherstone, historian of the portable stage, have been of especially invaluable assistance — the former for diligent research in newspaper libraries, the latter delving through her mental archive to pass on tit-bits from the pages of long forgotten theatrical periodicals. Professor Vanessa Toulmin, of the National Fairground Archive at the University of Sheffield, herself from a family of showfolk, has always been helpful in sharing knowledge of the history of popular entertainment. Bryony Dixon of the British Film Institute has been ever-ready to dive deep into the murky waters of early British silents to uncover precious pearls. Gerry Turvey, historian of British & Colonial, was the source of material about the lost Geoff Barlow film. Peter Yorke's history of his remarkable Haggar forebears is indispensable. Michael Diamond has been generous in sifting through his fabulous Victorian collection to uncover otherwise lost Peaceiana. In Brisbane Australia the great comic book illustrator Eddie Campbell finally submitted to stout-sodden entreaties for him to enter the uncharted terrain of theatre design. My greatest debt of gratitude is to my collaborator Giles Croft, Artistic Director of Nottingham Playhouse, whose fine production of *Charlie Peace — His Amazing Life And Astounding Legend*, played by a splendid company, has been a highlight of my professional life.

> *In Hell you'll meet Old Nick himself*
> *Playing cards with Charlie Peace,*
> *While all the devils round the fire*
> *Are eating whelks and bread and cheese.*

See you in Tartarus, comrades.